SECRETS OF COLOMBIAN COOKING

Expanded Edition

THE HIPPOCRENE COOKBOOK LIBRARY

SECRETS OF
COLOMBIAN
COOKING

Expanded Edition

Patricia McCausland-Gallo

HIPPOCRENE BOOKS
NEW YORK

I dedicate this book to my father, who got sick suddenly and passed away the same day my cookbook proposal was accepted. Many years ago, when I wanted to make cooking videos, he inspired me to study our Colombian foods and recipes.

I thank my very patient husband, Jorge, and my three girls, Isabella, Cristina, and Daniela, for helping me through many years of trial and error!

Book design by Acme Klong Design, Inc.
Cover design by Wanda España / Wee Design Group

For more information, address:
HIPPOCRENE BOOKS, INC.
171 Madison Avenue
New York, NY 10016
www.hippocrenebooks.com

original edition ISBN 0-7818-1025-6

ISBN-13: 978-0-7818-1289-4
ISBN-10: 0-7818-1289-5

Cataloging-in-Publication Data available from the Library of Congress.

Printed in the United States of America.

FSC
www.fsc.org
MIX
Paper from
responsible sources
FSC® C011935

CONTENTS

COLOMBIA

Our country, in the eyes of my 15 year old daughter Isabella Gallo.

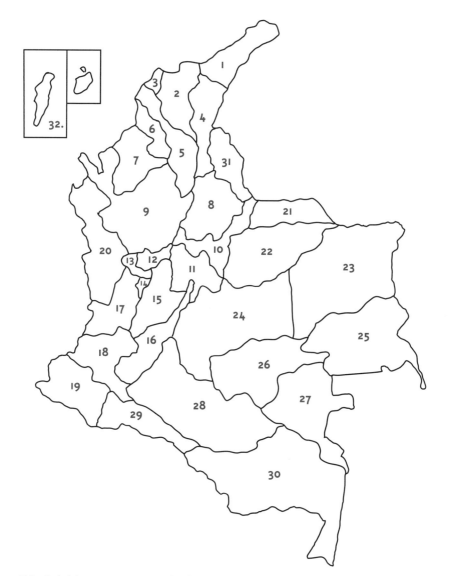

Political Division: Departments of Colombia

1	Guajira	12	Caldas	23	Vichada
2	Magdalena	13	Risaralda	24	Meta
3	Atlántico	14	Quindío	25	Guainía
4	Cesar	15	Tolima	26	Guaviare
5	Bolivar	16	Huila	27	Vaupez
6	Sucre	17	Valle	28	Caquetá
7	Córdoba	18	Cauca	29	Putumayo
8	Santander	19	Nariño	30	Amazonas
9	Antioquia	20	Chocó	31	Norte de Santander
10	Boyacá	21	Arauca	32	San Andrés y Providencia
11	Cundinamarca	22	Casanare		

INTRODUCTION

In *Secrets of Colombian Cooking*, I share with you some of the recipes and memories with which I, and many other Colombians, were brought up. We have hundreds of food preparations from all over the country—some similar, others very different, depending on where we live. I wish to introduce you to the variety, flavor, and delight of many of them.

Colombia's location is one of welcome: we are the first country in the South American continent, formed by the Andes Mountains together with volcanoes, valleys, forests and rivers. We are a spot on this earth with an abundance of resources, surrounded by both the Atlantic and Pacific oceans, with plains, highlands, beaches and deserts, and every sort of land form in between. Three mountain ranges cross the territory: the Oriental, Central, and Occidental *cordilleras*. Colombia is divided into five large areas: the "Zona Andina," which surrounds the Andes Cordillera, is by far the most populated, developed and greatest in economic importance. Santa Fé de Bogotá, the ultramodern capital of the country where our cultural and political organizations are all grouped, lies there. Medellín, the center of the "Paisa" territory, is a very industrialized town with the only subway, or rapid transportation system in the country, as well as the first intelligent building owned by the public services company; it is also the hometown of painter Fernando Botero and many others. Santiago de Cali, the capital of a large and developed agricultural department, hosts most of the country's sugarcane fields on its outskirts, along with refineries; for many years, it hosted the majority of the multinational corporations present in Colombia. Popayán, a historical pathway for the southern incursion in colonial times, has many architectural treasures that include churches and museums. Pasto, a city located at the skirts of the Volcán Galeras, is home to many colonial and archeological sites, including the beautiful Lake La Cocha, where the Andean, Amazonic and Pacific zones meet. The coffee-growing departments, Quindío, Risaralda and Caldas, are jewels of lands filled with hills of coffee plantations, beautiful houses with multicolored flowers and great foods offered on the roadways. Bucaramanga is called the city of the parks because of the perfectly maintained parks it has all over town. Tunja, the Chibcha capital that was later transformed by the colonists into a medieval European town, is a weekend haven for many. Ibagué, my grandmother's hometown, sits on the sides of the Magdalena River and embraces the Park of the Nevados, and many touristic places like Honda and Melgar. Neiva is the capital of the *bambuco* dance and of the department of Huila, which hosts the park of San Agustín and the peaks of Nevado del Huila too. The Andean zone has cooler climates and the majority of the coffee, corn, potatoes and cacao crops as well as fruit and vegetables are cultivated there.

The Caribbean zone, warm in climate year-round, is where I was born. In this region, there is great influence from all over the world since it has been a principal port of entrance for immigrants of all origins. Cartagena de Indias is a major tourist attraction, having the Fortresses and Walled City from the Spanish conquistador times, with many historical monuments, beautiful Islands and great places to stay. Barranquilla, my hometown, is a more industrial city; the warmth of our people brings the whole country here during Carnival season, when the people of all economic and social statuses meet and blend into one and show the rest of the country what sharing in peace really is all about. Santa Marta is a major tourist attraction too because of its beaches, and its closeness to the Sierra Nevada and to the Tayrona Park, both very important archeological and marine sites. La Guajira is a desertic peninsula that comprises Cabo de la Vela, one of the northern most place in the country, a majestic place where you can feel the softness of a white silky sand with the sunsets that bring about a beauty emanating from the perfection of a creator, and the territory of the Wayuu Indian community, which still stands strong in its traditions. Valledupar, the capital of Vallenato music and all their *parrandas* of festive get-togethers, is also the capital of the Cesar Department where many of our cotton and African palm is grown, and where many of our cattle farms are. Sincelejo is the capital of our typical sweets, *bollos* and *suero costeño*, our Colombian crème fraîche. Montería, with its typical Livestock or *Ganadería* Queen and the Mote de Queso, is a cattle raising territory. The Caribbean zone also holds the Islands of San Andres, Providencia and Santa Catalina. Off the mainland, in the midst of the Caribbean Sea, they offer more unusually natural territories, great for those who are looking for peaceful and ecological tourism, sailing, snorkeling and deep sea diving. The Caribbean people are said to be calm, cool and collected.

The Pacific zone is located on the Pacific Ocean and is made up of large extensions of rainforests and hot humid land. In the department of Chocó, many banana and coconuts are grown, and there is great fishing and hunting. Buenaventura, one of the biggest ports of the country, is located here.

The Amazonic and Orinoquía zones are far less developed, more natural territories in which Indian communities still reside. Forests in the Amazon mix with the great Amazon River in the city of Leticia, making it a very special ecological attraction and a wondrous tourist site. Sitting on the mainstream of the giant river, it is a departure point for tours to Indian reservations by boat and through the heavy jungles. The tropical rainforest jungle is home to much fauna and flora, including various kinds of monkeys, tigers, anacondas, tucans and orchids, which create a singular sight. The Amazon department borders Brazil and Perú. Villavicencio and Florencia are the center of great cattle farming plains or *llanos*.

Through our *cordilleras* travel huge rivers that bring abundant life and vegetation to our country. The Magdalena, Cauca and Atrato rivers, the largest ones, parent hundreds of small waterways that cross the land from one end to the other. On the northern part of the country, there is an independent mountain chain called the Sierra Nevada de Santa

Marta. This is an area that is still inhabited by two indigenous communities, the Arhuaco and the Kogi-Malayo, and that has a great ancient city called Ciudad Perdida or the Lost City. Even though it is a recent discovery, the city dates back to 500 B.C.; people can get there in two weeks by foot or helicopter. In my teen years, we spent many weekends in the Sierra Nevada; with no electricity or sewage systems and no cell phones in those years, the times we spent there were completely outdoors. In creeks and streams, and walking through colossal vegetation we dissected tarantulas and other insects for our school projects. Doctor Casas, a family friend, would drive for two hours in his jeep over dirt roads to take us there to spend weekends and take a glance at the highest peak at over 18,000 feet above sea level from where we could see the both Caribbean Sea and the snowy mountain tops. In the Cordillera Central, in the department of Huila, the San Agustin and Tierradentro Park is another outstanding Pre-Colombian archeological site of giant monoliths and stone statues that date back to the first century, representing gods, humans, animals, and showing the advanced civilization of that time. Colombia is a country of great archeological and historical value, as can be seen in the cities of Santa Cruz de Mompox, Cartagena de Indias, and Popayán to name a few.

Our crops are immense in variety, our animals diverse in type, shape, and size. Tropical vegetation covers more than half our territory: our land is in great part natural, untouched forests filled with the color and perfume of native plants and orchids and a rainbow of birds and animals. Carnations, chrysanthemums, dahlias, and roses give Colombia the title of second largest flower exporter in the world. Mango, guava, papaya, palm, and many other fruit trees fill the air with a sweet aroma. Plantations of coffee bushes, bananas, plantains, rice, sugarcane, potatoes, corn, and cacao are few of the hundreds of plants that we grow. Coffee is our principal crop, and we are proud owners of the title to the best coffee in the world: the mild Arabica coffee. We produce the highest quality of coffee, and the second largest quantity of it after Brazil. Coffee is grown high in the Andes, in what we call the *zona cafetera*, a beautiful area that comprises more than three departments that could be called little Switzerland for the beauty and color of the crops, flowers and farms. Rich and intense, yet soft and mild, perfection is reached in every grain of Colombian coffee. Our cultivators handpick each grain of coffee when it is the right time, rich red in color, to be later soaked in cool mountain water. The beans are always checked for quality, guarantying our uniquely high standards. Even though traditionally few foods are prepared with coffee, we start drinking it at an early age. Colombians have no restrictions on coffee drinking for children—I remember as a young child drinking a cup of *café con leche* (coffee with milk) with eggs and fruit as breakfast before going to school. Our black coffee (called *tinto* or "tinted") is a pure, non-sweetened drink with no added flavors or oils, served in 2-ounce cups. *Pintao* or *perico* is what we call *tinto* with just a teaspoon or two of milk.

Bananas are grown on the Pacific and Caribbean coasts. Colombia is the only country to harvest sugarcane year-round, thus having great yields. Corn and cacao beans are staples throughout the basic Colombian diet; our fine chocolates are exported throughout the world; we have excellent baking, drinking, and candy bar varieties.

The gigantic Amazon River hosts the largest of snakes, the pinkest of dolphins, the smallest and most colorful of decorative fish, and the deadliest piranhas. Colombian fauna includes crocodiles, parrots, large Galapagos and Carrey turtles, jaguars, pink flamingos, hundreds of birds including eagles and condors, one of our national symbols, monkeys of many types, and even spectacled bears. In the plain lands there is a lot of cattle ranching, the largest industry in animal farming in Colombia. The dairy business is very industrialized and diverse. Poultry, pork, and sheep are too.

Colombia is a country of celebration and queens. We have festivities for almost every occasion you can think of, both religious and not. Most of the country starts its holidays on New Year's Eve, when some of us burn the old year—a large cloth doll—followed by the Three Kings Day, when candy is given to children. In Cartagena de Indias, Cali, Santa Fé de Bogotá, Medellín, and Manizales, bullfights are also held along parties and city fairs. Carnival is celebrated mainly in Barranquilla during the five days before Ash Wednesday, but celebrations run every Friday starting the first week of January. Holy Week is held with large processions and pageantry in some cities like Popayán, Mompox, and Guamal. We have beauty queens not only for the national and international pageants, but also for coffee, cotton, sugar, barley, *butiffarra*, typical sweets, salt, *cachama* fish, coconut, pinapple and more. We have festivals for sweets and music like the accordion and the Vallenato music festivals. All over the territory, some kind of celebratory event is always taking place, keeping the people connected with their roots and ancestry as well as with their crops and surroundings. Mother's and Father's Day, Love and Friendship Day, and most professions have a day too. The end of the year finishes with the Holy Mary Day, which is beautifully celebrated by of lighting hundreds candles outside of houses and buildings, and Christmas Eve. Young Jesus or El Niño Dios comes during the night and children open their gifts on the morning of December 25.

The cultural richness of the thirty million people of our land is just like the nature of our country. We are a country of differences, not only in traditions, but even in our speech patterns. There are still many Indian reservations who have kept their own languages, while the Spanish-speaking rest of the country is distinguishably different in every region. *Costeños* like me speak very differently from the *Paisas* (my in-laws), or the *Pastusos*, or the many other cultural groups of Colombia. The customs of the people who live near the sea are more relaxed and calm: there is no rush in our lives and we always seem to be thinking of parties, rarely making it on time to places. The Andean zone people are early birds, who work long days and are said to be hardworking and more active. All over the territory, the people change as the land sculpts into their lives different environmental settings and ambience.

We make full use of the bounty our land gives us and thus create very colorful, tasty, and aromatic dishes. Our foods are a mixture of the indigenous cultures entwined with the Spanish, African, and later Asian and American influences. From the Spanish, we gained sugarcane, which happened to sweeten the spices and mixtures native to our soil and those brought to us by Africans. Mixed with sugar, our cacao beans became one of the most popular drinks in our country, hot chocolate. In newer recipes, we find the use of curry and saffron, as well as cumin seeds and cinnamon, and even dishes prepared with Coca-Cola. Deep in the mountains of Nariño you find ginger and chanterelles; the possibilities in our local food supply are almost infinite, and each region does its best to use the products grown on its own land. Food markets in Colombia are a joy to shop in; nowadays, there is nothing you will not find in them, and all is natural, beautiful, and filled with color and taste.

The influence of other cultures is diversely marked in the country. On the Pacific Coast, the cooking is more pure, traditional, with African influence; it includes many fried foods and *masas*. In the Andean region, the Spanish traditions have a more pronounced effect on culinary preparations, whereas in the Caribbean coastal areas, which have had greater trade with the rest of the world, Asian and American customs come through.

Sweets are central to our culture. We celebrate every occasion with dessert; one *dulce* for the Christmas holidays, another one for Easter, the other for birthdays. Whether from the most elegant and sophisticated bakeries or from street vendors, sugary concoctions are imbedded in our souls. Delicacies are prepared at home and sold by vendors on street corners and outside supermarkets, out of wooden boxes or aluminum *poncheras*, wrapped in transparent papers like the colored sugar candy we call *pirulí* and gelatin prepared with real bone marrow named *gelatina de pata*, or in brown paper like the sugarcane toffee candy called *melcochas* or *arropillas*. Even at the beach, we buy sweets from *pailas* on top of lady vendors' heads as they travel smoothly through the salty air, weightless-seeming pictures of beauty and color. The variety of forms and textures is fantastic, ranging from candied fruits like papaya and figs, guava jams and jellies to coconut *cocadas*, cookies, and nougats. We can stop the car and buy cashews, *pandeyucas*, and *galleta griega* or wafer rolled cookies in many stoplights and corners.

Food is essential to Colombians; it brings us together culturally, especially when we are away from our land. Colombians are always looking for traveling friends to bring foods or ingredients that are hard to find. For example, I now live in Panamá, where yuca corn starch is not available, so every time a family member wants to bring me something I ask for *yucarina*. In the United States, it is readily available in Latin American grocery stores and on the Internet. Every time I fly to visit family and friends overseas they want me to cook *deditos de queso*, *pandebonos*, and, especially, *arroz con coco*. As expatriate Colombians, we are constantly finding places that sell our traditional foods like *arepas* and white farmer's cheese; in group conversation we compare the best ones in the market. I usually invite my friends to share afternoon coffee and *pandebonos*, or to evening buffets with miniature *arepas* with crème fraîche and caviar. Food, our ethnic identity, is what gives away each person's hometown. In the variety of foods and ingredients that make up our abundant gastronomy, we distinguish and differentiate our fellow Colombians into groups. *Paisas* are expected to make the best *arepas* and *frisoles*. *Costeños* have to serve the crispiest *deditos* and *sancocho*; *Bogotanos* should prepare the tastiest *ajiaco*; and *Tolimenses* the best *tamales* and *lechona*. We describe characters and personalities along with eating habits, making analogies between the people of a territory and their fare.

Throughout the book, you will find pictures of my family and friends, as well as landscapes of places in Colombia we've been to recently. And, of course, some of the dishes I will show you how to make here. I want you to feel a bit of what the life of a Colombian family is like, and to bring you closer to our hearts. Colombia is a civilization that uses food as social currency; and like the rest of the world, we try to bring up healthy, loving families who care about our country and the future it holds for generations to come.

NOTE: Ingredients and mixtures marked with an asterisk (*) are discussed in the Glossary, starting on page 257.

BREAKFAST FOODS AND SNACKS

Many of these breakfasts and snacks are finger foods sold on the streets of our cities. The vendors and street cooks are always willing to show and talk about their methods of preparation and the stories of their family traditions. It is great to see how many generations of people have survived financially by preparing the same recipe throughout the years and passed their heritage on with great pride and respect.

Arepas of all sizes and types, with and without fillings, slightly sweet and not; breads and cookies of cassava starch; *bollos*, and more, are all part of what make us feel closer to our country, especially when we are far away. Nothing captures our attention more than to run across some of this romanticized fare.

You will find white farmer's cheese in many of these recipes. This cheese is sold from thirty-pound blocks at many supermarkets, loose for people to buy as much as they want, or pre-packaged in the dairy sections. I buy it in three-quarters of a pound vacuum-sealed squares. Also called *queso blanco*, this fresh cow's milk cheese ranges in consistency from soft to very hard, but can be grated in both cases. If yours comes with excess whey or milk residues, discard them. They range from mild to salty. While in Colombia it is sometimes very salty, the cheese packaged to be sold abroad is not; these recipes are adapted to the less salty type, which could be eaten on its own. If you think that the recipes need more salt, add some. In American supermarkets, it is also called Colombian style white cheese and creamy white cheese, and it can be found in Mexican supermarkets too.

*Cuajada** is another variety of white farmer's cheese prepared with fresh, raw, non-pasteurized milk, and served alongside many sweets (see the Sweets chapter, page 178), but also cooked with corn or yuca starch to make some of these snack foods. Another of our most versatile ingredients is corn meal, which comes in yellow or white forms; whether to use yellow or white cornmeal depends on the dish. They can be used interchangeably, but it is the color and the tradition that makes us differentiate them in recipes. Nowadays you can purchase them in many ethnic food stores. It is a very helpful shortcut for the long and tedious recipes for which our elders ground their own.

Cassava starches are characteristic of our quick breads. They come in three types: regular cassava starch or *almidón de yuca* for *pandebonos*, sweet cassava starch or *almidón dulce* for *panderos*, and sour cassava starch or *almidón agrio* for *pandeyucas*. Each is slightly different, even in appearance: the sweet one is a shade of yellow; the regular is more powdery white; and the sour one looks more homemade and has large particles in it. The regular one can be used for both *pandebonos* and *pandeyucas*, but not for *panderos*; for those you need the sweet kind, which can be bought on the Internet or in Colombian markets.

Breakfast foods in small towns differ from every region depending on the climates and the foods available in the close surroundings. In large cities where the influx of people from different zones of the country and chain supermarkets make all foods available, the whole array of breakfast foods are served. For example, in the Caribbean coast *bollos* and sweet fried arepas or egg-filed arepas are very commonly eaten with coffee with milk and farmer's cheese; in the Andean region, ground corn arepas are the most typical type along with hot chocolate and dark coffee. In the Pacific region, *panela* water is very commonly served with sweet corn arepas and the cheese.

The Andean zone is the one with the greatest quantities of side dishes or *parva*. *Parva* are sweet or salty bakery goods, while *mecato* are the foods we would eat to satisfy our souls, which would be like healthful junk food. That area cultivates so much corn that there is where the majority of the corn recipes come from: *arepas* of all styles, *almojábanas, pandequeso, buñuelos, envueltos, tamales, chicha*, are traditionally *paisas; empanaditas, hojaldras, marranitas, pandebonos* and *panderos* from the Cauca, Viejo Caldas and Valle del Cauca region.

I think these are the foods we eat the most in my house because children—and we have three—are always looking for something good to eat. These tasty items satisfy even the hungriest and most finicky of them all.

ALMOJÁBANAS

Cheese and Corn Cakes
Twelve 1½-inch cakes

Did this recipe give me trouble! I think I tried at least twelve different versions before I got this one right. It came from Amparo, a Colombian friend in Panamá. She asked her mother for the recipe, and I adjusted it to be made with white farmer's cheese. It is traditionally made with *cuajada** (fresh, raw non-pasteurized milk cheese, page 178).

½ pound (1¼ cups) grated white farmer's cheese*
½ cup precooked yellow cornmeal*, sifted twice
1 teaspoon sugar
½ teaspoon baking powder
½ teaspoon salt
1 egg
¼ cup milk

Vegetable oil spray or melted butter

1. Preheat the oven to 300°F. Place the cheese, cornmeal, sugar, baking powder, and salt in the food processor and mix for 15 seconds. Add the egg and milk and process 2 minutes more. The mixture will leave the sides of the food processor bowl after 1 minute; continue mixing for the full 2 minutes, until you don't feel or see the cheese, and the mixture is soft.

2. Take 1½ tablespoonfuls of dough and form little balls with your hands.

3. Spray or lightly butter a cookie sheet or mini-cupcake molds, and place the almojábanas there.

4. Place the baking sheets or molds on the upper rack of the oven, and bake for 20 to 25 minutes, or until they are lightly golden.

AREPAS CON HUEVO

Egg-filled Arepas

Twelve 6-inch arepas

From my hometown on the Caribbean coast of Colombia, this is hearty breakfast fare! Eat them on days when you need extra energy. My husband first ate one of these in the streets of Cartagena de Indias, and was so surprised that he had to stand and watch how they got the egg into the *arepa*.

3 cups precooked white cornmeal*
1½ teaspoons salt
3 cups hot tap water
4 cups oil for frying
12 whole eggs

1. In a bowl, mix the cornmeal and salt with a fork. Add the water and mix with your hands for about a minute, or until you have a soft yet firm homogenous mixture; this is the arepa dough. Let it rest uncovered at room temperature for 15 minutes.

2. Divide the dough into 12 equal balls, leaving a small piece of dough aside for use later in the recipe. Lay a piece of plastic wrap on the work surface, place a ball of dough in the center, cover with another piece of plastic, and with a heavy pan or pot cover flatten it until it forms an even round about ⅙-inch thick.

3. Place the oil in a heavy, deep pot, and bring to a temperature of 325°F. Add the arepas one by one so that they don't stick to each other; don't put too many at the time. Cook for 1½ minutes on each side and remove them very carefully with a slotted spoon so they don't crack. They should have puffed up in the oil. Drain over paper towels on a rack with the inflated side up.

4. Take scissors or a knife and cut a 1-inch opening in the edge of the arepa; go all the way in to reach the pocket of air formed on one side of it. Crack a whole egg into a small espresso cup and pour it into the arepa. Close the opening with a piece of uncooked dough, and immediately place in the hot oil again. Fry for 2 more minutes on each side. Repeat with the remaining balls of dough.

5. Drain briefly on paper towels. Serve immediately, very hot.

AREPAS DE CHOCLO

Sweet Corn Arepas
Six 5-inch arepas

You would not believe how good these *arepas* taste just from the list of ingredients. They are not too sweet, they are just perfect. These *arepas* are from the Andean zone of Colombia, where most of the corn is grown. People stop along highways to buy and enjoy these wonderfully moist, slightly sweet and cheesy corn *arepas*. They are filled with cheese, baked in brick ovens, and served with butter.

2⅓ cups fresh corn kernels (from about 2½ large ears of corn)
1 pound (2½ cups) white farmer's cheese*
3 tablespoons *melado* (page 191)
1 teaspoon sugar
¼ teaspoon salt

Oil spray or butter for cooking
Butter for serving

1. Place the corn kernels in a food processor and process for 1 minute. Set aside in a nonreactive bowl.

2. Grate a little less than ½ pound of the cheese (about 1 cup) and add to the bowl of corn together with the melado, sugar, and salt; mix with a fork.

3. Spray a 5-inch nonstick pan with cooking oil, or butter it. Heat over medium heat. Pour in ½ cup of the mixture; flatten it with the back of a spoon to form a pancake. Cover and cook for 4 minutes; uncover, cover with a dessert plate, flip over and slide back into the pan to finish cooking another 4 minutes. (The arepa will be very delicate.) Decrease the heat if the arepas are too dark when you turn them.

4. Slice the rest of the cheese and place on top in the middle of each warm arepa.

5. Serve warm with butter on the side.

AREPAS DE MAÍZ

Yellow or White Corn Arepas

Sixteen 4-inch arepas

These are traditional *arepas* made from dried corn kernels, nowadays prepared that way mostly on farms. They are served with cheese on top, added after cooking. They are cooked on the grills directly over the heat, or on an *asador de arepas**, a special cooking pan that is basically a flat-surfaced pan made of very thin metal, which has over it another very thin metal rack.

You can also form *arepas* with cheese already mixed into the dough. In that case, add about 1 cup (½ pound) of grated white farmer's cheese to the corn after it has come out of the grinder, and before forming the balls.

Maíz peto is what we call the corn that is dried and sold in bags at the market.

2½ cups (1 pound) white or yellow dried corn kernels* (maiz peto)
½ teaspoon butter
¼ teaspoon salt plus more for cooking
White farmer's cheese* for serving
4 tablespoons melted butter

DAY 1

1. Wash the dried corn kernels with plenty of water. Place in a bowl with enough water to cover them, and let sit for 24 hours. This will rehydrate the corn a little.

DAY 2

2. Drain the corn and discard the water.

3. Place the corn in a medium pot or pressure cooker, and add 8 cups of water. If using a regular pot, cover and simmer over medium-low heat for 2½ hours; keep adding water, 1 cup at a time, if it dries out. If using a pressure cooker, cover and cook under pressure on medium heat for about 1 hour. The corn should be very soft; if not, return the pot to the stove and cook 20 minutes more. Let cool, uncover, and drain the corn; you will have about 8 cups of corn.

4. Pass the corn through a *molino** or meat grinder into a bowl. Add the butter and salt; mix well to blend evenly.

5. Form the ground corn mixture into a log; divide it into 16 pieces. Form each piece into a ball.

6. Place the arepa balls between 2 sheets of plastic and with a heavy pan or pot cover, flatten to the thickness you desire, from ¼ to ½ inch.

7. To cook the arepas, place them on a rack directly over a very low flame and cook about 5 minutes, until they look dry on the outside; brush melted butter and sprinkle salt, turn and cook 5 minutes more on the other side.

8. Serve with white farmer's cheese.

AREPAS DE QUESO

Cheese Arepas
Four 6-inch arepas

Nowadays these are the *arepas* made in homes in the cities, because they are much easier to prepare for everyday breakfasts. These are what I give my daughters Daniela and Cristina for breakfast.

⅔ cup precooked white cornmeal*
⅔ cup warm water
4 teaspoons butter, soft
1 teaspoon salt
½ pound white farmer's cheese, * grated (about 1⅓ cups)
Oil or butter for cooking

1. Place the cornmeal, water, butter and salt in a bowl; mix with your hands for about 30 seconds until it has taken the consistency of a paste. Let it rest 5 minutes. Knead with your hands about 1 more minute until a ball of dough forms.

2. Make an indentation in the ball with your hand, add the cheese, and knead 1 minute more. Divide and form into 4 small balls.

3. Place the balls between 2 sheets of plastic and with a heavy pan or pot cover flatten to the thickness you desire, from ¼ to ½ inch.

TO COOK ON A RACK:
4. Place an oiled rack on a flat pan over medium heat. When the rack is hot, put the arepas on it. Cook them about 2 minutes on each side, until they are golden brown. Serve immediately.

TO COOK IN A SAUTÉ PAN:
4. Melt ¼ teaspoon of butter in a pan set over medium heat. Place the arepas in the pan, and cook about 2 minutes on each side until they have a golden color.

NOTE: For an hors d'oeuvre, make mini-arepas, about 1 inch in diameter, and serve them with sour cream and caviar. A total delicacy!

AREPAS DULCES CON ANIS

Sweet Arepas with Aniseed
1 dozen to fourteen 6-inch arepas

These are also from the Atlantic coast, and are similar to the Egg-filled Arepas (page 10), but with a little sugar and no egg. Delicious with hot chocolate or *café con leche*—that is how we had them before school as children.

3 cups precooked white cornmeal*
1 tablespoon sugar
1½ teaspoons salt
3 cups hot tap water
1 teaspoon anise seeds, crushed
4 cups oil for frying

1. Place the cornmeal, sugar and salt in a bowl and mix with a fork. Add the water and anise seeds, and mix with your hands for about 1 minute, or until you have a soft homogenous mixture.

2. Divide into 12 to 14 equal balls of dough.

3. Place the balls between 2 sheets of plastic and with a heavy pan or pot cover flatten to ¼ inch.

4. In a deep heavy pot, heat the oil to 325°F. Add the arepas one by one so that they don't stick to each other.

5. Cook about 2 to 3 minutes on each side. Remove them from the pot with a slotted spoon and drain over paper towels. They should look golden brown.

6. Serve immediately.

BOLLOS DE MAZORCA

Mazorca Cakes

4 cakes

These wrapped corn cakes are sold on the streets of many cities. You can buy them warm in the mornings outside the doors of supermarkets, hundreds of them in large aluminum pans, sold for just dimes. Serve them warm, spread with butter, and cheese on the side. They are normally cooked in huge *calderos** over log fires, in batches of twenty-five. About fifty large ears of corn yield twenty to twenty-five *bollos*.

8 cups fresh corn kernels (from 6-8 large ears of corn)

1 tablespoon sugar

1 teaspoon salt

Aluminum foil strips or corn husks for cooking

Butter and white farmer's cheese* for serving

1. Pass the raw corn kernels through the finest disc of a *molino** or meat grinder into a bowl. You will get about 2 cups of a smooth paste.

2. Add the sugar and salt, and mix well with a fork or wooden spoon.

3. Cut 8- by 6-inch aluminum foil strips, or arrange corn husks in the palm of your hand. Place one-quarter of the corn mixture (½ cup) on each strip. Wrap as you would an envelope, folding in the top and bottom; use more than one husk if necessary to complete the task. Roll into log forms, and cover completely with the aluminum foil. Seal the foil carefully before rolling them to prevent leakage of water into the bollos or of the corn mixture into the cooking water.

4. Place the bollos standing up in the bottom of a 2-quart pot. Tie all the bollos together to keep them standing. They should fit tightly. Pour in enough boiling water to completely cover all the bollos and simmer, covered, for 45 minutes to an hour. They should feel set or hard to the touch.

5. Let rest for 5 minutes before serving. Peel the foil off and serve with butter and white farmer's cheese on the side.

BOLLO DE YUCA

Cassava Cakes
4 cakes

Bollos de Yuca are sweet, with the aroma of aniseeds and coconut. They are eaten alone or with *Chorizos* (page 61) and *Butifarras* (page 56). These are not sold as widely as *Bollos de Mazorca* (page 15), but I believe they are easier to prepare, so go ahead and try them!

2½ pounds peeled yuca*
or cassava
1 teaspoon salt
1 teaspoon anise seeds,
ground
¼ cup fresh unsweetened
grated coconut (optional)

Oil for shaping,
if necessary

1. Place the yuca or cassava in a medium pot and cover with water. Simmer for 15 minutes. The tip of a knife should enter easily about ¼ of the way into the yuca, which should be just a little under-cooked. Remove from the pot, drain, and set aside. Cool for 10 minutes.

2. Pass the yuca through a *molino** or meat grinder into a bowl.

3. Add the salt, anise seeds, and coconut, if using. Divide the mixture into 4 portions of approximately ¾ cup each; add some oil to your hands if the dough feels hard to manage.

4. Cut 8- by 6-inch aluminum foil strips, or arrange corn husks in the palm of your hand. Place one portion of the yuca mixture (¾ cup) on each strip. Wrap as you would an envelope, folding in the top and bottom; use more than one husk if necessary to complete the task. Roll into log forms, and cover complete-ly with the aluminum foil. Seal the foil carefully before rolling them to prevent leakage of water into the bollos or of the corn mixture into the cooking water.

5. Place the bollos standing up in the bottom of a 2-quart pot. Tie all the bollos together to keep them standing. They should fit tightly. Pour in enough boiling water to completely cover all the bollos and simmer, covered, for 45 minutes to an hour. They should feel set or hard to the touch.

6. Let rest for 5 minutes before serving. Peel the foil off and serve with Chorizos or Butifarras.

BOLLO LIMPIO

White Corn Cakes
6 cakes

These bland *bollos* are served with strong tasting foods like *Chorizos* (page 61) and *Butifarras* (page 56).

2½ cups (1¼ pounds or 2 large cobs) dried white corn kernels*
¼ pound (⅔ cup) grated white farmer's cheese*
½ cup butter
1 teaspoon salt
Oil for shaping, if necessary

Aluminum foil strips or corn husks for cooking

DAY 1

1. Wash the dried corn kernels with plenty of water. Place in a bowl with enough water to cover them for 24 hours. This will rehydrate the corn a little.

DAY 2

2. Drain the corn and discard the water.

3. Place the corn in a medium pot or pressure cooker, and add 8 cups of water. If using a regular pot, cover and simmer over medium-low heat for 2½ hours; keep adding water, 1 cup at a time, if it dries out. If using a pressure cooker, cover and cook under pressure on medium heat for about 1 hour. The corn should be very soft; if not, return the pot to the stove and cook 20 minutes more. Let cool, uncover, and drain the corn; you will have about 8 cups of corn.

4. Pass the corn through a *molino** or meat grinder into a bowl. Add the cheese, butter and salt; mix well to blend evenly.

5. Divide the mixture into 6 portions of approximately ¾ cup each; add some oil to your hands if the dough feels hard to manage.

6. Cut 8- by 6-inch aluminum foil strips, or arrange corn husks in the palm of your hand. Place one portion of the corn mixture (¾ cup) on each strip. Wrap as you would an envelope, folding in the top and bottom; use more than one husk if necessary to complete the task. Roll into log forms, and cover completely with the aluminum foil. Seal the foil carefully before rolling them to prevent leakage of water into the bollos or of the corn mixture into the cooking water.

7. Place the bollos standing up in the bottom of a 2-quart pot. Tie all the bollos together to keep them standing. They should fit tightly. Pour in enough boiling water to completely cover all the bollos and simmer, covered, for 20 to 30 minutes. They should feel set or hard to the touch.

8. Let rest for 5 minutes before serving. Peel the foil off and serve with Chorizos or Butifarras.

BUÑUELOS DE LA TÍA ISABELITA

Tia Isabelita's Buñuelos

30 large 1½-inch buñuelos, 2-inch finished size

Buñuelos are a traditional food served to friends and family who come to pray the Novenas to the Virgin Mary during the Christmas holidays, from December 15 to 24. In many of the central departments in Colombia, we serve them with *Hojaldras* (page 26) and *Natilla* (page 192). You can buy them in bakeries all around the country. These *buñuelos* are the original ones prepared with a yellow cornstarch called *harina de maiz capio*, which is an indigenous corn grown from the family of the yellow corn with large kernels and cob. You can also prepare them with Maizena or regular cornstarch. These *buñuelos* are so easy because you can prepare them ahead of time and serve them at room temperature. When you fry your *buñuelos*, they should fit loosely because they expand as they cook. This way they will turn themselves and cook evenly on all sides.

2 cups (¾ pound) very finely grated white farmer's cheese*
¼ cup capio corn flour or cornstarch
1 tablespoon sugar
¼ teaspoon salt
1 egg
4 cups oil for frying

1. Place the cheese in a large bowl.

2. Add the cornstarch, sugar, salt and egg and mix well with your hands. Form into about 30 1½-inch balls. The mixture is so soft that it feels like making balls out of cotton.

3. In a deep heavy pot, heat the oil to 325°F. To test the temperature of the oil in a traditional way we do the following: Form a ½-inch ball of masa and place it in the oil. It should fall to the bottom of the oil and float back up after 30 seconds. If it floats immediately, lower the heat of the oil. Place about 6 to 8 buñuelos at a time in the oil, decrease the heat to low, about 300°F for 5 minutes, cover and turn the heat off, leave covered for 5 minutes. They will grow, watch carefully!

4. Uncover and turn the heat up again to 350°F and keep cooking for 5 minutes more, turning if they don't turn themselves.

5. Remove from the oil and drain over paper towels.

6. Serve immediately, or store in airtight containers.

BUÑUELOS DE MAÍZ OR MASITAS

Corn Fritters
16 masitas

Even though these are also called *buñuelos*, they are different from the ones in the previous recipe. These are sweet tasting corn fritters with a bit of sugar mixed in; they are served as snacks or as side dishes. In some parts of the country, they add cheese to the mixture; mix with a fork after blending the corn, egg, sugar, and salt and fry in the same manner.

3 cups fresh corn kernels (about 3 large ears)
1 egg
3 tablespoons sugar
¾ teaspoon salt
¼ pound (½ cup) finely shredded white farmer's cheese* (optional)
2 tablespoons minced scallion (optional)
2 cups oil for frying

1. Place the corn kernels, egg, sugar, and salt in a blender and puree to a homogenous but rough consistency. Place in a bowl.

2. Add the cheese and scallion, if using, and mix with a fork.

3. In a deep heavy pot, heat the oil to 350°F. Drop tablespoonfuls of mixture into the oil; do not let them touch. Fry until lightly golden (about 20 seconds); turn and fry on the other side.

4. Remove with a slotted spoon and drain well over paper towels.

5. Serve warm.

DEDITOS DE QUESO

Cheese Fingers
Twelve 4-inch-long deditos

You could almost say that *deditos* are the national party snack of Colombia! These are also great for lunch boxes; in schools and cafeterias all over the country, they sell *deditos* in large sizes for kids to have as a mid-morning snack or even lunch. Just make sure they have plenty to take. In this recipe, I have made extra dough; the first time you make *deditos* you will probably use it all up and as you become and expert you will probably make the dough thinner and have some leftover dough.

2 cups flour, plus extra for rolling
2 teaspoons sugar
1½ teaspoons baking powder
1 teaspoon salt
4 tablespoons butter
⅓ cup ice water
1 egg white or yolk, lightly beaten, to brush the dough
10 ounces white farmer's cheese*
Oil for frying

1. Place the flour, sugar, baking powder, and salt in a food processor and mix for 10 seconds.

2. Add the butter and mix 10 seconds more.

3. Add the ice water and mix 30 seconds more or until the mixture leaves the sides of the bowl and forms a ball.

4. Wrap in plastic and refrigerate 30 to 45 minutes to rest. This resting time will let you roll the dough very thin with little resistance.

5. Cut the cheese into sticks about ⅓ by ⅓ by 4 inches.

6. Take the ball out of the refrigerator. Sprinkle some flour over the work surface. With a rolling pin, roll the dough out to a rectangle about 16 by 12 inches. Cut into 1-inch wide strips, and brush the dough with egg.

7. Wrap each strip around each piece of cheese, and carefully press on the ends so that they are well sealed. When you finish, roll each stick between your hands to be sure they are well sealed. At this point, you can place them on a baking sheet and set them in the freezer. Once they are complelety frozen, save them in plastic bags and fry them frozen.

8. In a heavy deep pan, heat the oil to 350°F degrees. Carefully drop the deditos into the oil one by one, so that they don't stick together. Fry for 30 to 40 seconds on each side or until golden.

9. Remove from the oil with a slotted spoon and place on paper towels to drain. Serve immediately.

ENVUELTOS DE MAZORCA

Corn Wraps
8 to 12 wraps

These corn cakes are like the *Bollos de Mazorca* (page 15) of the center of the country, Cundinamarca, where our capital is. Although they differ in ingredients and cooking procedure, they are similar in form and taste. This is another recipe from my friend Amparo in Panamá.

Kernels from 12 – 16 large ears of corn, about 16 cups
½ pound (1¼ cup) grated white farmer's cheese*
8 tablespoons butter
2 tablespoons Aguardiente* or aniseed liqueur
2 tablespoons sugar
1 tablespoon vanilla extract
1 tablespoon baking powder
1 pinch salt

Aluminum foil strips or corn husks for cooking

1. Pass the raw corn kernels through the finest disc of a *molino** or meat grinder, into a bowl. You will get about 4 cups total of a smooth paste of milled corn.

2. Add the cheese, butter, Aguardiente, sugar, vanilla, baking powder, and salt, and mix well with a fork or wooden spoon.

3. Divide the mixture in 8 to 12 portions, about ½ cup each.

4. Traditionally, these are cooked in fresh corn husks. You can also prepare them in foil. Cut 8- by 6-inch strips of aluminum foil. Place one portion of the corn mixture (½ cup) on each strip. Wrap as you would an envelope, folding in the top and bottom; use more than one husk if necessary to complete the task. Roll into log forms, and cover completely with the aluminum foil. (If using corn husks, tie with string.) Seal the foil carefully before rolling them to prevent leakage of water into the cakes or of the corn mixture into the cooking water.

5. Pour in the bottom of a large stockpot enough water to cover to a depth of 1 inch. Place a rack over the water; place the wrapped cakes on the rack standing up. They will hold each other upright. Simmer over low heat, covered, for 2 hours. Check every so often to make sure the water has not evaporated out, and add more if necessary.

6. Let rest for 5 minutes before serving. Peel and serve.

EMPANADITAS DE CARNE

Meat Turnovers
26 turnovers

These *empanadas* are round in shape and fried; sold around the cities in bakeries and *tiendas* (home mini-markets). They are generally found in glass cases or stands that keep them warm. We used to sell many of these to schools and universities when I had a bakery called Honey in Barranquilla.

DOUGH
2 cups flour, plus extra for rolling
1½ teaspoons sugar
1½ teaspoons baking powder
1 teaspoon salt
¼ cup butter
½ cup ice water
1 egg yolk for brushing border, beaten
2 cups oil for frying

1. Place the flour, sugar, baking powder and salt in the food processor and mix for 10 seconds. Add the butter and mix 10 seconds more. Add the ice water and mix 30 seconds more, or until a ball is formed which separates from the sides of the bowl.

2. Place in a bowl, cover, and refrigerate 30 to 45 minutes.

3. While the dough is chilling, MAKE THE FILLING: In a heavy sauté pan, over medium-high heat, heat the oil. Add the green onion, carrot, red pepper, scallions, celery, cilantro, bouillon cube, pepper, Adobo, cumin, garlic and salt, and sauté over medium-low heat for 15 minutes. Stir the mixture occasionally so it doesn't burn.

4. Add the meat and cook 5 minutes, stirring. Add the broth and potatoes and cook 15 to 20 minutes more or until the potatoes are soft and the broth has evaporated into the meat mixture.

5. Set aside to cool before filling the empanaditas.

6. Take the ball of dough out of the refrigerator and divide in half. Sprinkle the work surface with some flour, and roll the dough into two 9x15-inch rectangles.

7. Cut about thirteen 3-inch circles from each rectangle. Place 2 tablespoons of filling on one side of each circle. Moisten the borders of the circles with egg yolk. Fold the circles in half to cover the filling with the dough, and close by pressing the edges together so that they are well-sealed and the filling doesn't ooze out.

8. In a heavy deep pot, heat the oil to 325°F and fry the empanaditas for 3 minutes on each side. Take out with a slotted spoon and drain on paper towels. Serve hot.

NOTE: Toasted whole cumin seeds give an aroma that is hard to beat.

MEAT FILLING

- ¼ cup oil
- ½ cup minced green onion*
- ½ cup grated carrot
- ½ cup diced red pepper
- ¼ cup minced scallions
- ¼ cup diced celery
- ¼ cup minced cilantro
- 1 beef bouillon cube
- ¼ teaspoon pepper
- ¼ teaspoon Adobo* seasoning
- ¼ teaspoon whole cumin* seed, toasted
- 2 cloves garlic, minced
- 1 teaspoon salt
- ½ pound ground meat
- 2 cups beef broth
- 2 cups diced potatoes

EMPANADITAS VALLUNAS

Beef and Pork Turnovers
Ninety 2-inch empanadas

I have in my home a person who can eat more *empanadas* than anyone else in the world: my husband. We used to sit beside the pool at the club in his hometown of Cali, and order so many *empanadas* they even prepared the *ají* especially for him. They are a staple in his diet on weekends. These *empanadas* can be served with any of the *ajíes* from the Salsas and Sauces chapter (page 153) as well as with lime wedges. They are sold frozen in supermarkets in miniature one-inch *empanadas* for parties, and regular two-inch *empanadas* to be served as snacks, sent in lunchboxes, or served at lunch or dinner.

Even though the *masa* or dough for these *empanadas* is rarely used with any other filling, my daughter has them fried flat (with no filling) to be served as chips.

HOGAO

2 tablespoons oil

1¾ cups minced green onion*

1½ cups peeled and diced tomatoes

3 tablespoons minced garlic

½ teaspoon salt

½ teaspoon ground cumin*

¼ teaspoon color* or turmeric

4 tablespoons minced cilantro

1. **MAKE THE HOGAO:** In a medium sauté pan over medium-low heat, place the oil, green onion, tomatoes, garlic, salt, cumin, and color. Cook for 15 to 20 minutes, until the onion flavor has completely blended in. Remove from the heat and add the cilantro. Set aside.

2. While the hogao is cooking, **START THE FILLING:** Combine the pork, beef, salt, pepper, cumin and color in a bowl; set aside for 10 minutes.

3. In a medium pressure cooker, place 3 cups of water, the onion, garlic, bouillon cube and seasoned meats. Cover and cook over medium-low heat for 30 minutes. Let cool to release the steam, and uncover. Remove the meats, leaving the cooking liquid in the pot; chop the meats as small as you can. Add to the hogao.

4. Add the potatoes to the meat-cooking liquid, cover, and cook without pressure for 20 minutes. The potatoes will have overcooked and some of them will look mashed. That is the way it is supposed to be. Add the potatoes to the meats and hogao mixture.

5. While the meats are cooking, **MAKE THE DOUGH:** Place the cornmeal in a large bowl. Add the water, and mix until all the flour is moistened. Set aside for 5 minutes. Add the oil and salt, and mix with your hands for 1 minute, then form into a ball or log and place into a large 5- to 7-quart *caldero** or heavy pot. Cook over medium heat for 10 minutes turning continuously. Remove from the pot and set aside to rest uncovered at room temperature for 10 minutes.

6. Divide the dough into about 54 tablespoonfuls; roll each portion into a ball.

7. Place the balls of dough between two pieces of plastic. With the tips of your fingers or a flat pot cover, flatten to ⅛ inch. Remove the top plastic and place about ½ tablespoon of filling in the center of the flattened dough. Holding the plastic underneath, fold over the dough to form a half-moon shape, and press the edges of the dough together with a small coffee cup to seal. Repeat until you have flattened, filled, folded, and sealed all the dough.

8. Heat the oil in a heavy, deep pot, to 350° to 375° F. Deep fry the empanadas a few at a time in the hot oil for 2 to 3 minutes, moving them around in the oil as they fry, for an even distribution of the heat. They should be crunchy and hard on the outside. Remove from the oil with a slotted spoon and drain over paper towels. Repeat until all empanadas have been cooked and drained.

9. Serve with any of the *ajíes* in this book (pages 155 to 162) and lime wedges.

NOTE: Fry each batch with a smallish (1-inch) piece of carrot in the oil. Grandma said it keeps the empanadas from coming out greasy.

GUISO OR FILLING
1 pound pork,
  cut in ½-inch dice
1 pound beef skirt steak,
  cut in ½-inch dice
½ teaspoon salt
¼ teaspoon pepper
¼ teaspoon cumin*
¼ teaspoon color* or
  turmeric
1 small onion, cut in ½
3 cloves garlic
1 beef bouillon cube
1¾ cups peeled, diced
  russet potatoes, ½-inch
  dice
2¾ cups peeled, diced
  yellow or Yukon gold
  potatoes, ½-inch dice

**MASA* OR DOUGH FOR
EMPANADAS**
4 cups precooked yellow
  cornmeal*
5 cups hot tap water
6 tablespoons oil
1 tablespoon salt
2 quarts oil for frying
Ají and lime wedges, for
  serving

HOJALDRAS DE LA
TIA ISABELITA

Tia Isabelita's Flour Pastries
48 pastries

> *Hojaldras* are another Christmas holiday specialty. Nowadays you can buy them in supermarkets ready to fry, but I believe that they are so easy to make it'd be a shame not to prepare them myself. They are really worthwhile. I prepared these with my daughter Isabella at her great aunt Isabelita's house in Santa Fé de Bogotá, and I think we ate half of the platter. They are crunchy, tender, and flaky, sweet and light, and you can't get enough of them.

2 cups flour, plus extra for rolling
½ teaspoon salt
1 tablespoon sugar
2 tablespoons butter
6 tablespoons orange juice
2 cups oil for frying
½ cup powdered sugar for sprinkling

1. In the bowl of a food processor, place the flour, salt, and sugar and process for 10 seconds. Add the butter and process 20 seconds. Add the orange juice and 2 tablespoons of water, and process 15 seconds. If the dough does not form a ball and separate from the sides of the processor, then add another tablespoon of water, and process until the dough forms a ball. Remove the dough from the bowl and wrap in plastic. Let rest for 15 to 30 minutes.

2. Sprinkle flour lighly on the work surface. Remove the dough from the plastic and sprinkle with more flour if you feel it is a little sticky. Roll with a rolling pin to ¼ inch thickness and cut into 1-inch-wide strips. Cut again crosswise into 1-inch diamond shapes. Place all the 1-inch diamond-cut pieces on the side, and roll each one to ⅛ inch thick. Don't worry, they won't stick to the table; just peel them off the counter and fry.

3. In a heavy, deep pot over medium heat bring the oil to a temperature of 350°F, add the pieces of dough a few at a time and deep fry for 20 to 30 seconds per side.

4. Remove from the oil with a slotted spoon and drain on paper towels.

5. Sprinkle with the powdered sugar and serve immediately.

NOTE: You can keep them for a couple of days in airtight tins.

MARRANITAS O PUERQUITAS *Piglets*

Marranitas are typical from the Valle del Cauca region of the Pacific zone of Colombia. They are fried green plantains filled with *Chicharrones* (page 60), and refried into crispy balls. When I asked my friend Claudia from Tentenpié Restaurant in Cali the secret to hers being so crispy, she gave me this recipe, which dips them into chicken and garlic stock right before the second deep fry. Try it; it also helps seal them to a really round finish. These *marranitas* are great for parties, and can be stuffed with chicken and other surprise fillings.

½ recipe of Chicharrones (page 60)
8 green plantains*
½ chicken bouillon cube
3 cloves garlic, mashed
1 teaspoon salt
Oil for frying

1. Prepare the chicharrones and cut them into ¼-inch dice.

2. Cut the ends off the plantains and peel. Cut into 3-inch chunks.

3. Place 1 cup of water in a shallow, microwaveable bowl and heat on high for 1 minute. Add the bouillon cube, garlic, and salt. Mix and set aside.

4. In a heavy, deep pot over medium heat, bring the oil to a temperature of 300°F, add the pieces of plantains and fry 10 to 12 minutes. (If the oil doesn't cover the pieces, fry for 6 minutes, turn and fry for 6 minutes more.) Remove the plantains from the oil with a slotted spoon. Increase the heat of the oil to 350°F.

5. Place a piece of plastic wrap on the work surface; put a piece of plantain on it and cover with another piece of plastic. With a heavy, flat-bottomed pot or a meat pounder, press the pieces of plantain until they become very thin (¼-inch) and flat. Dip each thin slice of plantain in the garlic water for a couple of seconds; place it in the palm of your hand; top with some chicharrón bits, and close your hand to form a ball. Press to make the plantain close tightly on itself. If it is a little dry and hard to close, sprinkle with some of the garlic water to help you out.

6. Fry again in the same oil at 350°F for 4 minutes total. Take out with a slotted spoon and drain on paper towels. Sprinkle with more salt, if desired.

7. Serve hot.

SALCHICHITAS EN COCA-COLA

Wieners in Coke
24 pieces

These small appetizers are normally prepared with the party-size wieners that are sold in Colombia (like U.S. cocktail franks, not canned Vienna sausages). They can be prepared with regular hot dogs; just cut them in half before crisscrossing the ends. This is a typical Caribbean coast dish; we like to mix sweet and sour flavors in many of our dishes.

**12 hotdogs (wieners) or
24 "cocktail franks"
12 cups (3 quarts)
Coca-Cola**

1. If using full-size hot dogs, peel and cut wieners in half to yield 2 small wieners. Crisscross cut the ends of the cocktail franks or the hot dog halves.

2. In a medium, heavy pot or *caldero**, place the wieners and the Coca-Cola. Boil over medium-high heat for about 30 to 45 minutes, until the Coke has reduced to a dark caramel, and the wieners have opened up at the ends.

3. Serve.

PANDEBONO

Originally from the Valle del Cauca, these are my favorite food in the world. I learned to eat them while living in Cali, the city where all my children were born. Every afternoon I would have them for my afternoon snack. With my friend Connie from Barranquilla, I would visit every place where they sold *pandebonos* to buy only the best.

¾ pound (2 cups) finely grated white farmer's cheese*
½ cup cassava starch, yuca flour, or yucarina*
2 tablespoons precooked yellow cornmeal*
2 teaspoons sugar
1 teaspoon salt
1 egg
Vegetable oil spray or butter for the baking pan

1. Place the cheese, cassava starch, cornmeal, sugar, and salt in the food processor and mix 15 seconds. Add the egg and process 2 minutes more. The mixture will leave the sides of the food processor after 1 minute; continue mixing until you don't feel or see the cheese and the mixture is soft.

2. Take dough by tablespoonfuls and form with your hands into little balls.

3. Preheat the oven to 475°F. Spray or lightly butter a baking sheet or mini-cupcake mold, and place the pandebonos there.

4. Place the baking sheets or molds on the upper rack in the oven, close the door and immediately lower the temperature to 425°F. Bake for 10 to 15 minutes, or until the bottom is golden. (If they are getting too dark on the bottom, place a second sheet underneath.)

5. Serve warm from the oven.

PANDEROS

Panderos are cookies prepared with *almidón dulce** (sweet cassava starch or yuca flour). Originally from the Valle del Cauca region, they are sold by the highways there, in the Viejo Caldas area of the country, and the rest of the Andean highlands.

1³/₄ cups sweet cassava starch*
¹/₃ cup sugar
¹/₄ cup grated panela*
1 teaspoon baking powder
¹/₈ teaspoon salt
1 egg
2 tablespoons Aguardiente* or aniseed liqueur
4 tablespoons lard, shortening, or butter, plus extra for greasing the baking sheet
Extra starch or flour for rolling

1. Preheat the oven to 375°F. Place the starch, sugar, panela, baking powder, and salt in the food processor and mix for 10 seconds. Add the egg, Aguardiente, and the fat of your choice, and process for 2 minutes.

2. Remove the dough from the processor and place on a work surface sprinkled with starch or flour. The dough will look very shiny; if you have trouble rolling it, add 1 tablespoon more starch and mix by hand.

3. Turn 2 or 3 times until you have formed a log. Cut into 4 pieces and roll each one into a log 1 inch wide by 10 inches long. Cut into 1-inch squares and mark each cookie with a fork pressing horizontally.

4. Butter a baking sheet and place the cookies on it. Bake for 15 minutes. The cookies will look pale on top and lightly golden on the bottom.

5. Let cool. Serve or store in airtight tins.

PANDEYUCA

Pandeyucas are airy, hollow balls of yuca or cassava starch, mixed with lots of cheese and baked in a very hot oven to puff up. They are sold in many bakeries, but only a few can make them really well. On the coast, they are sold in a miniature one-inch size, baked so close to one another that they stick together and form strands. Packed into small plastic bags, they are sold by the dozen in the cities. These tiny ones are sold completely baked to a dry and toasted chip-like consistency. In bakeries in the innermost parts of the country, they are baked into three-inch round large *pandeyucas*; these are sold soft on the outside but will harden after they cool completely. These great snacks are best when eaten right out of the oven. They should be light golden and very airy on the inside.

¾ pound (2 cups) grated white farmer's cheese*
1 cup almidón de yuca agrio* (sour cassava starch)
1½ teaspoons baking powder
1 teaspoon salt
1 egg
Butter, for preparing the baking sheet

1. Preheat the oven to 425°F.

2. Place the cheese, starch, baking powder, and salt in the food processor and mix for 10 seconds. Add the egg and process for 3 minutes or until the mixture forms a ball of dough.

3. Take dough by tablespoonfuls and form with your hands into little balls. Place on buttered baking sheets. Bake for 20 to 25 minutes.

4. Serve immediately.

SOUPS

Soups are a staple in the Colombian diet. Every single department of the country has its own *sancocho* or soup dish specialty. The Antioqueños prepare their *sancochos* with beans, the Costeños with meat, pork and chicken, the Vallunos with free range hens and the Amazonian, Pacific and Caribbeans with fish and sometimes coconut milk.

We have hot soups even when it's close to 90°F—we love soups. Many of the Colombian celebrations are shared with *sancochos* and other heart-warming concoctions. The word *sancocho* comes from *sancochar*, which means to cook with some water or for a long time or parboil. Traditionally prepared over wood or coal stoves in huge pots that would only fit a restaurant-size stove top, *sancochos* contain many ingredients and are cooked in the gardens or patios where people gather to socialize and share with family and friends while they cook; they bring wonderful memories to many brothers and sisters around the world.

Soups are different depending on the area of the country, and even some that share similar names are prepared differently, depending where you are. In the Pacific region, *sancochos* are lighter soups that include broth and *seco* or dry foods: chicken, corn, yuca* and rice. The broth and the seco are served and eaten on separate plates. In the Atlantic region, *sancochos* are heartier and prepared with more than one meat. When served, meats and tubers are removed from the pot and placed in platters separately; each person cuts them into bite-size pieces and places them back into his or her individual soup. In the Caribbean coast, fish soups are prepared with lighter consistency than in the Pacific, where thicker stews are more common. In the Andean region, where the climates are colder, soups resemble stews and are prepared with potatoes and corn, and smaller quantities of beef.

The *sancochos* prepared with *gallina* are the ones from Valle del Cauca, Caquetá, Putumayo and Vichada, Guaviare, and Quindío. The beef-only *sancochos* are prepared mainly in the departments of Cauca, where they are served with *ají de maní*, and Antioquia, where they are served with *arepas*. Other departments that have different *sancochos* are Arauca, with the armadillo *sancocho*; the Caribbean departments that have many types prepared with pork and chicken, *guandú* beans, and fish *sancochos* with *bocachico* and *sábalo*, cooks in Risaralda serve three meats *sancochos*; in Cesar they cook goat *sancocho*, three meats, ribs, and *parranda vallenata sancocho*; in Caldas, they cook the whole head of a cow and call it *sancocho de cancana*, while in Casanare they prepare duck *sancocho*. In Chocó, the dish contains beef, smoked beef with cheese, or fish; the typical *sancocho* in Córdoba contains *bocachico*, a fish, and in Huila it contains hen and types of fish; and Santander has *sancocho ocañero*.

A sampler of soups from around the country would comprise *sopa de frijol* or bean soup from Antioquia; *sopa de guandú* or black-eyed pea soup from the Caribbean; *sopa de Indios*, a broth with cheese dumplings wrapped in cabbage, and *sopa seca*, our version of onion soup from Boyacá; *sopa de tortilla, carantanta* and *envueltos* from the Cauca and Valle departments; *sopa de cuchas* or onion soup from el Huila; corn soups from various departments, including Huila, Antioquia, Nariño and Norte de Santander; *ajiaco* or chicken soup and *sopa de pan* or potato and egg soup from Cundinamarca; *green plantain soup* from Risaralda; and *mondongo* or tripe soup from Sucre and Antioquia.

These soups are mostly made up of what we call ribs, not necessarily the long baby back ribs you imagine, but the ribcage center bones with the meaty and fatty tissues; when cooked for a long time, they become very tender and gelatinous and give the stocks great flavor, consistency, and color. Potatoes, yucas*, and plantains* give our soups the body and texture we enjoy so much. In some parts of Colombia, such as the coast, we add rice and lime juice to the soup right before eating it. In the Andean parts of the country, they serve and eat stock separately from the meats, roots, avocado and rice, without lime juice. On the coast too, we add sweet plantains to our soup; the plantain can be cooked in the soup or in another pot to keep it from sweetening the potage, and be later added to the serving platter at the table. Cilantro is served with almost all the soups throughout the country.

I hope you can get over the shock of having to buy so many ingredients, and enjoy preparing some of these succulent soups. Their preparation with a group of friend or family can be really exciting. And sitting down to eat and talk and remember, even more so.

AJIACO BOGOTANO
Chicken and Potato Soup
10 to 12 servings

This soup is a heartwarming concoction that everybody just loves. It is a chicken and potato soup flavored with an herb called *guascas**. It is typical of the country's capital city of Santa Fé de Bogotá and of the department of Cundinamarca. This is what my children have their grandmother prepare for them when we visit.

1 pound beef ribs or bones

6 whole ears of corns

1 tablespoon salt plus 1 teaspoon salt

¼ teaspoon pepper

4 whole chicken breasts, with excess fat and skin removed

2 whole green onions*

¼ bunch cilantro

36 small white potatoes, peeled and sliced

24 medium yellow or Yukon gold potatoes peeled and sliced

18 small red potatoes, peeled and sliced

2 cups julienned *guascas** (stems removed)

1 cup capers, for serving

1 cup heavy cream, for serving

1. In a medium stockpot or pressure cooker, place the beef, corn, teaspoon of salt and pepper. Add 4 cups of water. Simmer for 1½ hours, or cook under pressure for 20 minutes. Remove the beef and corn and set aside. Reserve the stock for later use.

2. In a separate large stockpot, place 10 cups of water, the chicken breasts, green onions, cilantro, and tablespoon of salt. Cover, bring to a boil over medium heat, and simmer for 20 minutes.

3. Uncover, remove and set aside the chicken breasts, and discard the green onions and cilantro. Add the white potatoes and the reserved beef stock, and simmer for 1 hour.

4. Add the rest of the potatoes and the guascas, and simmer, uncovered, for 30 minutes more. Season with more salt and pepper and serve with the chicken and corn (cut in half).

5. Serve with the capers and cream on the side.

CREMA DE MAÍZ O CHOCLO

Cream of Corn Soup
6 to 8 servings

Crema de Choclo is typical of the zone of Nariño, Cauca, and Valle del Cauca, even though it is prepared in the entire Andean Zone. This is a hearty winter soup to enjoy with the children or a large group of family members.

4½ cups beef stock
5 sprigs cilantro
2 cups corn kernels
(about 2 large ears)
6 whole ears of corn
1 pound yellow or Yukon
gold potatoes, peeled
and quartered
3 cups milk
½ recipe Hogao del
Pacífico (page 165)
1 teaspoon salt
½ teaspoon color*
¼ teaspoon pepper
2 eggs
½ cup heavy cream, for
serving
Cooked white rice, for
serving
Patacones (page 143) for
serving
Avocado slices, for serving

1. Place the beef stock and cilantro in a 7-quart pot. Bring to a boil.

2. Puree 1 cup of the corn kernels in a blender; leave the rest whole. Add the pureed corn kernels, whole corn kernels and corn ears, potatoes, 2 cups of the milk, hogao, salt, color, and pepper and simmer covered for 30 minutes.

3. Make small holes in the eggshells and drizzle the whites into the soup, stirring at the same time to create thin streams of white.

4. Combine the egg yolks with the remaining 1 cup of milk. Add ½ cup of the hot soup into this mixture, and pour it back into the pot. Stir continuously for 1 minute to ensure a smooth texture. Decrease the heat to low and cook for 10 minutes more.

5. Serve with the cream, white rice, patacones, and avocado on the side. Enjoy!

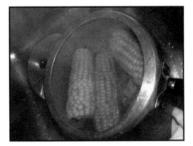

CREMA DE ZAPALLO O AHUYAMA

Cream of Pumpkin Soup
4 servings

> *Crema de Ahuyama* is what this soup is called in the northern part of Colombia, and *Crema de Zapallo* in the rest of the country. This is a soup that is prepared the same way everywhere and is given to babies as well as grown-ups. Some people put cooked white rice in it when serving.

1½ pounds pumpkin (about 2½ cups of diced pumpkin)
1½ cups chicken or vegetable stock
¼ of a white onion
1 clove garlic
½ teaspoon salt
1 pinch pepper
½ cup milk
¼ cup heavy cream

1. Peel and dice the pumpkin, discarding the seeds. Place the pumpkin, stock, onion, garlic, salt, and pepper in a medium pot over medium heat, and cook for 15 minutes, or until the pumpkin has softened.

2. Remove from the heat and blend until smooth. Return to the pot.

3. Add the milk and cream; reheat gently (do not allow to boil). Taste for salt and add more if necessary.

4. Serve hot.

CUCHUCO DE CEBADA

Pearl Barley Soup
8 to 12 servings

Cuchuco de Cebada is a typical soup from Nariño; it is very similar to the next recipe, which is prepared with wheat. This is a very flavorful soup with vegetables and small pieces of pork.

1. Rinse the barley with plenty of water and soak, covered with water, overnight.

2. Drain the barley and discard the water. Place the barley in a medium stockpot, with 4 quarts of water, and the pork meat, ribs, onion, green onion, garlic, bay leaves, bouillon cube, salt, pepper, and color. Simmer uncovered for 1 hour and 15 minutes.

3. Add the potatoes, peas, and cabbage and simmer for 15 minutes more. (The yellow potatoes will soften to a point where you won't see much of them, but they will give body to the soup.)

4. Add the parsley, cilantro, and hogao.

5. Taste for more salt and serve with the avocado on the side.

1 cup pearl barley
1 pound pork meat, cut in ¼-inch cubes
1 pound pork ribs or bones
1 cup diced onion
½ cup minced green onion*
4 cloves garlic, minced
3 bay leaves
2 beef bouillon cubes
1 teaspoon salt
¼ teaspoon pepper
¼ teaspoon color*
1 cup diced yellow or Yukon gold potatoes (about 3 small)
2 cups diced red potatoes (about 7 small)
1 cup fresh peas
1 cup shredded cabbage
2 tablespoon minced parsley
2 tablespoon minced cilantro
½ recipe of Hogao del Pacífico (page 165)
2 to 3 avocados, quartered, for serving

CUCHUCO DE TRIGO

Wheat Soup
8 to 12 servings

Cuchuco de Trigo comes from the Cundinamarca and Boyacá departments, where we find fava beans and a great variety of potatoes.

1. Rinse the wheat with plenty of water and soak, covered with water, overnight.

2. Drain the wheat and discard the water. Place the wheat in a medium stockpot with 4 quarts of water and the pork meat, ribs, onion, green onion, garlic, bay leaves, bouillon cube, salt, pepper, and color. Simmer uncovered for 1 hour and 15 minutes.

3. Add the potatoes, peas, carrot, fava beans, and cabbage, and simmer for 15 minutes more. (The yellow potatoes will soften to a point you won't see much of them but they will give body to the soup.)

4. Add the parsley, cilantro, and hogao.

5. Taste for more salt and serve with the avocado on the side.

NOTE: To clean fava beans, remove them from the pod, blanch in boiling salted water for 20 to 30 seconds, drain and place immediately in ice water. Press on each bean and the peel will come off very easily.

1 cup whole wheat berries
1 pound pork meat, cut in ¼-inch dice
1 pound pork ribs
1 cup diced onion
½ cup minced green onion*
4 cloves garlic
3 bay leaves
2 beef bouillon cubes
1 teaspoon salt
¼ teaspoon pepper
¼ teaspoon color*
2 cups diced yellow potatoes (about 7 small)
2 cups diced red potatoes (about 7 small)
1 cup fresh peas
1 cup diced carrot, ¼-inch dice
1 cup fava beans, cleaned (see note below)
1 cup shredded cabbage
2 tablespoon minced parsley
2 tablespoon minced cilantro
½ recipe of Hogao Del Pacífico (page 165)
2 to 3 avocadoes, quartered, for serving

MONDONGO

Tripe Soup
8 to 10 servings

Mondongo is one of the countries favorite dishes and my mother-in-law María Elena's best recipe! She is a native of Antioquia and loves tripe soup. When my mother visits her, she always asks María Elena to prepare it for her. Mondongo is a tripe soup that even though it contains *chorizo* and potatoes, is hearty in ingredients but soft in flavor. I think this is one of the country's favorite dishes. Nowadays you find tripe perfectly cleaned and ready-to-use in neat packages. There is a characteristic smell when preparing the tripe, which goes away as the first water is discarded.

1. Wash the tripe well with plenty of water. Remove any excess fat. Add the lime juice, rub it all over, let sit for 10 minutes, and wash again. Cook covered with water and the baking soda over medium heat, in a pressure cooker for 30 to 45 minutes, or in a regular pot for 1½ hours. Remove from the pot, drain, and discard the water.

2. In a large stockpot, place the mondongo, pork, chorizo, onion, green onion, tomatoes, garlic, bouillon cubes, bay leaves, cumin, 2 teaspoons of salt, and pepper. Cover with about 4 quarts of water and cook over medium-low heat for 1 hour.

3. Add the yuca, potatoes, and ½ teaspoon of salt and simmer for about 20 minutes or until they have completely softened.

4. Add the cilantro and parsley, taste for salt and serve.

2 pounds mondongo* or callos (tripe), cleaned and cut in 1-inch cubes
Juice of one lime
¼ teaspoon baking soda
1 pound pork meat, cut in ½-inch dice
3 chorizos (page 61), sliced ½ inch thick
1 cup diced onion
1 cup minced green onion*
1 cup peeled, diced tomatoes
4 cloves garlic, minced
2 beef bouillon cubes
2 bay leaves
½ tablespoon ground cumin*
2½ teaspoons salt
¼ teaspoon pepper
2 cups peeled and diced yuca*, ¾-inch dice
2 cups diced potatoes, ¾-inch dice
4 tablespoons minced cilantro
4 tablespoons minced parsley

MOTE DE QUESO

Ñame and Cheese Soup
8 to 10 servings

Mote de Queso is a delicious chowder; it is a little thick, flavored by the *guiso* and topped by the almost-melted cheese. It comes from the department of Córdoba. *Ñame** is the main ingredient in this recipe and therefore it cannot be replaced by anything else. *Ñame blanco espino* is the best variety for this recipe, but any kind of *ñame* will do.

If you have had *ñame* in soups before and think it is a little bland, please try it this way: I guarantee it is a delicious potage.

5 pounds ñame* blanco espino or other ñame

1. Peel and quarter the ñame lengthwise. Slice into 2-inch chunks.

2. Place half of the ñame in a large stockpot and cover it completely with water. Simmer over medium-low heat for 1 hour, add the rest of the ñame and continue to cook for another hour.

3. In the meantime, **PREPARE THE GUISO:** In a large sauté pan over medium heat, place the oil, scallion, onion, tomato, garlic, bouillon cube, and salt. Cook over medium heat for 15 minutes. Remove from the heat and set aside.

GUISO
3 tablespoons oil
1½ cups diced scallion
1 cup diced onion
1 cup diced tomato
2 cloves garlic, minced
1 chicken bouillon cube
3 to 4 teaspoons salt
2 pounds white farmer's cheese*, cut in ¼-inch dice

4. When the ñame mixture has thickened and the pieces are cooked through, add the guiso and the cheese. Simmer for 10 minutes more and taste for the salt; add more if necessary.

5. Serve hot.

SANCOCHO COSTEÑO

Caribbean Sancocho
12 servings

This is a dish to be served for a crowd ready to treat itself with some real slow home cooking. I love it, and prepare it with the ripe plantain and lime juice cooked within the soup, not separately. On the coast, we cut all the roots and vegetables, cook them in the soup, and add rice and lime juice at the end. Kale is the green we deem essential in any good *Sancocho Costeño*.

1. Wash the beef and hen pieces well. Rub with 3 tablespoons of the lime juice, and drain. Place in a very large bowl; add 1½ cups of the minced scallion, the kale, carrot, peppers, garlic, black pepper, color, cumin, 1 bouillon cube, and 1½ tablespoons of the salt. Rub all the seasonings into the meats, and set aside for 2 hours.

2. In a large stockpot, place the seasoned beef and chicken, and cook covered over high heat for 30 minutes, stirring occasionally to keep it from sticking.

3. Add 10 quarts of water to the meats, cover, and simmer for 1½ hours. Remove the chicken and set aside.

4. In the meantime cut the yuca, 1 of the green plantains, the potatoes, ñame, pumpkin, and corn into pieces about 2 inches by 1 inch; grate the other green plaintain and set aside.

8 pounds beef ribs, cut up
2 free-range hens, cut in serving pieces, without skin
6 tablespoons lime juice
2¼ cups minced scallion
1 cup chopped kale
¾ cup diced carrot
½ cup minced ají dulce (sweet green peppers)
1½ tablespoon minced garlic
½ teaspoon black pepper
½ teaspoon color* or turmeric
½ teaspoon ground cumin*
3 chicken bouillon cubes
4 tablespoons salt
3 pounds peeled yuca or cassava,
2 peeled green plantains*
3 pounds russet potatoes
2½ pounds peeled ñame*
1½ pounds peeled pumpkin
2 pounds corn on the cob (4 ears)
¾ cup minced cilantro, plus extra for serving
¼ cup chopped celery
1 tablespoon whole allspice berries
2 unpeeled ripe plantains*, cut into 1½-inch pieces
3 cups white rice, cooked to yield 6 cups, for serving
Sliced limes, for serving

5. When the meats have simmered for 1½ hours, add the yuca and the plantains to the pot and cook covered for 30 minutes.

6. Next add the remaining 2½ tablespoons of salt and 2 chicken bouillon cubes, the potatoes, ñame, pumpkin, corn, ¼ cup of the minced cilantro, celery, and the allspice. Continue to cook for 45 minutes more.

7. Add the ripe plantains and 3 tablespoons of lime juice, and keep simmering for 30 minutes more. (You can also cook the ripe plantains in water separately so that your soup doesn't taste too sweet and then add them right before serving.)

8. Finally, add the remaining ¾ cup of minced scallion and ½ cup of the minced cilantro and simmer for 15 minutes.

9. Serve the meats and vegetables on different platters, the broth in another serving dish, and white rice, lime slices, and minced cilantro on the side.

PUCHERO

Hearty Pork, Beef, and Chicken Soup
12 servings

> *Puchero* is a soup from the Andean zone, a bit like *Sancocho Costeño* (page 42). It is a hearty soup with a lot of roots, tubers, and vegetables, on the facing page, as well as beef, chicken, and pork, which makes it perfect for a one-dish meal for a family gathering or winter dinner party. If you cannot find *arracacha**, add some ripe plantain* in its place. Wash the skin of the plantain well, cut into 1½-inch pieces with the skin, and add to the soup in place of *arracacha*.

1. In a large stockpot, bring 4½ to 5 quarts of water to a boil. Add the chicken, beef bones, pork ribs, brisket, salt, and garlic. Tie the cilantro sprigs and green onions together like a bouquet garni and add. Cover and let simmer for 1 hour and 15 minutes.

2. Remove the chicken, cut into serving pieces, and set it aside. Remove and discard the cilantro and green onions.

3. Add the green plantains, yuca, and potatoes, and simmer for 10 minutes. Add the corn, arracacha and cabbage, cover and simmer for 20 to 30 minutes. Add the hogao and test to see if the meats, plantains, and yuca are tender. Cook a little longer if not.

4. Serve each bowl of puchero with a teaspoon of minced cilantro in the center. To each plate add: 1 piece of each of the meats, a couple of yuca and arracacha pieces, a potato half, some plantain pieces, ½ cup of rice, and a piece of avocado.

1 chicken, cut into serving pieces
1½ pounds beef bones with meat
1½ pounds pork ribs with meat
1 pound beef brisket cut into 2-inch pieces
1 tablespoon salt
1 teaspoon minced garlic
5 sprigs cilantro
3 whole green onions*
3 peeled green plantains, halved lengthwise and cut in 1½-inch pieces
2 pounds peeled,yuca*, quartered lengthwise and cut in 2-inch dice
2 pounds (about 6) peeled and halved medium potatoes
2 pounds (4 ears) corn on the cob, cut into 1½-inch pieces
2 pounds peeled arracacha*, quartered lengthwise and cut in 2-inch pieces
½ pound (½ small head) cabbage, sliced
¼ cup minced cilantro, for serving
½ cup Hogao del Pacífico (page 165)
3 cups white rice, cooked to yield 6 cups, for serving
3 avocados, quartered, for serving

SANCOCHO DE GUANDÚ O GUANDUL

Pigeon Pea Soup
10 to 12 servings

This *sancocho* is a bean, beef and salted beef jerky, and pork soup typical of the Caribbean coast. Pigeon peas may be called *guandú* or *guandul* depending on the region. Traditionally this soup is made with two pounds each of salted beef and salted pork, which are soaked in water at room temperature for the whole morning, with the water changed three times to remove the saltiness, and then prepared as follows. If using dry *guandú* beans, first soak them in water overnight to soften. These cannot be substituted; that would be a totally different recipe.

1. If using beef jerky, soak it in water overnight or boil it in water for 20 minutes. Discard the water.

2. In a large stockpot place 1 tablespoon of the oil, the beef and pork ribs, onion, peppers, garlic, mustard, bouillon cube, adobo seasoning, and cumin. Rub the meats to coat them, and place the pot over medium-high heat to brown for 10 minutes. Add 3 quarts of water, cover, and simmer for 3 hours. Add the salt.

3. While the meats are cooking, in a large pot or *caldero**, simmer the guandú beans in 5 cups of water for 2 hours over medium-low heat. After the first 2 hours have passed and the beans feel softened, add the yuca, pumpkin and ñame. Cover and simmer for another 40 minutes.

4. In a large sauté pan place the remaining 2 tablespoons of oil and fry the ripe plantains for 4 to 5 minutes; set aside.

5. Add the vegetables, their liquids, the plantains, and the minced scallion and cilantro to the meats, and simmer for 15 minutes more.

6. Serve.

3 tablespoons oil
4 pounds beef ribs, cut into 2-inch pieces or 2 pounds ribs and 1 pound soaked beef jerky
2 pounds pork ribs
½ cup diced onion
½ cup minced ají dulce* (sweet green peppers)
2 tablespoons mashed garlic
2 teaspoons prepared mustard
1 beef bouillon cube
1 teaspoon Adobo* seasoning
1 teaspoon ground cumin*
3 tablespoons salt
6 cups fresh guandú* beans, washed
2 pound peeled yuca* or cassava, cut into 2- by 1-inch pieces
1 pound peeled pumpkin, cut into 2-inch pieces
1 pound peeled ñame*, cut into 2- by 1-inch pieces
2 ripe plantains*, peeled and cut in ¼-inch dice
½ cup minced scallion
½ cup minced cilantro

SANCOCHO DE PESCADO AL COCO

Fish Sancocho with Coconut Milk

4 servings

This *sancocho* is typical of the Atlantic and Pacific coasts; both prepare many of their seafood dishes with coconut milk. Adding the lime juice right before eating greatly enhances the flavor, so we usually do it in the Caribbean coast. Try adding it to a little soup on the side before you add it your whole bowl, as it might be an acquired taste!

1. Mix 2 tablespoons of the olive oil, garlic paste, 2 tablespoons of the minced cilantro, lime juice, and ¼ teaspoon of the pepper, and rub on the fish pieces, heads included. Set aside for about 10 minutes while you prepare the rest of the ingredients.

2. In a a large pot over medium heat, heat the remaining 2 tablespoons of oil and sear the fish steaks for 2 minutes on each side. Remove and set aside. Leave the fish heads in the pot.

3. Add the remaining 2 tablespoons of olive oil, onion, tomatoes, cilantro, and whole garlic cloves and cook for 10 minutes. Add 4 cups of water, the coconut milk, yuca, green and ripe plantains, ñame, salt and remaining ½ teaspoon pepper. (Add the bouillon cube if your fish is not a strong tasting one.) Reduce the heat to medium-low and simmer covered for 20 minutes.

4. Remove the ripe plantains and simmer, covered, for 10 minutes more. Add the fish steaks and simmer covered 10 minutes more. Add the remaining 2 tablespoons of minced cilantro and serve.

5. Serve the soup in bowls, and the fish and vegetables on a separate platter, with white rice, patacones, and pieces of lime alongside.

4 tablespoons olive oil
1 tablespoon garlic paste (page 166)
4 tablespoons minced cilantro
1 tablespoon lime juice
¾ teaspoon pepper
2 (1½-pound) white fish, cleaned, and cut into steaks (including the heads)
2 cups sliced onion
1½ cups sliced tomatoes
5 sprigs cilantro
3 cloves garlic
1¾ cups coconut milk (freshly made, page 107, or canned)
¾ pound peeled and cubed yuca* or cassava
1 peeled green plantain*, quartered lengthwise and cut into 2-inch pieces
1 unpeeled ripe plantain*, cut crosswise into 1-inch chunks
½ pound peeled ñame* or yam
1 teaspoon salt
1 fish bouillon cube (optional)
Cooked white rice, for serving
Patacones (page 143), for serving
2 limes, quartered, for serving

SANCOCHO VALLUNO

Hearty Chicken Soup
12 servings

Sancocho Valluno comes from the Valle del Cauca department and is usually prepared with free-range hens; you normally find eggs from the hen in the *sancocho* when it is served. You can prepare it with chicken; just remove it from the soup earlier as the hen is tougher to cook and is left in the pot the whole time. This dish is cooked over log fires at farms and restaurants on the outskirts of the large cities of the Valle, giving it a defined smoky taste and aroma that we usually drive hours to savor.

10 sprigs of cilantro
1 whole green onion*
4 leaves cimarrón* or culantro
2 chicken bouillon cubes
1 tablespoon salt
1 teaspoon minced garlic
2 free-range hens or chickens, cut in serving pieces
3 peeled green plantains*, halved lengthwise and cut into 1½ -inch pieces
2 pounds peeled yuca, quartered lengthwise, and into 2-inch pieces
6 medium potatoes, peeled and halved lengthwise

1. In a large stockpot, bring 3½ quarts of water to a boil. Tie the cilantro, green onion, and cimarrón like a bouquet garni and add to the water. Add the bouillon cubes, salt, and garlic; cover and let simmer for 15 minutes.

2. Add the hen or chicken, cover and simmer for 45 minutes. If using chicken, remove the pieces from the pot; if using free-range hens, just keep simmering in the sancocho. Add the plantain, yuca, and potatoes, and cook for 45 minutes more.

3. Meanwhile, **MAKE THE GUISO**: In a medium pot over medium heat, place the oil, green onions, tomato, garlic, cilantro, bouillon cube, color, and pepper, and cook for 15 minutes. Add the chicken stock, cook for 5 minutes more. Set aside.

GUISO
4 tablespoons oil
1½ cups minced green onions*
1 cup diced tomato
1 tablespoon minced garlic
1 tablespoon minced cilantro
1 chicken bouillon cube
1 teaspoon color* or saffron powder
½ teaspoon pepper
¾ cup chicken stock

4. Remove the hen or chicken, potatoes and yuca from the soup pot and add to the guiso. Cook covered for 10 minutes on low heat.

5. Serve each bowl of sancocho with a teaspoon of minced cilantro in the center. To each plate add 1 chicken piece, a couple of yuca pieces, a potato half, some plantain pieces, ½ cup of rice and a piece of avocado.

¼ cup minced cilantro
3 cups white rice, cooked to yield 6 cups
3 avocados, quartered

SOPA DE CARANTANTAS

Corn Fritter Soup
8 servings

Another very unique soup, this one comes from the Cauca department. *Carantantas* are the leftover material in the bottom of the pot that is peeled off after cooked corn *masa* is prepared, for *empanadas* for example. It is sold as a snack, fried like chips, or sold for the preparation of soup. Take the *carantanta* pieces and fry in 375°F oil for 30 seconds. Drain and serve as chips or in the soup as follows. If you cannot find them, prepare some *Masa de Empanaditas Vallunas* (page 24) and fry them as you would the *carantantas* (see note below).

1. In a medium stockpot or *caldero**, place the ribs, 3½ quarts of water, the bouillon cubes, salt, and garlic; tie the green onions, cimarrón, oregano, thyme and cilantro into a bouquet garni and add to the pot. Bring to a boil over medium-high heat, lower the heat to medium, cover and simmer for about 2 hours.

2. Add the potatoes and hogao, and simmer for 15 to 20 minutes or until the potatoes are done.

3. Remove the bouquet garni and bones from the pot.

4. Fry the carantanta pieces in 375°F oil for 30 seconds. Drain well. Add the fried carantantas and simmer for no more than 2 to 3 minutes.

5. Add the cilantro and serve.

STOCK
3 pounds beef ribs
2 beef bouillon cubes
1 tablespoon salt
1 teaspoon minced garlic
4 whole green onions*
4 leaves cimarrón* or
  culantro
4 sprigs oregano
4 sprigs thyme
4 sprigs cilantro
1 pound (about 8) very
  small potatoes, halved
½ cup Hogao del Pacífico
  (page 165)
¼ pound carantantas*
Oil for frying
¼ cup minced cilantro

NOTE: Instead of carantantas you can use fried masa from the Empanaditas Vallunas recipe (page 24). Take tablespoonfuls of masa and place each in the middle of two plastic bags; press or roll until you can almost see through it. You can press with the cover of a pot and then with your own hands make it thinner by spreading it with both index fingers. Don't be afraid the masa peels of easily if you lift up one of the bags and then let the masa fall of the other one. If it breaks into pieces, then better because real carantantas are not round or triangular they are free formed in shape.

SOPA DE TORREJAS O MASITAS

Dumpling Soup
8 servings

This is a soup from the Cauca River region. You can also try the *masitas* on their own. They are good as a side dish with any other soup. This is a light soup.

1. In a medium stockpot, place the ribs, steak if using, 3½ quarts of water, bouillon cubes, salt, and garlic. Tie the green onions, thyme, oregano, and cilantro into a bouquet garni and add it in. Bring to a boil. Lower the heat, cover, and simmer for about 1 to 2 hours or until the meat pieces are tender; if not yet tender, simmer until they are, 30 minutes more at most.

2. Add the potatoes and hogao and simmer for 10 to 15 minutes or until the potatoes are done.

3. To prepare the dumplings, place the eggs, flour, cilantro, salt, color, and baking powder in a bowl. Mix well to break up any lumps. Drop by table-spoonfuls into 350°F oil in a heavy pot for 1 minute on each side or until light golden. Set to drain over paper towels.

4. Remove the bones and bouquet garni from the soup pot.

5. Add the masitas and simmer for no more than 2 to 3 minutes.

6. Add the minced cilantro and serve.

STOCK
2 pounds beef ribs
1 pound skirt or flank steak, cut in ½-inch dice (optional)
2 beef bouillon cubes
1 tablespoon salt
1 teaspoon minced garlic
4 whole green onions*
4 sprigs thyme
4 sprigs oregano
4 sprigs cilantro
1 pound yellow potatoes, cut in ¼-inch dice
½ cup Hogao del Pacífico (page 165)

MASITAS OR TORRIJAS
18 dumplings

2 eggs, beaten
½ cup flour
2 teaspoons minced cilantro
1 teaspoon salt
¼ teaspoon Sazón Goya Color*
¼ teaspoon baking powder
1 cup oil for frying
1 cup minced cilantro, for serving

SOPA DE TORTILLA

Corn Tortilla Soup
8 servings

From the Valle del Cauca, this is a light soup that can be served as a starter or a light meal, with cut-up *White Corn Arepas* (page 12).
Remember that you have to start the corn for the *arepas* a day ahead.

1. In a medium stockpot, place the ribs, flank steak, 3½ quarts of water, bouillon cubes, salt, and garlic. Tie the green onions, thyme, oregano, and cilantro into a bouquet garni and add it to the pot. Bring to a boil. Lower the heat, cover, and simmer for about 1 to 2 hours or until the meat pieces are tender; if not yet tender, simmer until they are, 30 minutes more at most.

2. Add the potatoes and hogao and simmer for 10 minutes or until the potatoes are done.

3. Cook the arepas on a rack over a gas or electric burner for about 8 minutes on each side, or until crispy. Cut them into sixths and add to the pot together with the plantain coins and simmer for no more than 2 to 3 minutes.

4. Remove the beef bones and bouquet garni from the pot, add the cilantro and serve.

2 pounds beef ribs
1 pound flank or skirt steak, cut in ½-inch dice
2 beef bouillon cubes
1 tablespoon salt
1 teaspoon minced garlic
4 whole green onions*
4 sprigs thyme
4 sprigs oregano
4 sprigs cilantro
1 pound potatoes, cut in ¼-inch dice
½ cup Hogao del Pacífico (page 165)
4 (4-inch) White Corn Arepas, unsalted (page 12)
½ cup Plantain Coins (page 134)
1 cup minced cilantro

MEATS AND POULTRY

In general, we eat all the parts of chickens, cows, and pigs, for example in sausages such as *butiffarras, chorizos,* and *rellenas.* The organ meats we eat are found in dishes like *pinchos de corazon y hígado de pollo, lengua de res,* and *sobrebarriga.* This group of foods carries a wide variety of preparations. From sausages to *tamales, cuy* or guinea pigs to stuffed drunken turkey, we find succulent dishes that take us on a journey across the beautiful landscapes of Colombia.

Our cuts of beef are very different than those in the United States; the beef filet is one of the few cuts that is similar. We eat the organs, heart, liver, kidney, brain, tongue, tail, and tripe, as well as the rest of the beef; one of the favorite dishes is onioned liver. Children are given beef organs for their high iron contents and for their cheap price. If people can afford it, meat is eaten more than five times a week. We are a meat-loving population, and we usually season our meat for hours before taking it to the heat. It is rare to find a person placing a piece of meat on a pan without it being seasoned beforehand. Veal, lamb and goat are usually found in farms or in specialized markets. Veal is prepared in the Llanos area on wooden sticks arranged teepee-style over fire and is called *ternera a la llanera.* One-year-old calves are prepared in festive settings to feed thirty to forty people anxiously waiting and watching the whole preparation. Some restaurants do this in their entrances or patios to bring people into their places with the aroma and display it brings. Goat is stewed, roasted, prepared in *sancochos,* and in a special way called *pepitoria,*  which includes the organs and the meat in the head of the animal and is served along the roasted goat. Leftover beef is reheated for breakfast with white rice and plantains.

In general, we also eat all the parts of a chicken. We have a chicken rice dish that is prepared solely with entrails; *sancochos* with the legs and necks; livers and hearts are eaten like a delicacy; free range hens are placed in the soup pots with their eggs inside, which are then enjoyed as a special treat. These chicken parts are much cheaper, making it easier to afford poultry. In Colombia, chicken is a highly priced protein and the dark meat is eaten much more as it is less expensive. Free-range animals are eaten in farms for economical reasons, but in large cities, hormone-free or organic chickens are sold for very high prices to the few people who are still interested in buying them nowadays.

In recent years, the pork industry has become so specialized that we have wonderful farms growing beautiful animals that are now available throughout the country. Tender pieces of fresh ham, chops, and large loins as well as delicious small tenderloins are now eaten more than ever. People are very comfortable with the processing procedures that industrialization has brought to the pork industry. Processed pork meats are also a large business, both in production and consumption; sausages, *butiffarras*, *chorizos* and *rellenas* sell not only nationally but also overseas and are very high in quality.

Many other animals eaten include the iguana's eggs, although now very restricted, the *guagua*, which is like a miniature pig that only comes out at night, the turtles that are now prohibited from being caught or sold, and ants called *hormigas culonas*, which actually look like large peppercorns and taste like salty peanuts.

BANDEJA PAISA

Paisa or Antioqueño Platter
8 servings

You would think that *Bandeja Paisa* is only for special occasions, since it involves so many preparations. But no, it is a very common dish in the regions of Antioquia and Viejo Caldas. Much of the country's coffee is grown in those parts of the country, and people need lots of energy to cultivate the land and work. *Bandeja Paisa* is served very often and eaten even during the evening meals. The *carne en polvo*, beans and *hogao* can be prepared the day before and refrigerated. I keep the beef and beans frozen at home because I use them in other dishes or just with white rice when I am in a hurry for a meal. Typically, all the recipes are prepared the same morning or afternoon that the platter is served.

1. Prepare the carne en polvo, frisoles and hogao in advance (can be done the day before). About one hour before serving, prepare the chicharrones.

2. As you are ready to serve, fry the plantains and prepare the eggs.

3. Mold the rice in coffee cups, and place in the center of every platter. Add a ladle of frisoles, and one of the beef. Around the sides place the tajadas de maduro, chorizo, and chicharrones.

4. Over the frisoles place a dollop of hogao, and over the beef and rice place the egg.

5. Enjoy!

1 recipe Carne En Polvo (page 59)
1 recipe Frisoles Antioqueños (page 131)
1 recipe Hogao del Pacífico (page 165)
1 recipe Chicharrones (page 60)
1 recipe Tajadas de Plátano Maduro, made without the cheese and sugar (page 147)
8 eggs fried sunny side up
2 cups of white rice, cooked to yield 8 servings of ½ cup each
8 Chorizos (page 61), cooked through

BISTEC A LA CRIOLLA

Creole Beefsteak
8 servings

Bistec a la Criolla are steaks served with a delicious sautéed onion and tomato sauce. You can prepare them with any piece meat but we prepare them with *bistec relajado*—a piece of meat cut thick and then butterflied to a thickness of a quarter of an inch. This makes them very quick to cook, and larger to the eye than they really are, normally no more than six ounces in weight.

1. Place the beef in a nonreactive container.

2. Combine the oil, mustard, garlic, bay leaves, cilantro, cumin, and pepper. Rub over the beef slices. Cover and refrigerate overnight, or at least 1 to 2 hours.

3. In a large sauté pan over medium heat, cook the beef slices for 2 minutes on each side for medium rare, 3 to 4 minutes for medium, and 5 minutes for well-done. Add the salt while cooking.

4. Serve with hogao sauce over it.

NOTE: There is a world of difference between ground cumin and cumin seeds. Try to use the whole seeds. Place them in a small, dry sauté pan over medium heat and swirl the pan for 20 to 30 seconds. The aroma is just divine!

3 pounds thinly sliced beef (skirt steak, flank steak, or filet)
2 tablespoons oil
2 tablespoons prepared mustard
2 cloves garlic, minced
2 whole bay leaves
1 tablespoon minced cilantro
½ teaspoon cumin* seeds, toasted (see note below)
¼ teaspoon pepper
1½ teaspoons salt
1 recipe Hogao del Caribe (page 164)

BISTEC ENCEBOLLADO

Onioned Beef Filet
4 to 6 servings

This is definitely my husband's favorite dish—although anything else that has lots of onions is, too! This recipe is somewhat elegant compared to other beef recipes. Using wine and beef filet it is still very typical; it could be prepared with skirt or flank steak instead. Many of our dishes have Asian or European influences, as does this one.

3 to 4 pounds filet of beef, cut into 1½-inch thick steaks
2 tablespoons red wine
4 cloves garlic, minced
1 teaspoon prepared mustard
¼ teaspoon pepper
4 tablespoons olive oil
3 cups thinly sliced onions
5 whole allspice berries
5 whole cloves
2 teaspoons salt
½ cup sliced tomatoes
2 tablespoons cognac or brandy
Butter or oil, for cooking the meat

1. Place the beef in a nonreactive container.

2. Combine the wine, 2 of the garlic cloves, the mustard, and pepper. Add 2 tablespoons of the oil and whisk well. Keep one teaspoon of this mixture aside for the onions; rub the rest over the beef slices, and set aside for 30 minutes.

3. In the meantime prepare the onions. Tie the allspice and cloves in cheesecloth for easier removal. Heat the remaining 2 tablespoons of oil in a large sauté pan, add the onions, the remaining 2 garlic cloves, the allspice and cloves, and ½ teaspoon salt. Cook over very low heat, covered, for 15 minutes.

4. Increase the heat to medium, add another ½ teaspoon of the salt, the tomatoes, 1 tablespoon of cognac, and reserved mustard mixture, and cook uncovered for 5 more minutes. Remove the allspice and cloves. Set aside.

5. In a large sauté pan over medium heat, cook the beef slices for 4 minutes on each side for medium-rare, 6 minutes for medium, and 8 minutes on each side for well-done. Add 1 teaspoon of salt while cooking.

6. Add the remaining tablespoon of cognac to deglaze the pan, and add the cooked onions.

7. Mix and serve.

BUTIFARRAS

Spicy Beef Sausages
Fourteen 1½-inch sausages

These small, oval-shaped sausages are charming and delicious even though they are grayish in color. They smell of peppery heat and when you bite into them, you can taste the heat of the coast, with the music and the salty air of the sea. They are served at many parties and social events.

Butifarras are typical from the Atlantic or Caribbean coast of Colombia; slowly they have spread to the rest of the country. When you buy them, they are completely cooked so you can eat them as is; you can also heat them to serve them hot. They are traditionally served with *Bollo Limpio* (page 17) and *Bollo de Yuca* (page 16).

1 pound flank steak, diced
¼ pound pork belly, diced
4 cloves garlic, minced
1½ teaspoons salt, plus
　extra for cooking
1½ teaspoons ground
　pepper
¼ teaspoon ground
　cumin*
Pork casings (about 3
　feet), cleaned and ready
　to use

1. In a food processor, process beef, pork, garlic, salt, pepper and cumin for 3 minutes. You can also pass these through the finest disc of a meat grinder.

2. Stuff the pork casings with the mixture and tie carefully every 1½ inch and at the ends.

3. In a medium pot, place 8 cups of water with some salt added and bring to a boil. Add the sausages and cook for 15 minutes. Remove from the water, and drain. If there is water in the sausage casing, pinch it to release it.

4. Cool and refrigerate overnight.

5. Serve cold or hot, with Bollo de Yuca or Bollo Limpio.

6. To serve warm, place the butiffarras on a grill or on a pan with cooking spray and cook over medium heat for 10 minutes or until heated through to the center.

CARNE ASADA SOBRE AREPAS

Steak and Arepas
6 to 8 servings

This beef preparation is sold in many *asaderos* around the country. These are places where meats are prepared over wood fires or coals. Beef, veal, pork, *Butifarras* (facing page), *Chorizos* (page 61), and *Morcillas* (page 70) are sold there, accompanied by *Yuca Frita* (page 150) and *Patacones* (page 143) as well as *Papa Salada* (page 136) or *Papita Amarilla Asada* (page 140). Served also are many of the sauces or *ajíes* that appear here in the Salsas and Sauces chapter (page 153). From where I am now, many hundred miles away, I can smell the hot coals and the meat smoking into the cold air of the *asaderos* on the outskirts of Bogotá.

2 tablespoons red wine
2 cloves garlic, minced
1 teaspoon prepared mustard
$\frac{1}{4}$ teaspoon pepper
2 tablespoons oil
3 pounds beef (skirt steak, flank steak, or filet), in one piece or cut into portions
$1\frac{1}{2}$ teaspoons salt

1 recipe for Arepas de Maíz (page 12) or Arepas de Queso (page 13)
1 recipe of Chimichurri (page 163)

1. Combine the wine, garlic, mustard, and pepper; add the oil and mix well. Rub over the beef slices or the whole piece of beef. Refrigerate overnight or at least 1 to 2 hours.

2. In a large sauté pan over medium heat, cook the beef slices for 4 minutes on each side for medium rare, 6 for medium, and 8 for well-done. Add the salt while cooking. If cooking a whole beef strip 1 to $1\frac{1}{2}$ inches thick, the times are the same; if cooking a whole filet (2 to 3 pounds), sear on the outside, and transfer to a preheated 350°F oven for 20 more minutes for medium-rare, 25 for medium, 30 for well-done. Let it rest a few minutes before slicing.

3. Serve over arepas with a tablespoon of chimichurri sauce on top of each serving.

CARNE DESMECHADA

Stripped Beef
8 servings

Carne Desmechada is a staple in most Colombian homes. It is a delicious, saucy, very tasty dish that can be prepared with inexpensive cuts. It can be prepared with or without the eggs. I personally love it with them, and my children prefer it without. This is a great food to make a lot of and keep frozen for the kids!

When you pack this dish for the freezer, place it in bags that are no more than an inch thick so that it thaws out easily and in a shorter period of time. Always thaw it out in your refrigerator by leaving it there overnight, or over running cold tap water. Beef keeps frozen for nine to twelve months if the temperature of your freezer is kept at 0°F.

2 pounds beef skirt steak in one piece
½ cup grated white onion
1 minced ají dulce* (sweet green or red pepper)
3 cloves garlic, minced
1 recipe of Hogao del Pacífico (page 165) or Hogao del Caribe (page 164)
2 whole eggs, beaten
Cooked rice, for serving

1. In a medium pot, over medium heat place the beef, 10 cups of water, the onion, ají dulce, and garlic. Cover and cook for 1 hour. Uncover and cook for 15 to 20 minutes more. You know the meat is done when you can rip off strips with a fork. Almost all the water should have evaporated, but in case it hasn't, remove the beef, and boil it down to 1 cup. Place the beef back in the pot and let it stand for 10 to 15 minutes to relax and cool off so you can handle it.

2. Remove the beef from the pot. Cut across the grain into 1-inch-wide strips.

3. Take each strip, and with 2 forks or with your fingers shred the meat.

4. Place the beef back in the pot, bring the heat to medium-high, and mix it with 1 cup of the reduced cooking liquid; add the hogao and mix.

5. Pour the beaten eggs into the pot, and cook for 2 minutes or until the egg is cooked.

6. Serve over rice.

CARNE EN POLVO

Powdered Beef
8 to 10 servings

This meat is usually served with saucy dishes like *Machorrusio* (page 68) or *Frijoles Rojos* (page 132) and rice, or as part of *Bandeja Paisa* (page 53), but you can just serve it with *hogao* (pages 164-165) and rice. It is a bit bland to the taste if eaten alone, which could be great for young children.

2 pounds beef skirt steak in 1 piece
3 cloves garlic, minced
2 cups peeled and diced tomatoes
1¾ cups minced scallion
¼ cup minced cilantro
1 teaspoon Worcestershire sauce
1 teaspoon salt
½ teaspoon ground cumin*
¼ teaspoon pepper

1. In a large, nonreactive bowl mix the beef with the garlic, tomatoes, scallion, cilantro, Worcestershire, salt, cumin, and pepper. Set aside for 30 minutes.

2. In a medium pressure cooker, place the seasoned beef and 3 cups of water. Cover and cook for 30 minutes, turn the heat off and leave as is for 15 minutes more. Release the pressure and open. If using a regular pot simmer over medium-low heat for 2 to 3 hours or until the beef has softened. Add more water if it boils out.

3. Remove the meat from the liquid. (Pass the liquid though a sieve to strain, and freeze for later use as beef stock.)

4. Cut the beef into 1-inch cubes. Let cool completely.

5. Place in the bowl of a food processor, and process for 1 minute to a very fine, powder-like consistency.

6. Serve.

CHICHARRONES

Pork Fritters
8 chicharrones

Chicharrones are prepared all over Colombia, although the Paisas seem to hold their origins. The best are the ones that are very crisp and have lots of meat, too. I found that the piece of meat that comes along the ribs is a great way to get a piece of pork that gives a hearty *chicharron* with a crunch, and at the same time leaves you with bones to flavor a good pot of *Frisoles Antioqueños* (page 131) or a delicious *Arroz Atollado* (page 108).

3 pounds piece of pork ribs with 1½ inch of meat and fat on it (6 to 8 ribs)
1 tablespoon baking soda
1 teaspoon salt

1. Lay the ribs flat, and cut the meat horizontally from the bones. (Save the ribs to prepare beans.)

2. Cut the meat and fat lengthwise into ½-inch-wide strips.

3. Next take each strip and cut it crosswise without cutting completely through, or you will end up with squares. You want to have strips with cuts that open up but are held together by the thick pork fat skin.

4. Rub the baking soda over all the pork strips.

5. Place in a medium, heavy pan with just enough water to cover them. Cook over medium heat until all of the water evaporates. Watch that it doesn't burn.

6. Remove from the pan; wash the pork well with a lot of water.

7. Sprinkle the pork with salt and put it back in the pot. Cook over medium heat for 10 to 15 minutes, until the fat has all rendered out and you have crispy pieces of pork.

8. Serve, or put aside to use in other recipes.

CHORIZOS

Chorizos are typical of the Antioquia and Viejo Caldas regions of Colombia. If you travel from the Medellín airport into the city, you will see *chorizos* hanging from wooden farmer's markets along the way. There are different kinds or *chorizos* nowadays, some with beef, others with beef and pork; these are said to be the best. My father-in-law was born in a very small town called Sonsón in Antioquia, and he said they made the best *chorizos* there. Every time we traveled to the region of Rio Negro to visit my mother-in-law's family, we would stop at these street markets to enjoy the homemade *chorizos* of the region.

Colombian *chorizo* is much milder than the Mexican kind and usually not as red as the Spanish one. Like the Spanish, it is sold dry and fresh but both types need cooking.

1 pound finely diced pork meat
¼ pound finely diced pork belly or bacon
½ cup minced chard
½ cup minced ají dulce* (sweet green pepper)
½ cup minced scallion
1 tablespoon minced garlic
2½ teaspoons salt
¾ teaspoon black pepper
5 tablespoons oil
2 tablespoons achiote* seeds
Pork casings (5 to 6 feet), cleaned and ready to use

1. Place the pork, pork belly, chard, sweet peppers, scallion, garlic, salt, and pepper in a nonreactive bowl and mix well.

2. In a very small pot over low heat, cook the oil and achiote together for 3 to 5 minutes. The oil will turn very red. Strain the oil through a fine sieve and discard the seeds. Add the oil to the pork and mix thoroughly; set aside, covered, in the refrigerator overnight.

3. Stuff the pork casings with the mixture and tie carefully every 4 inches and at the ends.

4. Refrigerate uncovered for 2 days.

5. Cook over coals on a grill, or fry in a pan in its own oil until fully cooked, about 5 to 7 minutes.

CURÍ O CUY

Guinea Pig
2 servings

Nariño is the department where *cuy* or *curí* (guinea pig) is eaten. It is a delicacy of the region, and is typically prepared over coals or log fires in the outside beautiful gardens of the locality. Nariño is a mountainous land full of green and color, with both warm and cold climates and many striking views.

4 tablespoons oil
4 tablespoons minced
  scallion
1 tablespoon minced
  garlic
2 teaspoons color*
1 (1½ to 2 pounds)
  guinea pig, skinned and
  eviscerated
2 teaspoons salt

1. In a blender mix the oil, scallion, garlic, and color to a puree consistency.

2. Rub the inside of the belly and the outer skin of the guinea pig well with the mixture; refrigerate overnight.

3. Rub with the salt 1 hour before cooking and place back in the refrigerator. Remove from the refrigerator 30 minutes before cooking.

4. Place over hot coals, and grill, turning every 15 minutes for a total of about 1 hour. It will be done when the juices from the thigh run clear when pinched. The outside should be very crispy.

5. Instead of grilling, the cuy can be baked in a preheated 350°F oven. It will take about 1½ hours.

LENGUA DE RES

Tongue
6 to 8 servings

Tongue is a very common dish in Colombia; you can buy it clean and ready to cook, in large markets. It is typically cooked in a pressure cooker, like many of our dishes, and then seasoned with *hogao*. Either of the two *hogaos* in this book will go with it. As I was testing recipes in Bogotá, I cooked *lengua* for my children, but they heard what it was and were a bit shocked! But so many homes serve it regularly that children get used to it before knowing what it is.

1 (3-pound) beef tongue, cleaned by your butcher
¼ teaspoon baking soda
⅔ of a 12-ounce can of beer (8 ounces)
1 cup diced onion
1 cup peeled and diced tomato
4 tablespoons minced cilantro
4 tablespoons red wine
2 bay leaves
1 tablespoon butter
1 tablespoon oil
1 tablespoon brown sugar
½ tablespoon Worcestershire sauce
1 teaspoon salt
½ recipe of Hogao del Pacífico (page 165) or Hogao del Caribe (page 164), for serving (optional)

1. Cook the clean tongue covered with water and the baking soda in a pressure cooker for 40 minutes to an hour, or for about 2½ hours in a regular pot. Remove from the pot and peel off the outer skin; it will peel off easily.

2. Discard the water, and put the peeled tongue back in the pressure cooker or pot. Add the rest of the ingredients plus 1 cup of water, cover and cook for another 45 minutes in the pressure cooker, or 1½ hours in the regular pot. Remove from the pot, let cool, and slice.

3. Remove any excess fat from the liquid in the pot, and taste for salt. Serve with the meat and juices as is, or add the half recipe of *hogao* if desired.

HAYACAS DE POLLO

Chicken Hayacas
Forty 3- by 1½-inch hayacas

Hayacas vary throughout different regions in Colombia, from the coast, to the Santanderes, the plaíns of Arauca, and the Llanos Orientales. They are eaten especially on festive occasions like Christmas, New Year and Carnival. Some *hayacas* are prepared with pork and others with chicken; some have peas and potatoes and other don't. Here's a great *hayaca* recipe for you to enjoy.

FILLING

2 whole chicken breasts, skins removed
¾ cup diced onion
5 tablespoons diced green pepper
1 teaspoon prepared mustard
2 teaspoons minced garlic
3 tablespoon butter
1 cup grated carrots
¼ cup minced green onion
¼ cup minced red bell pepper
3 tablespoon minced celery
1 chicken bouillon cube
1 teaspoon salt
¼ teaspoon pepper
¼ teaspoon curry powder
½ cup minced scallion
¼ cup minced cilantro

1. Place the chicken breasts and ¼ cup of the diced onion, 1 tablespoon of the green pepper, the mustard, and 1 teaspoon of the minced garlic in a bowl. Mix well and let sit for 30 minutes.

2. Transfer to a medium pot; add 6 cups of water and simmer, covered, over medium-low heat for 30 minutes. Remove the breasts and set aside to cool; cut into small dice. Pass the liquid through a strainer and set aside for the masa.

3. In a large sauté pan place butter and carrots, cook over low heat for 20 minutes. Add the remaining ½ cup diced onion, green onion, red pepper, remaining ¼ cup green pepper, celery, remaining garlic, bouillon cube, salt, pepper, and curry powder, and continue to cook for 15 minutes more. Add the scallion and cilantro and cook 3 minutes more.

4. Add the diced chicken and set aside to cool.

5. While the chicken is cooking, **MAKE THE MASA**: mix cornmeal, chicken stock, oil, bouillon cube and salt with your hands for 2 to 3 minutes. Cover and set aside until ready to use.

6. Wash the leaves well on both sides, dry, and cut into forty 8-inch squares.

7. Place one 8-inch square piece of bijao leaf on the work surface. In the center of the leaf add ¼ cup of masa; spread it into a 2- by 4-inch rectangle and flatten it with a fork. Place 1 tablespoon of filling on the masa. Wrap the leaf around the "pie" or tamal in the form of an envelope. Repeat until all the masa and filling are used.

8. Stack the filled leaves in the basket of a 9-quart pasta pot. In another pot bring to a boil enough water to cover the tamales. Pour the hot water over the tamales. Place a pan with weight on top of them so the water does not penetrate the leaves (these are not tied with string).

MASA
3 cups yellow cornmeal
5½ cups chicken stock
 (use the broth from
 cooking the chicken for
 the filling and top up
 with commercial broth)
½ cup oil
1 chicken bouillon cube
2 teaspoons salt

ASSEMBLY OR WRAPPING
12 bijao* or plantain
 leaves

9. Bring the water to a boil, reduce the heat to medium-low and simmer for 1 hour.

10. Remove from the pot, drain, and discard the liquid in the pot. Let the hayacas sit 5 minutes before unwrapping.

11. Serve.

LECHONA EN BOLSA

Whole Piglet or Pig in a Bag
12 servings

Lechona is a very typical large-event dish in Colombia. The most typical is the *Lechona Tolimense*: the whole pig bakes in a huge brick oven for eight to ten hours, enough for at least sixty to eighty people to eat from the smallest ones. The pig is bled and the blood used to make *Morcillas* (page 70); the rest of the meat is cut, seasoned, and placed back into the pig's skin with rice, potatoes, and peas. The cooked pig is displayed and served whole. My husband's aunt and I prepared a small version of *Lechona*, making a "bag" from the skin of the animal, instead of cooking it whole.

1 teaspoon baking soda
1 whole skin of pork, cleaned, ½-inch thick and large enough to cut into an 18- by 24-inch rectangle (ask your butcher to prepare it)

DAY 1

1. Rub baking soda all over the pork skin. Remove the excess fat with a sharp knife. Refrigerate overnight or at least one hour.

DAY 2

2. Wash the skin well to remove all the baking soda. Place the skin in a large pot of boiling water and cook until it has softened and is easier to bend and handle, about 15 minutes. Discard the cooking water.

3. Fold the skin in half, and with a large needle and butcher's twine, sew two of the open sides to make a sort of pillow case or bag with one side still open. Set aside to fill later.

4. In a large bowl place the pork, scallion, garlic, cumin, and salt. Mix well and set aside until ready to fill the bag.

PORK MEAT AND SEASONING
3 pounds pork, cut in ½-inch dice
1 cup minced scallion
2 cloves garlic, minced
½ teaspoon ground cumin*
1 teaspoon salt
1 cup white rice, cooked with 2 cups of water
1 cup green peas, cooked
2 cup raw diced red potatoes, ½-inch dice

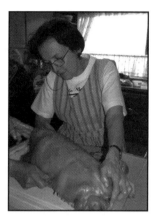

GUISO
2 tablespoons pork fat
3 cups minced scallions
8 cloves garlic, minced
1½ teaspoons ground
    cumin*
1 teaspoon salt
1 teaspoon color* or
    turmeric
1 teaspoon pepper
4 cups peeled and diced
    tomatoes

2 sour oranges, for baking

5. **PREPARE THE GUISO**: In a large sauté pan or *caldero** over medium-low heat, melt the pork fat, and sauté the scallions, garlic, cumin, salt, color, and pepper for 5 minutes. Add the tomatoes and cook for 20 to 25 minutes more; set aside.

6. In a very large bowl or pan, mix together the raw seasoned pork, rice, peas, potatoes and guiso; mix them all together.

7. Fill the pork skin bag with this mixture, and sew the end shut.

8. If you have pork mixture leftover, place it in a baking dish and cover it with foil or wrap it in plantain leaves.

9. Preheat the oven to 325°F.

10. Place the filled pork bag in a baking dish. Rub all over with half a sour orange.

11. Cover and bake for 1½ hours.

12. Uncover, turn, rub with more orange, re-cover, and bake another 1½ hours.

13. Turn again and rub the second orange over the pork bag.

14. Remove the foil, increase the heat to 475°F and cook for 10 to 15 minutes more on each side or until the skin bursts with bubbles and is really crispy.

15. Let rest for 30 minutes. Carve and serve.

MACHORRUSIO

Dried Corn "Risotto"
8 servings

This is a sensational dish with an odd name, even for Colombians. The words *macho* and *russio* would translate as a gray, not shiny, macho man's dish! It is a typical dish from old Antioquia, but is new to the younger generations. Prepared with *cuchuco de maíz**, which was probably leftover cut pieces of dry corn in old times, the corn is transformed into a creamy, risotto-type dish. Then all the goodies are added and a great meal full of contrasting flavors comes together: soothing *Carne en Polvo*, sweet and delicious *Tajadas de Plátano*, scrumptious crackling *Chicharrones*, and flavorful *Hogao del Pacífico*.

1 pound cuchuco de maíz*
8 cups beef stock, or
   more as needed
½ cup minced scallion,
   white part only
3 sprigs cilantro
2 cloves garlic, minced
1 beef bouillon cube
¼ teaspoon salt
¼ teaspoon pepper
¼ teaspoon ground
   cumin*

1 recipe of Carne en Polvo
   (page 59)
1 recipe Chicharrones
   (page 60)
1 recipe Hogao del
   Pacífico (page 165)
1 recipe Tajadas de Plátano,
   without the cheese and
   sugar (page 147)

1. Wash the corn pieces well, and drain. Soak in 3 cups of water overnight.

2. Drain the corn and discard the water. Place the corn in a medium pressure cooker together with beef stock, scallion, cilantro, garlic, bouillon cube, salt, pepper and cumin. Cover and cook over medium-low heat. After 1 hour, turn off the heat and let the pot cool down enough to release the steam and open. If the corn has completely softened, continue the recipe at the next step; if not, add 1 more cup of stock, cover, and put back on the heat for 15 to 20 minutes more. The corn should look like a risotto when it's almost done, very moist but not watery. Simmer uncovered if it needs to dry out some more. In a regular pot follow the same guide but initially simmer over low heat for 2 to 2½ hours.

3. Prepare the rest of the recipes, leaving the tajadas de plátano for last, as they should be prepared just before serving time.

4. When ready to serve, fry the tajadas de plátano, which in this case can be diced for ease of serving, although traditionally they are served long and each person cuts them into pieces.

5. Serve the corn in soup bowls, and pass the other foods to be added into the bowl with the corn.

MOLDE DE PURÉ DE PAPA Y CARNE

Beef and Potato Puree Pie

8 servings

My sister in New York City wonders why she can't get this dish there. It is so simple, she thinks; why does every meal have to be so complex? Actually, it *is* simple, and we ate it at least twice a month all through our childhood. I think the seasoning for the meat and the combination with eggs are what make this dish so good.

POTATOES

1½ tablespoons salt
2 eggs, at room temperature
4 pounds potatoes, peeled and cut in quarters
1 tablespoon butter
½ cup minced scallions
2 tablespoons minced parsley

BEEF FILLING

3 tablespoons oil
1 cup minced scallion
¼ cup peeled and diced tomatoes
1 chicken bouillon cube
1 teaspoon minced garlic
¾ teaspoon color* or turmeric
½ teaspoon ground cumin*
½ teaspoon salt
1 pound ground beef
Oil or butter for the baking pan

1. In large pot place 10 cups of water, the salt, and the eggs; bring to a boil.

2. Add the potatoes, cover and simmer for 15 to 20 minutes, until the potatoes are tender when pricked with a fork.

3. While the potatoes are cooking, in a small sauté pan over low heat place the butter and scallions. Cook for 8 minutes, add the parsley and set aside.

4. Drain the potatoes and eggs and discard the water. Mash the potatoes with a fork or potato masher and add the sautéed scallions. Peel and dice the eggs. Set both aside for assembly.

5. In a large sauté pan, over medium heat place the oil, scallion, tomatoes, bouillon cube, garlic, color, cumin, and salt; sauté for 5 minutes.

6. Add the beef, decrease the heat to low and cook for 10 minutes, breaking up the meat to remove chunks.

7. Remove from the heat and set aside.

8. Preheat the oven to 350°F. Butter or oil an 8 by 8-inch square Pyrex mold. Place ½ of the mashed potatoes in the bottom and spread it evenly.

9. Spread the beef filling and the diced eggs over the potatoes, and cover with the rest of the potatoes.

10. Bake for 20 minutes or until completely heated.

11. Serve.

MORCILLAS O RELLENAS

Blood Sausages from Isabel Gelpud

2 pounds of sausages

On the coast, we call these *morcillas*, while in the interior of the country they call them *rellenas*. For this recipe, I traveled to the small town of Candelaria on the outskirts of Cali, where supposedly the best *rellenas* are prepared. Isabel Gelpud invited us in to watch, learn, and take lots of pictures. After seeing the whole process done in a very homey style, handmade and very clean, I was positively surprised. These sausages are mostly herbs, and the raw mixture is beautifully colored. They are definitely an acquired taste, but once you do like them, they are great! On the third floor of her house, Isabel grows many of the herbs we used, and there for the first time I saw large leaf oregano (about 2 inches long!) that she says is called *oreganon*.

Pork blood can be ordered through your butcher or meat market.

8 teaspoons pork belly or fat
1 pound scallion, minced
2 cups minced chard
½ cup pork fat (from the casings or bought separately)
1 tablespoon salt
1 tablespoon garlic
1 beef bouillon cube
1 teaspoon color* or turmeric
¾ cup white rice
1 whole scallion
1 tablespoon lard or oil
1 teaspoon salt
2 tablespoons fresh thyme leaves
2 tablespoons minced cilantro
2 tablespoons minced cimarrón*
2 tablespoons minced mint leaves
2 tablespoons minced oregano
2 teaspoons minced poleo* or additional mint
2 cups pork blood
Pork casings (4 to 5 feet), clean

1. In a medium pot place the pork fat and sauté the scallion for 5 minutes. Add the chard, pork fat from the casings, salt, garlic, bouillon cube, and color. Cook for 5 minutes more. Set aside and cool.

2. In a small pot, over medium heat place the rice, whole scallion, lard, and salt; sauté for 1 minute. Add 1½ cups of water, bring to a boil and simmer until you can see the rice on the surface. Lower the heat to minimum, cover, and cook for 15 minutes. Uncover, fluff with a fork, remove the whole scallion, and set aside to cool completely.

3. In a very large mixing bow, mix the cooked scallions, prepared rice, thyme, cilantro, cimarrón, mint, oregano, and poleo with the blood. The amount of blood is only enough to moisten all the other ingredients; the mixture should be wet but not runny.

4. Fill the casings with the mixture. Tie carefully with string.

5. In a large pot place 3½ quarts of water, the 2 bouillon cubes, cilantro, cimarron, oregano, and salt, and bring to a boil. Simmer for 15 minutes.

6. Drop the sausages into the simmering stock and cook for 30 minutes or until they release clear juices when poked.

COOKING STOCK
2 beef bouillon cubes
4 sprigs cilantro
4 leaves cimarron*
4 sprigs oregano
2 tablespoons salt

7. Remove from the pot, discard the stock, and set aside to cool. Refrigerate for later use, or barbecue or fry just enough to reheat and serve.

PAVO RELLENO

12 to 14 servings

Pavo Relleno is what is served in many homes along with *Pernil de Cerdo* (page 76), *Tamales* (page 82) and *Hayacas* (page 64) for Christmas holiday season events. Normally turkeys were given Aguardiente* or rum to get them drunk before being killed to be prepared for the festivities.

I have used this filling for many years and changed it a bit over time, such as adding Dijon mustard, but otherwise it is the traditional beef and pork filling. Count one pound of raw turkey per serving.

One 14-pound turkey
Lime juice or vinegar, as needed

TURKEY SEASONING
1½ cup diced onion
1 cup butter
¼ cup minced parsley
½ cup minced cilantro
2 tablespoons Dijon mustard
3 cloves garlic, minced
1 tablespoon fresh thyme leaves
1 tablespoon minced scallion
1 tablespoon salt
1 tablespoon Worcestershire sauce
½ teaspoon pepper

1. If frozen, thaw the turkey in the refrigerator about 2 days without unwrapping from the original package. Remove the gizzards and any other giblets inside (discard or use for other purposes). Wash the turkey well inside and out with lime juice or vinegar.

2. Once the turkey has thawed, make the seasoning: Place onion, butter, parsley, cilantro, mustard, garlic, thyme, scallion, salt, Worcestershire, and pepper in the bowl of a food processor, and process for 30 seconds.

3. Spread the mixture under the turkey skin. Let the turkey rest in the refrigerator, covered, for 1 day.

4. Make the Pork and Beef Stuffing a day ahead if you will be stuffing the turkey with it; if you will be serving it alongside, you can make it the same day you cook the turkey: In a food processor place the beef, pork, onion, ⅓ cup of the raisins, scallion, cilantro, parsley, mustard, thyme, capers, garlic, and pepper, and process to a smooth consistency.

5. Cook the bacon until crispy. Set the fat aside and crumble the bacon into small pieces. The pork fat may be used if the beef is too dry and you want to add 2 tablespoons of it; otherwise discard.

6. Remove the meat mixture from the processor and place it into a medium pot or *caldero**. Add the crumbled bacon, prunes, and olives. Cook over medium-high heat, stirring to break up any clumps, about 15 minutes or until the beef and pork are completely cooked.

7. While the meat mixture is cooking, in a small pot place the remaining ⅔ cup of raisins and the cognac. Cook over medium heat until the raisins absorb the cognac and plump up. Add them to the meat mixture.

8. Reduce the heat of the pot to medium and add the Port, apples, and almonds. Taste for salt, and add more if necessary.

9. In the food processor bowl, place the bread slices and process to get crumbs. Remove from the processor and place them into a small bowl. Add the eggs and mix them together. Add to the meat mixture and cook for 4 to 5 minutes.

10. Remove the pot from the heat. If you will use it the next day, let the stuffing cool and then refrigerate it. Do not stuff the turkey with hot stuffing, and do not stuff the turkey the day before roasting it! Only stuff the turkey right before you roast it!

11. If serving the stuffing alongside the turkey right after cooking, place it on a nice platter and serve immediately. To reheat, place the filling in an ovenproof serving container and bake for 30 to 40 minutes a 375°F.

12. Remove the turkey from the refrigerator at least 1 or 2 hours before cooking, to bring it back to room temperature.

13. If stuffing the turkey, do it now. Truss the turkey, tying the legs last. Place it on a rack in a roasting pan. Pour the beer and 2 cups of water into the bottom of the pan.

ROASTING METHOD 1
14. Preheat the oven to 425°F. Put the turkey in, and decrease the heat to 325°F. Bake for 20 minutes per pound if stuffed, or 16 minutes per pound if not.

ROASTING METHOD 2
14. Preheat the oven to 400°F. Place the turkey in the oven and bake until golden brown, about 45 minutes; cover with foil and reduce the temperature to 325°F and cook 3 to 3½ hours more.

CONTINUED

PORK AND BEEF STUFFING
½ pound ground beef
½ pound ground pork or
   Italian sausage
1½ cups diced onion
1 cup raisins
½ cup minced scallions
¼ cup minced cilantro
¼ cup minced parsley
2 tablespoons Dijon
   mustard
2 tablespoons fresh
   thyme leaves
15 capers, rinsed
1 clove garlic, minced
1 teaspoon pepper
4 ounces bacon
¼ cup sliced pitted
   prunes
8 pitted green olives,
   sliced
½ cup cognac
1 cup port wine
3 green apples, peeled
   and diced
½ cup toasted almonds
5 slices white bread
2 whole eggs, beaten

1 (12-ounce) can of beer,
   for roasting the turkey
Juices from from the
   roasting pan, for the
   gravy
Butter, for the gravy
Flour, for the gravy

15. Whichever method you use to roast the turkey, it is done when after pinching the thickest part of the thigh, the liquid runs clear and not pink. The internal temperature at the thigh of the bird should be 160 to 180° F. Let rest 30 minutes before carving and serving. While the turkey is resting, make the gravy.

16. Remove all the fat from the juices in the roasting pan. Measure the liquid and place it in a pot.

17. For each cup of liquid, add 1 tablespoon of butter mixed with 1 tablespoon of flour. Cook to thicken, stirring occasionally, about 5 to 10 minutes.

18. Taste and season with salt and pepper and serve.

PECHUGAS DE POLLO AL COCO

Chicken Breasts with Coconut Sauce

6 to 8 servings

> Chicken in Coconut Sauce is a dish of the Pacific region usually prepared with free-range chickens. It is very good and can be prepared ahead of time: cook it the night before and refrigerate it, or freeze it up to a week in advance, only to reheat right before serving what will be a tastier chicken. Freeze in one-layer thickness to defrost overnight in the refrigerator.

6 tablespoons olive oil
1 tablespoon plus ½ teaspoon garlic paste (page 166)
½ teaspoon salt
½ teaspoon pepper
4 whole chicken breasts cut in 2, skin and bones included
2 cups sliced white onion
1 cup julienned red bell pepper
½ chicken bouillon cube
1 teaspoon color* or turmeric
2½ cups coconut milk (freshly made, page 107, or canned)
2 tablespoons flour
4 tablespoons minced parsley
Cooked white rice, for serving
Patacones (page 143), for serving

1. Combine 4 tablespoons of the oil, ½ teaspoon of garlic paste, and ¼ teaspoon each of the salt and pepper. Rub onto the chicken breasts. Set aside in the refrigerator to marinate for at least an hour or overnight if desired.

2. In a large sauté pan over medium-high heat, brown the breasts skin-side down for 3 to 5 minutes or until golden. Turn and brown the bone side for 3 to 5 minutes more. Remove from the heat and set aside.

3. In a large pot over medium heat, place the remaining 2 tablespoons of oil. Add the onion, red pepper, remaining garlic paste, bouillon cube, color, and the remaining ¼ teaspoon of salt and pepper. Sauté for 5 minutes.

4. Place the coconut milk and flour in a bowl and mix until free of lumps; pour into the pot. Add the chicken breasts; cover and simmer for 15 to 20 minutes. Check to see if the chicken is cooked through, and remove from the heat.

5. Sprinkle with parsley and serve over white rice with patacones.

PERNIL DE CERDO

Fresh Leg of Pork
20 to 25 servings

Another very festive dish, this is a delicious recipe prepared throughout the country for the Christmas season. Sometimes even prepared with Coca-Cola, the traditional way is to prepare it with the bone in and to leave the top layer of skin and fat on the leg. It is beautifully cooked to a golden brownish-red, with crisscross-cut skin that is crispy and delicious, and with tender meat inside. In my house we prepare both turkey and pork on Christmas Eve; *Hayacas* (page 64) are served the next morning. Then for lunch on Christmas Day, my sister Sylvia, who is a great cook, prepares a large outdoor barbecue with *Chorizos* (page 61), *Morcillas* (page 70), *Butifarras* (page 56), beef, and corn on the cob.

1 fresh ham or leg of pork
  (about 12 pounds)
2 cups orange juice
1 cup diced onion
1 cup Dijon mustard
½ cup minced cilantro
½ cup minced parsley
½ cup lime juice
8 cloves garlic, minced
2 tablespoons fresh
  thyme leaves
2 tablespoons
  Worcestershire sauce
2 tablespoons salt
4 bay leaves
1 teaspoon pepper
1 teaspoon minced fresh
  ginger

1. Buy the whole leg of pork with the bone, fat, and skin included. Ask your butcher to make crisscross cuts, 1 inch apart, on the skin.

2. Place the pork in a large nonreactive container; add the orange juice, onion, mustard, cilantro, parsley, lime juice, garlic, thyme, Worcestershire, 4 teaspoons of the salt, bay leaves, pepper, and ginger, and rub all over the leg. Refrigerate covered until the next day.

3. Remove from the refrigerator and let it come to room temperature, 1 to 2 hours. Rub with the remaining 2 teaspoons of salt. If you bought the pork already boned, tie it with twine to hold it together while cooking. (A leg with the bone will hold together on its own.)

4. Preheat the oven to 325°F. Place the leg on a rack in a roasting pan. Pour the leftover seasoning juices in the bottom of the pan together with 1 cup of water.

5. Bake, covered with foil, for 20 minutes per pound, about 4 hours.

6. While the meat is cooking, **PREPARE THE GLAZE**: in a small, heavy pot, mix the mustard, sugar, thyme, orange peel, cloves, ginger, and pepper. Bring to a boil, reduce the heat and simmer for 5 minutes. Stir occasionally so it doesn't burn. Set aside until needed.

7. Remove foil from the meat, brush all over with the glaze and cook uncovered 10 minutes more per pound, about 2 hours. When you add the glaze, check that the water on the bottom of the pan has not evaporated; keep checking and adding more if needed.

8. Remove the leg when the internal temperature is 160 to 180°F. Let it rest for 30 minutes before carving.

GLAZE
1 cup Dijon mustard
1½ cups brown sugar or panela*
4 tablespoons fresh thyme leaves
2 tablespoons grated orange peel
2 teaspoons whole cloves
2 teaspoons minced fresh ginger
2 teaspoons pepper

SAUCE
Pan drippings
Flour

9. **TO PREPARE THE SAUCE**, remove fat from pan drippings. Measure the remaining juices into a small pot and add 1½ teaspoons of flour per cup of liquid. Stir well and cook until thickened.

10. Serve and enjoy!

PINCHOS DE HÍGADO Y
CORAZÓN DE POLLO *Chicken Liver and Heart Kebobs*

6 kebobs

In the farms and mountains of Colombia, a lot of free-range chickens are raised to be part of the basic diet. This happens for practical and economical reasons: chickens in Colombia are pretty expensive and this way the farmers grow the hens in their yards instead of buying them; they eat their eggs and later on the animal's meat. The livers and hearts are usually used for this dish. The best way to cook them is over wooden fires or coals; they cook slowly and take the smoky taste and aroma of the surroundings. I think this is a dish that takes you back to the cool mountains, wet grass and pine and eucalyptus smelling lands of our country.

1 pound chicken livers
  with hearts attached
1 teaspoon minced scallion
½ teaspoon minced garlic
¼ teaspoon salt
¼ teaspoon ground
  cumin*
¼ teaspoon curry powder
½ cup diced red bell
  pepper, 1-inch dice
½ cup diced onion, 1-inch
  dice
2 tablespoons olive oil

1. Clean the chicken livers well by removing all the fat around them. Separate the livers from the hearts and cut each liver in half.

2. Place the livers and hearts in a bowl and mix with scallion, garlic, salt, cumin, and curry. Refrigerate for at least 1 hour, or overnight.

3. Place the livers, red pepper, hearts and onions on skewers, alternating with each other. Brush with oil.

4. Set on the hot barbecue or grill (400°F) and cook for 10 minutes; turn and cook for another 10 minutes. They usually shrink as they cook through.

TO COOK IN THE OVEN: Preheat the oven to 350°F, brush with olive oil, set on baking sheets and bake for 25 minutes.

TO COOK IN A SAUTÉ PAN: Brush them with oil and place in the pan over medium low heat cook for 5 minutes on each side; cover and decrease the heat to low and cook for 5 minutes more.

5. Serve.

POLLO SUDADO

Chicken Stew
6 servings

> This dish is prepared in my house once a week, or almost. Every time we run out of ideas, *Pollo Sudado* comes up in the air. It could be called a quick comfort food for us. It is very easy to prepare (even if all you have is frozen chicken pieces), and the kids really like it. They eat it with white rice, even though it has potatoes; the rice soaks up all the tasty sauce. Try it!

1. In a large, nonreactive bowl place the chicken thighs, minced onion, 2 tablespoons of the oil, mustard, garlic, 1 teaspoon of the salt, and the pepper. Mix well and set aside for 30 minutes.

2. In a large pot over medium heat, place the remaining 1 tablespoon oil and sauté the sliced onions for 4 minutes. Add the tomatoes, cilantro, parsley, the remaining 2 teaspoons of salt, Worcestershire, color, and bouillon cube, and sauté for 4 minutes more.

3. Add the seasoned chicken and 1 cup of water. Cover and cook for 30 minutes.

4. Add the potatoes and cover again, and cook until the potatoes are tender, about 20 minutes more.

5. Serve over white rice.

12 chicken thighs (thawed in the refrigerator if frozen)
⅓ cup minced onion
3 tablespoons olive oil
2 tablespoons prepared mustard
3 cloves garlic, minced
3 teaspoons salt
¼ teaspoon pepper
2 cup sliced onion
2 cups peeled and diced tomatoes
2 tablespoons minced cilantro
2 tablespoons minced parsley
2 teaspoons Worcestershire sauce
1 teaspoon color* or turmeric
1 chicken bouillon cube
1½ pounds (about 12) small yellow potatoes
Cooked white rice, for serving

POSTA NEGRA

Black Beef
8 servings

Posta Negra is prepared with different cuts of meat in different places around the country; some with rib eye, some with *bollo* or rolled rump or eye of round, most with *punta de anca* or top round and even sirloin. The flavor varies with the type of meat but they are all good. This traditional dish is often prepared with Coca-Cola.

⅔ cup sliced green onion*, 1-inch chunks
6 tablespoons oil
3 tablespoons prepared mustard
5 tablespoons Worcestershire sauce
3 cloves garlic, minced
¼ teaspoon pepper
3 pounds beef rolled rump, eye of round, or top round, in 1 piece
1 medium onion, quartered
3 cloves garlic
2 cups Coca-Cola
½ cup brown sugar
¾ cup red wine
2 tablespoons ketchup
2½ teaspoons salt

1. Place the green onion, 3 tablespoons of the oil, mustard, 3 tablespoons of the Worcestershire, minced garlic, and pepper in a blender and puree.

2. Place the beef in a nonreactive container and add the blended ingredients. Mix well to coat the meat all over. Cover and refrigerate for 1 to 3 days. (The longer, the more tender the beef will be.)

3. Thirty minutes before cooking, remove the meat from the refrigerator, and set aside to reach room temperature.

4. In a medium or large pressure cooker, over high heat place the remaining 3 tablespoons of oil. When it is hot, add the beef fat side down and brown for 7 minutes; turn and brown or seal the other side of the beef for 2 more minutes. Add 2 cups of water, the quartered onion, and whole garlic; cover and cook under pressure on medium heat for 25 minutes. If using a regular pot, cook for 2 to 3 hours.

5. In a large bowl place Coca-Cola, sugar, red wine, ketchup, the remaining 2 tablespoons of Worcestershire, and salt, mix and set aside.

6. Remove the pot from the heat; release the pressure, let stand for 10 minutes and open. Add the Coca-Cola mixture and put back on the heat. Simmer over low heat for 1 hour, with the cover ajar (this is the same in a regular pot).

7. Remove the meat from the pot, let it stand for 10 minutes, slice.

8. Pour the sauce from the pot and remove the fat. Serve over the sliced beef or on the side.

SOBREBARRIGA

Sobrebarriga* is translated as "belly beef," and is actually the piece of meat that surrounds the flank steak. Very typical of the Boyacá and Cundinamarca regions, this delicious cut of beef has to be cooked thoroughly to become tender, but has great taste and texture. The closest American cut is outer skirt steak, or diaphragm.

½ cup diced tomato
½ cup minced onion
¼ cup minced scallion
2 tablespoons minced cilantro
1 teaspoon salt
½ teaspoon powdered bay leaf
¼ teaspoon pepper
3 pounds sobrebarriga*, clean

HOGAO
2 tablespoons oil
1½ cup diced onion
1½ cup peeled and diced tomatoes
2 teaspoon minced garlic
¼ teaspoon Worcestershire sauce
¼ teaspoon salt
⅛ teaspoon pepper
1 teaspoon minced cilantro

½ cup bread crumbs

1. Combine the tomato, onion, scallion, cilantro, salt, bay leaf, and pepper and rub all over the meat; refrigerate for 1 hour or overnight if desired.

2. Cook the sobrebarriga in one of the two following ways:

IN THE OVEN
3. Preheat the oven to 250°F. Place the meat in a baking pan, add 1 cup of water, cover tightly, and bake for 2 hours or until tender.

IN A PRESSURE COOKER
3. Place the meat and 1 cup of water in a pressure cooker over medium-low heat and cook until tender, about 40 minutes. Remove from the pressure cooker, and place in a baking pan or ovenproof serving dish.

4. While the meat is cooking, **PREPARE THE HOGAO:** In a large sauté pan over medium heat place the oil, and sauté the onions, tomatoes, garlic, Worcestershire, salt, and pepper. Lower the heat to low and cook for 10 to 12 minutes. The raw onion flavor will have disappeared. Add the cilantro and set aside.

5. Remove the meat from the oven or pressure cooker. Turn the oven heat up to 475°F. Cover the meat with hogao and sprinkle with bread crumbs.

6. Bake for 10 minutes. Serve.

TAMALES

12 servings, 1 tamal each

Tamales are different as you travel around the country. Variations include *tamales vallunos*, from Valle del Cauca, like these ones with corn *masa* and chicken; rice tamales like the *tamales tolimenses* from the Tolima department and the Pacific Coast varieties; *tamales bogotanos* are found in Bogotá, the country's capital, and contain pork, chicken and *longaniza**; *antioqueños*, from the Valle de Aburrá, are made with *tocino** and tomatoes; and *nariñenses*, from the South, with hard-boiled egg and pork or chicken. This is a long recipe, but one I believe is worthwhile preparing, so I made it for twelve servings so you could invite people to share and enjoy your gastronomic expertise. *Tamales* can be frozen after they are wrapped and cooked the first time. Then they are set frozen into boiling salted water until heated through, about 20 minutes.

7 chicken thighs
1½ pounds pork leg, cut in 12 pieces
2 cups minced scallion
3 cloves garlic, minced
2 tablespoon Worcestershire sauce
1 chicken bouillon cube
1 teaspoon Adobo* Goya
1 teaspoon color* or turmeric

1. In a large bowl mix the chicken, pork, scallions, garlic, Worcestershire, bouillon cube, adobo, and color. Cover and refrigerate overnight.

2. Place the chicken and pork mixture and 1 cup of water in a large pot over medium heat. Bring to a simmer, cover, and cook over medium-low heat for 20 minutes.

3. Remove from the heat and set aside to cool. Remove the skin and bones from the chicken pieces. Strain the cooking liquid to use in the dough.

MASA*
6 cups (2 pounds) yellow corn masa flour*
¼ cup minced scallion
1 teaspoon minced garlic
1 chicken bouillon cube
1 cup cooking liquid from the chicken and pork
1 tablespoon salt
1½ teaspoons color*
1 teaspoon Adobo* Goya
1 teaspoon ground cumin*

4. **TO PREPARE THE DOUGH**: Place the masa flour with the scallion and garlic in a large bowl. Mix with a fork.

5. Heat ½ cup of water in the microwave for 1 minute. Add the chicken bouillon cube and dissolve.

6. Add the bouillon cube water, 8 cups of water, 1 cup of the meat cooking liquid, salt, color, adobo, and cumin to the masa flour mixture. Mix well with your hands or with a fork; make sure you have no lumps in the mixture. Set aside.

GUISO
⅓ cup oil
5 cups minced scallion
8 cloves garlic, minced
3 chicken bouillon cubes
1½ teaspoons color*
1½ teaspoons ground cumin*
½ teaspoon pepper

WRAPPING
24 bijao* or plantain leaves, each 24 inches long
Butcher's string for tying

VEGETABLE FILLING
2 cups sliced potatoes, ¼-inch thick (about 24 slices)
3 yellow potatoes cut in 8^{ths} (24 pieces)
1 cup sliced carrot, ¼-inch thick (about 24 slices)
1 cup fresh peas

4 tablespoons salt
4 chicken bouillon cubes

7. **TO PREPARE THE GUISO:** Place the oil, scallion, garlic, chicken bouillon cubes, color, cumin, and pepper in a 5-quart pot over medium heat. Cook for 12 minutes. Set aside.

8. **TO PREPARE THE LEAVES:** Wash the leaves well on both sides. Pass over the flame of your stove top to dry. They will change from dark green to bright green. Set aside.

9. **TO ASSEMBLE THE TAMALES:** Place a 24-inch-long piece of bijao leaf over your work surface. Place a second one perpendicular to the first, on top of it. (Make a cross with the two.)

10. In the center where the two leaves cross, add ½ tablespoon of guiso, and spread it over a 5-inch diameter. Add about 1 cup of dough and flatten it with a fork. On the dough place 1 piece of chicken, 1 piece of pork, 2 slices each of potatoes, yellow potatoes, and carrots, and about a tablespoon of peas. Add 2 tablespoons of guiso over the vegetables. Place another cup of dough over the whole thing. Flatten to cover all you can.

11. Wrap the leaves around the "pie" or tamal. Tie with string and continue until you have them all filled and tied.

12. Place 2 large pots of water over high heat, each with 2 tablespoons of salt and 2 bouillon cubes. Bring to a boil, decrease the heat to very low and place the tamales into the water. Cover and cook for 1 hour. Remove the tamales from the pot, drain them, and discard the liquid. Let sit for 5 minutes before untying.

13. Cut the string and serve.

TAMALES DE PIPIÁN

36 small tamales (4 by 2 inches)

Tamales de Pipián are typical of the Valle del Cauca region—and are something out of this world. They are smaller than other *tamales*, somewhat like an appetizer size. They contain a yellow potato mixture called *pipián*, and are served with an extraordinary hot *Ají de Maní* (page 159). They are not hard to prepare; just read the recipe several times to put some of the steps in order in your mind and go. Enjoy, as they are really worth it.

1. **PREPARE THE FILLLING**: In a bowl place the pork, oil, scallion, garlic, adobo, and pepper, mix well and set aside in the refrigerator for 1 hour.

2. In a medium pot over medium-low heat, place the seasoned pork and 1½ cups of water; cook covered for 30 to 45 minutes or until the pork is fully cooked and tender.

3. Remove the meat from the liquid. Strain the cooking liquid and discard the vegetables. Set aside both the meat and cooking liquid.

4. **FOR THE HOGAO**: in a medium pot over low heat cook the scallions in the oil for 8 minutes. Add the tomatoes, garlic, cilantro, bouillon cube, sugar, salt, pepper, and cumin, and continue to cook over low heat for 15 minutes more. Set aside.

5. **FOR THE POTATOES**: In a large pot, place 3 cups water, the bouillon cube, and salt. Bring to a boil and add the potatoes. Cover and cook for 10 to 12 minutes; the potatoes will be very soft and the water will have thickened. Remove from the heat and let cool a little. Add the pork filling, hogao, ground peanuts, and diced eggs; mix well and set aside.

PORK FILLING
1½ pounds pork, cut in
    ½-inch dice
1 tablespoon oil
4 tablespoons minced
    scallion
1 clove garlic, minced
½ teaspoon Adobo* Goya
¼ teaspoon pepper

HOGAO
1½ cups minced scallion
2 tablespoons oil
1½ cups peeled, diced
    tomatoes
1 clove garlic, minced and
    then mashed
2 teaspoons minced
    cilantro
½ beef bouillon cube
¼ teaspoon sugar
¼ teaspoon salt
¼ teaspoon pepper
¼ teaspoon ground
    cumin*

POTATOES
1 beef bouillon cube
1 teaspoon salt
2 pounds (4 cups) diced
    yellow potatoes, ½-inch
    dice
½ cup unsalted, roasted
    peanuts, ground

2 hard-boiled eggs, peeled and diced

MASA*
3 cups (1 pound) yellow corn masa flour*
2 tablespoons minced scallion
1 teaspoon minced garlic
½ beef bouillon cube
1 cup cooking liquid from the pork
1 teaspoon color*
½ tablespoon salt
½ teaspoon Adobo* Goya
½ teaspoon ground cumin*

12 bijao* or plantain leaves

6. **PREPARE THE DOUGH**: Place the masa flour with the scallion and garlic in a 4-quart bowl. Mix with a fork.

7. Heat ½ cup of water in the microwave for 1 minute. Add the bouillon cube and dissolve.

8. Add 4 cups of water, 1 cup of pork stock (the strained cooking liquid), color, salt, adobo, and cumin to the masa flour mixture. Mix well with your hands or with a fork. Make sure you have no lumps in the dough. Set aside.

9. Wash the leaves well on both sides, dry, cut into 8-inch squares and set aside.

10. Place one 8-inch square piece of bijao leaf on the work surface. In the center of the leaf place ¼ cup of masa; spread it into a 2- by 4-inch rectangle and flatten it with a fork. On the masa place 1 tablespoon of filling. Wrap the leaves around the "pie" or tamal in the form of an envelope. Tie with string.

COOKING
11. In a large pot, bring enough water to cover tamales to a boil. Put a rack on the bottom of another 7-quart pot and place the tamales on the rack. Pour in enough of the boiling water to cover the tamales. Bring the water to a simmer, cover and simmer for 40 minutes.

12. Remove the tamales from the pot (discard the liquid) and let them sit for 5 minutes before untying.

13. Cut the strings and serve with Ají de Maní (page 159).

SUDADO DE RES

Beef Stew
6 to 8 servings

Beef stew is a typical dish of all areas and with all families. A relatively inexpensive cut of meat is used and therefore cooked in a pressure cooker to soften. This recipe can be made in a slow cooker; just add the potatoes whole so they take as long as the meat and the yuca.

1. In a medium stockpot, place the beef, stock, and yuca strips; simmer over low heat, covered, for 30 to 45 minutes.

2. While the meat is cooking, prepare the hogao and set aside.

3. Add 1 cup of water and the potato halves to the beef. Simmer for 20 minutes, and let the water dry out so the beef browns a little. Add the last cup of water, hogao, salt, and pepper, and simmer 10 to 15 minutes more, covered. Check that the yuca and potatoes are completely cooked and soft when pierced with a fork.

4. Uncover, check that the beef is tender, and serve over white rice.

1½ pounds beef, cut in ¾-inch dice
2 cups beef stock or 2 cups water plus 1 beef bouillon cube
1 pound peeled yuca* or cassava, cut into ¼-inch strips
1 recipe of Hogao del Pacífico (page 165) or Hogao del Caribe (page 164)
1 pound red potatoes, peeled and halved
1 teaspoon salt
¼ teaspoon pepper
Cooked white rice, for serving

SEAFOOD

Colombia is bordered by both the Pacific Ocean and the Caribbean Sea, which provides us with a great diversity of seafood and many ways of preparing each type. I have wonderful memories of my children playing with the live lobsters and then helping out at the table, as well as fishing with their father and friends for the foods we would later prepare.

In Colombia, fishermen say that shellfish should not be eaten in the months that do not have an "r" in their name, which are May, June, July and August, for these are the months of *veda*, when they reproduce.

The Atlantic Coast has a variety of seafood from the Caribbean Sea and river fish from the Magdalena River, the largest river in the country that almost crosses it from north to south. From the ocean, we get a whole array of shellfish that includes shrimp, langoustines, lobster, crabs, and oysters, along with fish of many types like *pargo* or snapper, red snapper, *lisa*, a dried fish also called mullet, *robalo* or bass, *sierra* or Spanish mackerel, *mojarra (Eugerres plumieri)*, and even eel. Fish is usually served with coconut rice and plantains and eaten fully smothered in lime juice. From the river comes an abundance of *bocachico*, a small mouthed fish that is very popular, and the typical dish of the departments of Córdoba and Magdalena. We eat it mostly in *sancochos* and *viuda* dishes like *Viuda de Pescado* (page 104).

The department of Bolívar, hosting the beautiful Islas del Rosario, is one of the main sources of this abundance and variety of seafood. The Guajira, a semiarid peninsula located directly on the Caribbean, is the farthest department to the north in the country and also a vast source of sea ingredients and concoctions, especially ones including the turtle, which is now protected and cannot be caught or sold.

The Pacific region is by far the area where most seafood is eaten. The people here have a large African influence, from the times that the Spanish brought the slaves to cook and work for them. They have a lot of fried foods, *envueltos* or wrapped dishes, and spicy recipes that combine both cultures: the aboriginal and the African. Fish is eaten fresh, salted, dried, fried, stewed, made into balls or croquettes, their eggs eaten, their meats prepared into seviches or cocktails and made into paste forms.

The Andean zone is the farthest to the sea, but we still find there a lot of *viuda de pescado*, which is prepared with dry *bocachico* in parts like the departments of Huila, Caldas, Risaralda, Cauca and Nariño. Trouts and tilapia are also harvested in modern lakes and facilities.

In the Amazonía region, fish is the principal food source. With the majestic Amazon River, along the Casanare, Meta, Vichada, Guaviare, Guainía, Vaupés, Caquetá and Putumayo rivers, these great plain and forest territories are a large source of fish, including *dorado, sábalo* or *tarpon, cachama,* and other fish of the area called *pintadillo o rayado* (*Pseudoplatystoma fasciatum*), *baboso* (*Goslinea platynema*), *amarillo* (*Pauliceae lutkeni*), and *pujon* (*Brachyplatystoma viallantii*). They are prepared in soups, *sancochos,* or stews, with coconut, yuca and plantains as favorite accompaniments. In the departments of Caqueta, Guaviare and Guainía, in typical settings the fish is wrapped in plantains leaves and cooked underground over coals. Guainíans cook their fish with scales covered with leaves too, but the whole skin is later removed when ready to eat. *Cahama,* one of the most popular fish in the area, is a large black fish that can grow up to one meter long and has a large skeleton but great white meat and is much appreciated. I used to make *ceviche* from *cachamas* in el Valle del Cauca, as a friend of my husband, Alonso Villegas, had a lake full of them; he would feed them guavas from the trees around the lake. My kids would go and fish there and have the time of their life! Moving up to Arauca, they also eat *bagre* or catfish and turtle and corn fritters.

I had to choose my favorites from an extensive list of seafood recipes. The cocktails and *ceviches* can be quick light dinners if served over lettuce with a light lime vinaigrette, or beautiful appetizers for elegant sit-down dinner parties, or even fillings for tartlets at a buffet. The fish, either fried—my children's favorite; in coconut "aphrodisiac" sauce—my husband's; or Creole style, are all great ways to prepare whichever variety you find fresh where you live, whether whole or as filets. From simple to elaborate, these recipes show an array of our bountiful seafood. Many of the recipes here are for two or four servings, mainly because they are usually prepared like that, two at a time, to offer a chance to enjoy them at home in romantic settings. Try them, and find out how they can be exciting and provocative.

"In a nonreactive bowl" is a term I use a lot in this chapter. It refers to a bowl made of glass, plastic or stainless steel. Acidic ingredients can change the color and flavor of foods if mixed in aluminum or iron containers.

CALAMARES AL AJILLO

Garlic Squid
2 servings

This is a great way to cook a quick and elegant meal for family or friends using calamari. Enjoy this dish any day with freshly baked bread.

6 tablespoons butter
2 tablespoons garlic paste (page 166)
½ teaspoon salt
¼ teaspoon pepper
2 tablespoons dry sherry
3 teaspoons minced parsley, plus more for garnish
¾ pound clean squid rings, fresh or frozen but not precooked

1. Place butter into a small sauté pan over low heat. Add the garlic, salt and pepper and cook on low for 2 minutes.

2. Add the sherry and parsley; continue cooking for 2 minutes more.

3. Increase the heat to medium and add the squid, sauté in the sauce for about 55 seconds—no more than one minute. They turn from glossy grayish white to completely white in color and their consistency changes from jelly-like to harder and rounder but not tough.

4. Sprinkle with more parsley if desired and serve with bread to pick up the sauce.

NOTE: Fresh squid should be cooked for no longer than one minute; if you forget, keep on cooking it for about 1 hour, at which point it will soften again.

CAZUELA DE MARISCOS
Crustacean Chowder
4 to 6 servings

This dish is the perfect romantic dinner for two. It looks beautiful served in coconuts and adds a sensual feeling to the evening when the table is set with candles and maybe some real plantain leaves and earth-colored tableware. Have a handy person cut some coconut shells into basket-like forms, wash, and dry them well over a flame to warm before serving. I also like to add pieces of quartered plantain at the beginning of the recipe. Use a whole plantain that is neither green nor completely ripe, one you bought green and left unrefrigerated for two days. It will be just a little sweet and taste like nothing you have ever had before.

This idea for this recipe came from the Restaurant Pacífico, in Cali, whose owners have had restaurants in the Pacific city of Buenaventura for over thirty years.

1. In a large, heavy pot or *caldero** over medium-low heat, place the oil, onion, red pepper, seafood, bouillon cubes, garlic, color or saffron, salt, and pepper. Cook for 12 minutes.

2. Mix the coconut milk, milk and flour together to a smooth consistency. Add them to the pot; simmer over low heat for 15 minutes more.

3. Next, add the wine and simmer for 15 minutes.

4. Sprinkle with cilantro and parsley and serve.

NOTE: You can use a 2½ to 3-pound bag of mixed seafood in place of all the individual ones.

2 tablespoons olive oil
1 cup diced onion
1 cup grated red bell pepper (grated on the large holes)
2 pounds raw shrimp, cleaned and deveined
½ pound raw squid rings, cleaned
½ pound piangua* or clams, cleaned
½ pound raw conch pieces or oysters
1½ fish bouillon cubes
2 tablespoons garlic paste (page 166)
1 teaspoon color* or Sazón Goya with Saffron
1¼ teaspoons salt
¾ teaspoon pepper
4 cups coconut milk (freshly made, page 107, or canned)
2 cups milk
4 tablespoons flour
¼ cup white wine
1½ tablespoons minced cilantro
1 tablespoon minced parsley

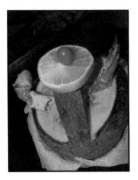

CEVICHE DE CORVINA

Corvina White Fish Ceviche
8 servings

Ceviche is such a popular food in the coastal areas of Colombia that we can even buy it at the beach. It is served as in this recipe, or with ketchup: all you would need to do is add a quarter cup of ketchup in step 2 of this recipe. I like to leave the fish overnight in the first lime juice to make sure it is fully cooked; in many places, it is left to marinate for just a few hours. I have added the tomato juice, not traditional in our Caribbean coast recipe, but it was an idea I adopted many years ago from a Mexican friend when I lived in Cali. If you cannot find corvina, any firm-fleshed white fish will do.

1 pound corvina fish, cut into ½-inch cubes
2¾ cups lime juice
1½ cups diced red onion
1½ cups peeled, seeded, and diced tomatoes
½ cup minced cilantro
¼ cup minced parsley
1½ tablespoons Worcestershire sauce
1 tablespoon tomato juice
2 teaspoons salt
1½ teaspoons pepper
Tabasco to taste
½ cup olive oil (optional)
Salted crackers or mini-tartlet shells, for serving

DAY 1
1. In a nonreactive container mix the fish with 2 cups of the lime juice. Refrigerate overnight.

DAY 2
2. Drain the lime juice from the fish, discard the juice and add the remaining ¾ cup of lime juice, onion, tomato, cilantro, parsley, Worcestershire, tomato juice, salt, and pepper to the bowl. Let marinate at least 30 minutes, or up to 8 hours for the best taste. (Flavors mature and soften after sitting together for so long.)

3. If desired, which a lot of people now seem to like, spike the heat up with some Tabasco sauce.

4. The olive oil is optional; if you leave it out the flavor will be crispier and more citrusy; if you add it, a mellower ceviche is the outcome. Both options are very good; just a matter of what works best for your taste.

5. Serve with salted crackers or in mini-tartlet shells.

CEVICHE DE PULPO

Octopus Ceviche
8 servings

Have your fishmonger clean and cut the octopus for you. After that, preparation is a breeze. This is a great Valentine's Day appetizer, because legend says octopus is an aphrodisiac. You can serve it in martini glasses and decorate them with red hearts and ribbons. Our Valentine's Day in Colombia is a holiday called Love and Friendship Day that is celebrated on the second Friday of September. Since we have the same climate year-round, we have all the seafood we need then, so I like preparing this for that occasion as well.

1 stalk celery, quartered
1 carrot, quartered
1 onion, quartered
3 to 4 sprigs cilantro
3 to 4 sprigs dill or thyme
2 bay leaves
½ teaspoon whole peppercorns
1 teaspoon salt
4 ½ pounds octopus bodies, heads and long tentacles removed
1 cup diced onion

DRESSING
¾ cup lime juice
6 cloves garlic, minced
3 tablespoons minced cilantro
2 teaspoons salt
½ teaspoon pepper
8 drops Tabasco sauce
4½ tablespoons olive oil
Crackers or mini-tartlets, for serving

1. In a medium pot or pressure cooker place 12 cups of water, the celery, carrot, onion, cilantro, dill or thyme, bay leaves, peppercorns, and salt. Bring to a boil and simmer covered for 15 minutes. Add the octopus and simmer covered over medium heat for 1 hour; if you use a pressure cooker you can cut the cooking time to 20 minutes.

2. Remove the octopus from the pot. Discard the liquid and flavorings.

3. Cut the octopus into ½ inch pieces and place in a nonreactive bowl.

4. In a small pot bring 2 cups of water to a boil. Add the diced onion and blanch for 15 seconds. Drain, dry on paper towels, and add to the octopus.

5. To **PREPARE THE DRESSING** mix the lime juice, garlic, cilantro, salt, pepper, and Tabasco in a nonreactive bowl. Add the oil and whisk well to incorporate.

6. Pour the dressing over the octopus and fold together with the onion. Refrigerate at least 30 minutes and up to 8 hours for the octopus to absorb the flavors of the sauce.

7. Serve cold with crackers or in mini-tartlets.

COCKTAIL DE CALAMARES   *Squid Cocktail*

Four 6-ounce servings

Squid Cocktail is another of those popular foods you can buy and enjoy near the beach in the Caribbean city of Cartagena de Indias. One of the tricks with squid is to either keep it over heat for less than one minute, or let it cook for a long time, about one hour, to delight in a soft and not chewy meal. After that trick is taken care of, you can enjoy one of the most versatile and delicious foods that is readily available year-round.

1 pound raw squid rings, cleaned
¾ cup lime juice
¼ cup minced onion
¼ cup minced cilantro
¼ cup olive oil
¼ cup ketchup
2 teaspoons minced parsley
1 teaspoon Worcestershire sauce
1 teaspoon garlic paste (page 166)
½ teaspoon salt
¼ teaspoon pepper
¼ teaspoon Tabasco sauce
Lettuce leaves, for serving
Saltine crackers, for serving

1. Place the squid and ½ cup of lime juice in a nonreactive bowl. Set aside in the refrigerator for 1 hour.

2. Drain the lime juice from the squid and discard the juice.

3. In a 1-quart pot, bring 3 cups of water to a boil. Turn off the heat and drop the squid in the pot. Cover and let them sit in the hot water for 30 seconds. Drain the squid and discard the water. Place the squid in a clean, nonreactive bowl.

4. Add the remaining ¼ cup of lime juice, the onion, cilantro, oil, ketchup, parsley, Worcestershire, garlic, salt, pepper, and Tabasco, and refrigerate for 15 minutes or more.

5. Serve over lettuce leaves and with saltine crackers.

COCKTAIL DE CAMARONES *Shrimp Cocktail*

Four 6-ounce servings

You can prepare this simple recipe for your family on a warm sunny day. Keep the cocktail refrigerated until ready to serve. I serve it in a bowl set over crushed ice, which keeps it cold and safe at the same time. Cocktails are regularly sold at the beach, and in the islands fishermen come by in canoes to offer the best of cocktails. It is very important that the shrimp be fresh and not precooked, because this way the lime juice cooks it through and flavors are really absorbed by them.

1½ pound fresh raw shrimp, peeled and deveined
⅓ cup lime juice
⅓ cup minced onion
¼ cup minced parsley
2 teaspoons olive oil
½ teaspoon salt
¼ teaspoon pepper
½ cup mayonnaise
½ cup ketchup
2 tablespoons lime juice
Lettuce leaves, for serving
Saltine crackers, for serving

1. Place the shrimp and ⅓ cup of lime juice in a nonreactive bowl. Set aside in the refrigerator for 1 hour.

2. Drain the shrimp and discard lime juice.

3. In a small pot, bring 3 cups of water to a boil. Turn off the heat, drop the shrimp, and cover. Let them sit in the hot water for 30 seconds. Drain off the water. Place the shrimp in a clean, nonreactive bowl.

4. Add the onion, parsley, oil, salt, and pepper. Set aside 5 minutes.

5. Combine the mayonnaise, ketchup, and 2 tablespoons of lime juice. Add to the shrimp and serve over lettuce leaves with saltine crackers.

COCKTAIL DE OSTRAS

Oyster Cocktail
Four 6-ounce servings

The oysters we have in Colombia are tiny. We buy the oysters shelled in one-pound bags in their juice when it's oyster season. Colombian fishermen say that we should not eat shellfish in months that don't carry an "r" in Spanish, which are May, June, July, and August, because they are the months of reproduction. You can also use large ones in the shell. Just prepare the seasoning sauce with all the ingredients except the oysters and their juice, and spoon a teaspoon of sauce on top of each one oyster.

1 pound shelled oysters, in their juice
¾ cup ketchup
¼ cup minced onion
¼ cup lime juice
2 teaspoons minced parsley
1 teaspoon Worcestershire sauce
1 teaspoon garlic paste (page 166)
¼ teaspoon pepper
¼ teaspoon Tabasco sauce
Salt
Lettuce leaves, for serving
Saltine crackers, for serving

1. Place the oysters and juice in a nonreactive bowl. Add the ketchup, onion, lime juice, parsley, Worcestershire, garlic, pepper, and Tabasco sauce and mix well.

2. Taste and add ¼ to ½ teaspoon of salt, according to your taste and the salinity of the oysters.

3. Refrigerate and serve cold over lettuce leaves and with saltine crackers.

ESTOFADO DE CORVINA AL COCO

Fish Etouffee
2 servings

Here you have a typical Pacific coast fish platter for two. Of course, you can make it for many more but to me, seafood is the ideal "Dinner for Two" meal. Try it: the coconut and fish go very well together and are considered aphrodisiacs by some!

1. Rub ½ teaspoon of garlic paste and ¼ teaspoon of salt into the fish steaks. Set aside in the refrigerator for 15 to 30 minutes.

2. In a large, deep sauté pan over medium heat, place the oil. Add the onion, red pepper, remaining garlic, bouillon cube, remaining salt, pepper, and color, and sauté for 5 minutes.

3. Mix the coconut milk and the flour to a smooth consistency. Next add the coconut milk mixture and plantains to the pan and simmer for 15 to 20 minutes. The plantains will be almost done; if you test them they will feel tender almost to the center.

4. Add the fish steaks and simmer for 5 minutes more. To serve remove the plantains from the sauce and divide them between 2 plates. Transfer each fish steak carefully to the platter. Cover with the sauce and enjoy. You can serve this with white rice on the side.

1 tablespoon plus
  ½ teaspoon garlic paste
  (page 166)
½ teaspoon salt
1½ to 2 pounds corvina
  steaks (2 large), or
  other firm, white fish
2 tablespoons oil
¼ cup diced onion
¼ cup grated red bell
  pepper
½ fish bouillon cube
¼ teaspoon pepper
1 teaspoon color* or
  Sazón Goya with
  Saffron
2½ cups coconut milk
  (freshly made, page
  107, or canned)
2 tablespoons flour
½ of a green plantain,
  peeled, quartered
  lengthwise and into
  2-inch-long pieces
Cooked white rice, for
  serving

LANGOSTA AL CARBON

Barbecued Lobster
2 servings

Lobster has been all my daughters' favorite food. I can remember as if it were yesterday when Isabella was a little girl in the Islas del Rosario, where she would carry the live animals by their "whiskers" to have them cooked and eaten as fast as they were caught. They are normally trapped in wire mesh boxes or cages that are dropped and kept on the surface of the ocean floor. Every day, lobsters would be brought in to cook and eat fresh.

1 onion, halved
1 carrot, halved
5 sprigs cilantro
1 whole scallion
4 bay leaves
1 teaspoon whole
   peppercorns
2 whole live lobsters
   (size depends on your
   appetite)
4 tablespoons butter
2 teaspoons mashed garlic
2 teaspoons minced parsley
3/4 teaspoon prepared
   mustard
1/2 teaspoon salt
1/4 teaspoon pepper
Patacones (page 143),
   for serving
White or brown coconut
   rice (pages 111-112), for
   serving
Tomato and onion salad,
   for serving

1. In a large pot put 4 quarts of water, the onion, carrot, cilantro, scallion, bay leaves, and peppercorns. Bring to a boil, cover and simmer for 15 minutes.

2. Add the live lobsters and cook until they turn red, about 8 minutes.

3. Remove them from the pot, cut in half lengthwise from head to tail, and discard the green tomalley and liver.

4. In a small saucepan place the butter, garlic, parsley, mustard, salt, and pepper and cook over low heat for 2 minutes.

5. Brush this mixture over the lobster meat and head, and cook cut-side down over hot coals until golden brown.

6. Serve with patacones, white or brown coconut rice, and tomato and onion salad.

LANGOSTA AL COCO
Lobster in Coconut Sauce
2 servings

The sauce for this recipe can be used with many kinds of seafood: shrimp, langoustines, squid, crayfish, and more. Just pick your favorite one and enjoy!

1 onion, halved
1 carrot, halved
5 sprigs cilantro
1 whole scallion
4 bay leaves
1 teaspoon whole
    peppercorns
2 whole live lobsters
    (size depends on your
    appetite)
4 tablespoons butter
¼ cup minced onion
1 tablespoon garlic paste
    (page 166)
½ teaspoon salt
¼ teaspoon pepper
¾ cup coconut milk
    (freshly made, page 107,
    or canned)
1 tablespoon flour
3 tablespoon minced
    parsley
½ tablespoon lime juice
Patacones (page 143),
    for serving
Salad, for serving

1. In a large pot put 4 quarts of water, the onion, carrot, cilantro, scallion, bay leaves, and peppercorns. Bring to a boil, cover, and simmer for 15 minutes.

2. Add the live lobsters and cook until they turn red, about 8 minutes.

3. Remove them from the pot, cut in half lengthwise from head to tail, and discard the green tomalley and liver.

4. In a large sauté pan place the butter, minced onion, garlic, salt, and pepper, and cook over low heat for 5 minutes.

5. Mix the coconut milk and the flour well to a smooth consistency. Increase the heat to high, add the lobsters, prepared coconut milk, parsley and lime juice and simmer for 5 minutes more.

6. Remove the lobsters and continue simmering to reduce the sauce to half, about 5 minutes.

7. Serve with patacones and salad.

MUELAS DE JAIBA

Crab Claws
2 servings

Crab claws can be purchased frozen and are great to keep on hand for an unexpected visit; they come precooked unless you buy the live crabs. They are very elegant and give the impression that you have made a very special meal for the guests you want to impress. I found this recipe on the menu of the Pacífico Restaurant in Cali and they showed me how it was done. Here it goes!

2 pounds precooked crab claws, thawed if frozen, and rinsed
6 tablespoons butter
2 tablespoons garlic paste (page 166)
1 teaspoon minced parsley, plus extra for serving (optional)
¼ seafood bouillon cube

1. Place the claws into a large sauté pan. Turn on the heat to medium and warm them up for 2 minutes.

2. Add the butter, mix, and cook 2 minutes more.

3. Add the garlic paste, parsley, and seafood bouillon cube, and cook for 3 minutes more.

4. Sprinkle with more parsley if desired and serve.

PESCADO A LA CRIOLLA

Creole Fish
4 servings

Another job for your fishmonger! Buy your fish head-on, but cleaned, gutted, and scaled. This is a typical Caribbean coast Creole-sauced fish; it is very good over white rice. Prepare fillets the same way if you prefer: sauté them in two tablespoons of oil instead of frying them; otherwise follow the same instructions.

5 pounds (4 individual) fish such as red snapper, cleaned, gutted, and scaled
4 tablespoons lime juice
2 tablespoons Worcestershire sauce
2 teaspoons mashed garlic
2 teaspoons color* or Sazón Goya with Saffron
2 teaspoons curry powder
2 cups oil for frying

GUISO
4 tablespoons oil
2 cups sliced onion, ¼-inch thick
1½ cups sliced tomatoes, ¼-inch thick
2 teaspoons mashed garlic
1 teaspoon color* or Sazón Goya with Saffron
1 fish bouillon cube
¼ teaspoon salt
¼ teaspoon pepper
Pinch curry powder
Cooked white rice, for serving

1. Make sure all the scales have been removed from the fish by passing your hands over them from tail to head. Make 3 or 4 slashes along the sides of the skin of each fish; they should go all the way down to the bones.

2. Combine the lime juice, Worcestershire, garlic, color and curry powder, and rub the mixture inside the cuts and in the belly of the fish.

3. Covered and set aside in the refrigerator for 15 minutes or until ready to fry.

4. Heat the oil in a large sauté pan or wok over medium heat to 350°F.

5. Carefully drop the fish into the oil and fry for 2 minutes. Turn and fry for 2 minutes more.

6. Remove from the oil and drain over paper towels.

7. While the fish are frying, in another large sauté pan **PREPARE THE GUISO**. Place the oil, onion, tomatoes, the garlic, color, bouillon cube, salt, pepper, and curry powder, over medium heat and cook for 12 minutes.

8. When all the fish have been fried, place them into the guiso sauce and finish cooking, 5 minutes on each side. Serve hot, with white rice.

PESCADO AL COCO

Coconut Snapper
4 servings

The coconut sauce in this recipe is so good you could make it alone to serve with rice. If you wish to bake or broil the fish instead of frying them, go ahead: bake at 450°F for eight minutes on each side or broil for five minutes on each side; otherwise follow the rest of the instructions. If you wish to prepare fish fillets, then you can prepare either less sauce, or more than four large fillets.

5 pounds (4 individual) fish such as red snapper, cleaned, gutted, and scaled
1 cup sliced onion
½ cup minced scallion
¼ cup lime juice
1 tablespoon minced parsley
1 teaspoon mashed garlic
1 teaspoon salt
2 cups plus 1 tablespoon oil for frying
2 cups coconut milk (freshly made, page 107, or canned)
½ fish bouillon cube
½ teaspoon curry powder
¼ teaspoon ground cumin*
¼ teaspoon pepper

1. Make sure all the scales have been removed from the fish by passing your hands over them from tail to head. Make 3 or 4 slashes along the sides of the skin of each fish; they should go all the way down to the bones.

2. Combine the sliced onion, scallion, lime juice, parsley, garlic, and salt, and rub them inside the cuts and in the belly of the fish.

3. Cover and set aside in the refrigerator for 15 minutes or until ready to fry.

4. When you are ready to fry the fish, remove the onion mixture from the fish and drain the lime juice out. Discard the liquid but keep the rest.

5. Heat 2 cups of oil in a large sauté pan or wok over medium heat to 350°F.

6. Carefully drop the fish into the oil and fry for 2 minutes. Turn and fry for 2 minutes more.

7. Remove from the oil and drain over paper towels.

8. While the fish are frying, in another large sauté pan place the onion mixture you removed from the fish with the tablespoon of oil. Cook over medium heat until the onion is translucent, about 7 minutes. Add the coconut milk, bouillon cube, curry, cumin, and pepper. Cook briefly to blend the flavors.

9. When all the fish have been fried, place them into the coconut sauce and finish cooking, 5 minutes on each side.

PESCADO FRITO

Fried Whole Fish
1 serving

This is my favorite way to eat fish; served with head and tail they are a delicacy. We eat the eyes too. I would have it every Sunday at the beach when I was a teenager. They sold the fish with plantains and coconut rice from small wooden houses right on the beach. Imagine the vendors walking around, selling mangos with salt and pepper, *mamoncillos**, coconuts with their water and a straw to drink it from them, and advertising their "fish of the day," which in my hometown was almost always *mojarra*, a kind of tilapia. *Mojarra* and red snapper are the most popular fried fish in Colombia.

One (1 to 1½ pound) whole snapper or mojarra, cleaned, scaled, and gutted
1½ teaspoons minced scallion,
1 teaspoon minced parsley
1 teaspoon lime juice
½ teaspoon salt
2 cups oil for frying
2 slices of lime

1. Make sure all the scales have been removed from the fish by passing your hands over them from tail to head. Make 3 or 4 slashes along the sides of the skin of each fish; they should go all the way down to the bones.

2. Combine the scallion, parsley, lime juice, and salt, and rub them inside the cuts and in the belly of the fish.

3. Cover and set aside in the refrigerate for 15 minutes or until ready to fry.

4. Heat 2 cups of oil in a large sauté pan or wok over medium heat to 325°F.

5. Carefully drop the fish into the oil and fry for 10 to 12 minutes. Turn and fry for 8 minutes more.

6. Remove from the oil and drain over paper towels.

7. Serve with lime slices.

PICADA DE CARACOL

Conch Appetizer
4 servings

Large conch is found all around the coasts of Colombia. It is very good to eat, and the shells are beautiful. It is a delicacy and is said to have powerful aphrodisiac properties. Since it is a large muscle, it is very tough and must be softened with a mallet. People in the islands and coastal regions hit conch with a rock and then simmer it for two hours.

You can serve this as an appetizer with toasts, on lettuce as a salad, or just as is, alone.

2 pounds conch, cleaned
1 onion, halved
1 carrot, halved
5 sprigs cilantro
1 whole scallion
4 bay leaves
1 teaspoon whole peppercorns
½ cup minced onion
¼ cup lime juice
4 tablespoons olive oil
2 tablespoons minced cilantro
2 teaspoons minced parsley
1 teaspoon garlic paste (page 166)
1 teaspoon Worcestershire sauce
½ teaspoon salt
¼ teaspoon pepper
¼ teaspoon hot sauce

1. Place the conch on a work surface where you can hit it hard with a small, heavy pot or meat pallet on all sides; this will soften it.

2. Cover with water in a medium pot, and simmer with the onion, carrot, cilantro, scallion, bay leaves, and peppercorns for 2 hours. Alternatively, you can cook it for 40 minutes in a pressure cooker with the same stock ingredients and enough water to cover. Release the pressure, open the pot and set aside to cool. Drain the conch and discard the cooking water and vegetables.

3. Place the minced onion, lime juice, olive oil, cilantro, parsley, garlic paste, Worcestershire, salt, pepper and hot sauce in a nonreactive bowl. Mix well and set aside until the conch is ready.

4. Cut the conch into ½-inch pieces and place in the bowl with the sauce. Mix well and set aside in the refrigerator for 30 minutes or up to 8 hours for the conch to absorb the flavors.

VIUDA DE PESCADO

Fish Widow
4 servings

I usually serve this dish without *ñame* or pumpkin. If you prefer to leave out some of the vegetables, just increase the other ones. For example, I use three-quarter of a pound each of yuca and potatoes in place of the ones I mentioned. This is a great dish to prepare on cold winter nights; it is heartwarming and delicious. The name of this recipe comes from the legend of a spirit dressed like a woman that lived near the fishing town of Buenaventura and smelled like fish; she would appear to men who cheated on their wives.

Different parts of the country use different kinds of fish, but the original recipe is with *bocachico*, which is a gray migratory river fish.

2 to 3 pounds whole white fish, cleaned, scaled, and gutted, or 4 (6-ounce) fish fillets
2 tablespoons olive oil
2 tablespoons minced scallion
2 tablespoons garlic paste (page 166)
¼ teaspoon pepper
½ onion, cut in quarters
5 sprigs cilantro
2 cloves garlic
½ teaspoon salt
½ teaspoon ground cumin*
1 small green plantain*, peeled and cut into 1½-inch chunks
½ pound peeled yuca*, quartered lengthwise
½ pound (3 small) peeled potatoes, halved
½ pound peeled ñame* or yam, cut in 1-inch cubes
1 small ripe unpeeled plantain*, cut into 1½-inch chunks
½ pound peeled pumpkin, cut in 1-inch cubes
½ cup Hogao del Pacífico (page 165)
Cooked white rice, for serving

1. Make sure all the scales have been removed from the fish by passing your hands over them from tail to head. Season the fish or fillets by rubbing with the oil, scallion, garlic, and pepper. Set aside in the refrigerator until ready to cook.

2. In a large pot over medium heat place 6 cups of water, the quartered onion, cilantro, cloves garlic, salt, and cumin. Bring to a boil and simmer for 15 minutes.

3. Add the green plantain, yuca, potatoes, and ñame, and simmer covered over medium-low heat for 20 minutes.

4. Add the ripe plantain and pumpkin, and simmer for 15 minutes more.

5. If using whole fish, add and simmer covered 15 minutes more; if using fillets, add and simmer covered for 10 minutes more.

6. To serve, place 1 or 2 pieces of each vegetable on each plate. Place the fish on top, pour on the liquid from the pot, and add 1 to 2 tablespoons of Hogao del Pacífico to each.

7. Serve with white rice.

Aji dulce (small, sweet peppers)

Arepas con Huevo
(Egg-filled Arepas), p.10

Masa or dough for arepas

Flor de Jamaica
(hibiscus flowers)

Arepas de Queso (Cheese Arepas), p. 13
with Chorizos, p. 61

Arepas de Maíz
(Yellow or White Corn Arepas), p. 12

Bollos de Mazorca (Mazorca Cakes), p. 15

Deditos de Queso
(Cheese Fingers), p. 20

Bollo Limpio (White Corn Cakes), p. 17
with *Bufitarras* (Spicy Beef Sausages), p. 56

Buñuelos de Maíz (Corn Fritters), p. 19

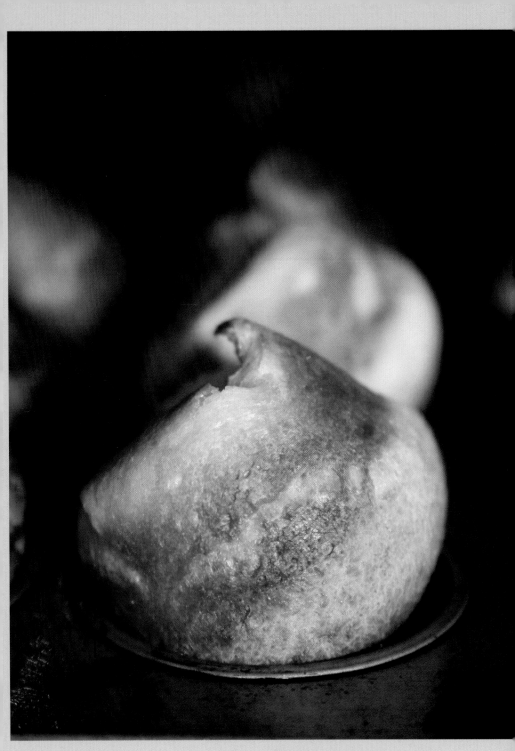

(above) Pandebono, p. 29

(right, top) Ajiaco bogotano (Chicken and Potato Soup), p. 35

(right, bottom) Crema de Zapallo o Ahuyama
        (Cream of Pumpkin Soup), p. 37

Carne Desmechada (Stripped Beef), p. 58

Morcillas o Rellenas (Blood Sausages), p. 70, for sale on street

Posta Negra (Black Beef), p. 80

Pernil de Cerdo (Fresh Leg of Pork), p. 76

Seafood Cocktails

(left) Cocktail de Calamares (Squid Cocktail), p. 93
(right) Cocktail de Camarones (Shrimp Cocktail), p. 94

Empanaditas Vallunas (Beef and Pork Turnovers), p. 24

Pescado Frito (Fried Whole Fish), p. 102

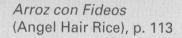
Arroz con Fideos
(Angel Hair Rice), p. 113

Arroz con Pollo
(Chicken and Rice), p. 117

Arroz con Coco y Pasas Titoté
(Brown Coconut Rice), p. 112

Plátano Asado (Oven-baked Plantains), p. 144

Chocolate Caliente (Hot Chocolate), p. 208

Bolas de Tamarindo (Tamarind Balls), p. 172

Moneditas de Plátano (Plantain Coins), p. 134

Mango seller preparing fruit

Colombian Street Vendors

(top, left) *Palenquera* (fruit vendor from Palenque, Colombia)

(top, right) Plantains being fried by street vendor

(below) Selling sweets on the streets of Colombia

RICE

Rice is Colombia's third crop in land extension after coffee and corn, but comes after potatoes in production volume. It is one of the most important staples in the country, with a per capita consumption of around 40 kilos a year. Rice has only recently started to be fortified with vitamins and minerals. Grown in many parts of the country, the largest production is in the departments of Tolima, Huila, and Valle; it is also grown in the Llanos Orientales, Bajo Cauca and Caribbean regions. Cesar Martinez, a rice planter at the International Center for Tropical Agriculture (CIAT) in Colombia, told me that the main rice varieties grown in Colombia are IR-22, CICA 8, Llanos 5, Oryzica 1, Oryzica3, Selecta320, Progreso, and Fedearroz50 and Tailandia. However, Fedearroz 50 is the leading variety planted in about 70 percent of the rice area of Colombia, mainly because of its high yield potential and resistance to major insect pests and diseases and good grain quality. This is a long-grain white rice that is sold in bags and that is not precooked or parboiled; some parboiled rice is sold but not a lot; also some brown rice, but it has very limited consumption, mainly for vegetarians and people with health-conscious mentality.

People in Colombia see rice as a staple to be eaten every day with lunch and dinner, and sometimes even breakfast. Rice was brought to the Americas from China during the Spanish Conquista years, and has been adopted as the most important single food source in the country. Eating this simple white grain of rice is transformed daily into a custom so hard to break that we even serve it alongside other starchy foods like potatoes and plantains. We add it to our soups, mix it with our fried eggs, and serve it alongside meats, poultry, beans, and seafood. It is an essential part of our diet as well as of our society, because it is an affordable foodstuff for most. Among the rice recipes prepared around the country are *arroz de lisa* or dried mullet fish rice, *arroz de chipi chipi* or tiny clam rice, corn rice, rice and eggs, turtle rice, armadillo rice, crocodile rice, rice *tamales*, and more.

We dress, color and surround rice with a vast array of ingredients, turning it from a simple white to enchanting shades of orange or green. One of the leading ingredients in this labor is *color**, a condiment that comes from the achiote* seed and gives a yellow to red color to our dishes; you can use turmeric in its place.

Coconut milk is another of the flavoring ingredients that we include, sometimes very subtly, as in the Coconut Rice with Lentils (page 114), and sometimes in a more intense form as in the Brown Coconut Rice (page 112). You can prepare coconut milk or buy it canned; make sure it's coconut milk and not coconut cream, which is sweetened. Herbs like cilantro, spices like cumin*, garlic and onions are also used to empower rice in the different dishes we prepare. Red and green peppers, vegetables like green beans and peas, and even different variety of beans are added to make heartier one-dish meals that offer low cost and great nutrition to the most needy population of the country.

COCONUTS AND THE PREPARATION OF COCONUT MILK

Coconuts come in all different sizes. When you go to buy one, first look at the three holes in the top to see that they don't look brown, moldy, or open, and smell them to make sure they smell fresh and not rancid. Second, shake the coconut. You should be able to hear that it has plenty of water inside.

In general, this is what I found that came in coconuts of different weights.

WEIGHT (POUNDS)	WATER (CUPS)	YIELD SHREDDED (CUPS)
1¼	⅓	3
1½	⅔	3¼
3	1¾	3½ to 4**

**Larger coconuts have more water but not a lot more coconut meat.

TO REMOVE THE WATER FROM THE COCONUT:
Pierce one of the three holes on the top of the coconut with a sharp pointed stick, or a clean ice pick. One of them will easily puncture. Turn up side down and pour the water from the inside of the coconut into a cup. Set aside.

TO BREAK OPEN AND REMOVE THE MEAT FROM A COCONUT:
Place the whole coconut in a 400°F oven for 3 minutes. Remove from the oven; hit hard with a hammer to break it open. With the tip of a knife, pry out the coconut meat. Peel the brown skin of the meat only if the recipe requires it. In the case of coconut milk, it is not necessary; in the case of *Cocadas Blancas* (page 175), it is.

COCONUT MILK PREPARATION:

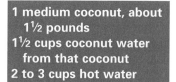
1 medium coconut, about 1½ pounds
1½ cups coconut water from that coconut
2 to 3 cups hot water

Shred or grate the coconut meat; you should have about 3½ to 4 cups. Place it in a blender with the coconut water and about 1 cup of the hot water. Blend for 1 minute. Pour into a cheesecloth-lined colander over a bowl and press to extract all of the milk from the coconut meat. Return the coconut meat to the blender and repeat with the remaining 2 cups of hot water. Add the milk from this pressing to the first one. Repeat with extra hot water if necessary, to yield a total of 4 cups of coconut milk. Discard the coconut meat and put the prepared coconut milk aside in the refrigerator for the preparation of the rice.

NOTE: Coconut milk is perishable; keep fresh coconut milk and open cans in the refrigerator for 2-3 days or freeze for as long as 6 months.

ARROZ ATOLLADO

Pork Risotto
8 to 12 large (16 ounce) servings

> *Arroz Atollado* is a typical dish from the Valle del Cauca region of Colombia. It can be prepared with chicken instead. I used to travel about one hour to the outskirts of Cali to get the best *atollado*, where it was prepared over log fires in a farm-like restaurant where the children could run around, ride horses, jump across a small river, and have lots of fun.
>
> For all my friends who are constantly on a diet, this is one of the best reasons to break it.

STOCK
5 to 6 pork rib bones
1 pound pork leg meat, cut in ½-inch dice
½ cup diced onion
½ cup diced tomato
2 cloves garlic
2 bay leaves
¼ teaspoon pepper

HOGAO OR GUISO
2 chorizos (page 61) or store bought, sliced ½-inch thick
2 tablespoons oil (if needed)
1½ cups minced scallion
1½ cups peeled, finely diced tomato
3 tablespoon minced garlic
1 teaspoon sugar
½ beef bouillon cube
½ teaspoon salt
½ teaspoon ground cumin*
½ teaspoon color* or turmeric
4 tablespoons minced cilantro

1. **PREPARE THE STOCK:** In a pressure cooker, over medium heat, brown the ribs and diced pork about 3 minutes on each side. Add 8 cups of water, the diced onion and tomato, garlic, bay leaves, and pepper. Cover and cook under pressure for 30 minutes. Turn the heat off, release the pressure, and open.

2. Remove the meats from the liquid and set aside. Strain the stock and remove any fat. Measure the stock; you should have 8 cups of liquid; if not, make up the difference with beef or chicken broth. Set aside the stock for later use (Step 7).

3. While the stock is cooking: In a large pot or *caldero** over medium heat cook the chorizos for 3 minutes. If too much fat is released by the chorizos, remove most of it and only leave 2 tablespoons; if not enough fat is released, add enough oil to make up the difference.

4. Decrease the heat to medium-low and add the scallion, tomatoes, garlic, sugar, bouillon cube, salt, cumin, and color, and cook for 15 to 20 minutes. The ingredients should have blended into a sauce consistency.

5. Add the cilantro and remove from the heat. Set aside, or continue if your stock is ready.

6. Return the hogao to medium-high heat and add the rice and 2 teaspoons of salt; sauté for 2 minutes.

7. Reduce the heat to medium-low, add the pork meat, and 8 cups of stock, and simmer uncovered for 15 minutes; the rice will plump up.

RICE
2 cups white rice
2 teaspoons salt
1 pound yellow potatoes, peeled and cut in ½-inch dice
2 tablespoons minced cilantro

8. Add the potatoes and continue cooking for another 15 to 20 minutes; the potatoes will be cooked and the rice will be very wet.

9. Sprinkle the cilantro, remove from the heat, and serve.

ARROZ CON CEBOLLA DE NANDA

Nanda's Onion Rice
8 servings

This rice is a little sticky, very aromatic, and simply delicious. The onions brown to a sweet yet savory taste that you could go on eating for days. This is my sister-in-law's recipe, which she makes for my daughter Isabella. It's Isabella's favorite dish. You can serve it in round forms, molded in empty tuna cans, as it will keep its shape. Serve it with meats or poultry on the side, and maybe some fried Plantain Chips (page 134).

3 cups thinly sliced
   onions
3 tablespoons oil
2 cups rice
1½ teaspoons salt
½ chicken bouillon cube

1. In a medium pot over medium heat, sauté the onion in the oil. Cook for 20 to 25 minutes until the onion has turned golden brown.

2. Add the rice, salt, chicken bouillon cube, and sauté 1 minute.

3. Add 4 cups of water, stir, and bring to a boil. Cook for 15 minutes, or until you see the rice very close to the surface of the water.

4. Decrease the heat to low, cover, and cook for 20 minutes more.

5. Serve.

ARROZ CON COCO BLANCO

White Coconut Rice
8 servings

Coconut rice is very popular on both the Pacific and Caribbean coasts of Colombia. This rice is typically served with fish and other types of seafood. In the city of Cartagena de Indias, it is eaten almost every day instead of the plain white rice that is eaten in the rest of the country.

1 tablespoon oil
2 cups rice
1 tablespoon sugar
2 teaspoons salt
4 cups coconut milk
   (freshly made, page 107, or canned)

1. Heat the oil in a medium pot over medium heat.

2. Add the rice, sugar, and salt, and stir for 2 minutes.

3. Add the coconut milk and bring to a boil.

4. After about 7 minutes, or as soon as you see the rice on the surface and most of the liquid has evaporated, cover the pot; reduce to minimum heat and cook covered for 20 minutes.

5. Serve.

ARROZ CON ÇOCO Y PASAS TITOTÉ

Brown Coconut Rice
8 servings

The name *titoté* refers to the brown curls that result after coconut milk is cooked long enough to "curdle" and separate. It has a concentrated, toasted, aromatic coconut flavor that nothing else equals. This is my favorite kind of rice, and one that my mother makes for me as a welcome-home dinner with *Posta Negra* (page 80) and *Torta de Plátano* (page 148). Nowadays you can buy the *titoté* in glass jars; if you find them in your neighborhood try them. A half-cup of commercial *titoté* will do for this recipe.

This is our traditional rice for the holidays in the Caribbean. And one I have to prepare every time I am in New York for some festive occasion.

4 cups coconut milk (freshly made, page 107, or canned)
⅓ cup raisins
2 cups rice
1 tablespoon brown sugar
2 teaspoons salt

1. In a medium pot or *caldero** over medium heat pour the coconut milk, and cook for 15 to 20 minutes; the milk will reduce to the point of separating into coconut oil and brownish crumbs. Scrape the bottom of the pot as soon as you see the milk has turned into oil, and continue to do so until the crumbs look light brown. These crumbs are called titoté.

2. Add the raisins and sauté in the coconut oil and crumbs for 2 minutes, until they plump up.

3. Add the rice, brown sugar, and salt. Stir for 2 minutes.

4. Add 4 cups of water and bring to a boil.

5. As soon as you see the rice on the surface, and most of the water has evaporated, cover the pot; reduce to minimum heat and cook for 20 minutes.

6. Serve.

ARROZ CON FIDEOS

Angel Hair Rice
4 servings

This is indeed one of the most popular rices in all of the country; you will find that almost all Colombians have it on their regular menu. Children love it because the pasta in the rice softens as it cooks and gives them something to play with as they eat! You can prepare it without the garlic if you have finicky children like mine—they prefer their rice without the aromatic flavor garlic gives it. I like it just as it is, and sometimes prepare it with chicken stock instead of water and add a tablespoon or two of minced cilantro right before serving.

2 tablespoons oil
½ cup broken angel hair pasta, in 1-inch pieces
1 cup rice
2 cloves garlic
1 teaspoon salt

1. In a small pot over medium heat, place the oil and pasta. Sauté for 2 minutes or until the pasta turns brown.

2. Add the rice, garlic, and salt and sauté 1 minute.

3. Add 2 cups of water, stir, and bring to a boil over medium heat. Cook about 7 minutes, or until you see the rice very close to the surface of the water.

4. Decrease the heat to low, cover, and cook for 20 minutes more.

5. Serve.

ARROZ CON LENTEJAS Y COCO

Coconut Rice with Lentils
8 servings

Coconut goes well with anything, as far as I'm concerned! I just love it and lentils, too. We have two typical rice dishes we prepare with coconut, this one and one with black-eyed peas (page 120). They are both served with beef, ground meat or steak and plantains prepared in all ways.

2 tablespoons oil
½ cup diced white onion
1 cup lentils
2 cups rice
2 teaspoons salt
4 cups coconut milk
(freshly made, page 107, or canned)

1. Heat the oil in a large pot over medium heat.

2. Add the diced onion and sauté 2 minutes.

3. Add the lentils and 1 cup of water and simmer for 30 minutes, or until the lentils have softened and absorbed most of the water.

4. Add the rice and salt, and stir for 2 minutes more.

5. Pour the coconut milk and bring to a boil.

6. As soon as you see the rice on the surface, and most of the liquid has evaporated, cover the pot; reduce the heat to minimum and cook for 20 minutes.

7. Serve.

ARROZ CON MARISCOS

Seafood Rice
8 to 10 servings

Serve this to a large crowd; your guests will be impressed and delighted. It is great for parties or get-togethers. It has a lot of ingredients but is very easy to prepare. Have the seafood prepared by your fishmonger ahead of time and keep it frozen. You can add large prawns and mussels to decorate the top if you are having a very special and elegant dinner or lunch party. We usually serve it with plantains, either sweet *Tajadas de Plátano* (page 147) or fried green *Patacones* (page 143), and a salad or bread.

4 tablespoons oil
2 cups white rice
2 fish bouillon cubes
½ teaspoon curry powder
½ teaspoon color* or turmeric
½ teaspoon salt
1 ½ cups fresh peas
1 ½ cups diced green beans, ¼ inch dice
1 ½ cups diced carrots, ¼-inch dice
¼ cup diced red bell pepper, ¼-inch dice
1 cup diced scallion
2 tablespoons minced garlic
1 teaspoon color* or turmeric
½ teaspoon curry powder
2 pound bag of seafood mix (shrimp, calamari, octopus, clams)
3 tablespoons parsley, chopped
Tajadas de Plátano (page 147), or Patacones (page 143), for serving
Avocado Ají (page 156), for serving

1. In a large pot over medium heat, place 2 tablespoons of the oil and the rice; sauté for 3 minutes. Add 1 bouillon cube, curry, color, and salt, and stir; sauté 3 more minutes.

2. Add 4 cups of water and the peas, and bring to a boil; continue to cook for 7 minutes or until you see the rice very close to the surface of the water. Cover and cook for 5 minutes more.

3. While the rice is cooking, START THE SEAFOOD: In a large sauté pan over medium heat, place the remaining 2 tablespoons of oil. Add the green beans and carrots, and cook for 5 to 7 minutes. Add the red pepper and cook for 3 minutes more. Add the scallions, garlic, color, curry, and the remaining bouillon cube, and sauté for 3 to 5 minutes. Reduce the heat to low, add the seafood, stir and cook covered for 15 minutes. Uncover.

4. Pour the seafood mixture into the rice, and using one or two large forks fold it in. Cover again; cook everything together over low heat for 20 more minutes.

5. Add parsley and serve with Tajadas de Plátano or Patacones, and Avocado Ají.

ARROZ CON PIMENTÓN

Red Pepper Rice
8 servings

This is a very convenient way of adding veggies to your children's diet. In Colombia, we eat rice twice a day so adding vegetables to it is a way of introducing our children to them in a mild and subtle way.

2 tablespoons oil
½ cup diced onion
2 cups julienned red bell pepper
2 cups rice
2 teaspoons salt
4 cups vegetable stock

1. In a medium pot over medium heat, place the oil. Add the onions and sauté for 2 minutes; add the red peppers, rice, and salt and sauté 2 more minutes.

2. Add the stock and bring to a boil.

3. As soon as you see the rice on the surface, and most of the liquid has evaporated, cover the pot; reduce to minimum heat and cook covered for 20 minutes.

4. Serve.

ARROZ CON POLLO

Chicken and Rice
8 to 10 servings

Arroz con Pollo is one of our staples; I think we had it every Saturday for lunch or dinner. It is what cooks leave prepared ahead of time so the family can eat when they are off on weekends, and therefore there is only one dish to reheat. It is also what many families serve when they have a lot of children to feed!

COOK THE CHICKEN AND PREPARE THE STOCK:
1. Place the chicken, 7 cups of water, onions, carrot, red pepper, cilantro, garlic, bouillon cube, Sazón Goya, and pepper into a large 5- to 7-quart pot and bring to a boil. When the water reaches a full boil, cover the pot and turn off the heat. Leave the breasts in the covered pot for 20 minutes, do not peak or open the lid. After the 20 minutes, remove the breasts from the stock, cool and shred. Set the chicken aside; strain the stock for later use.

PREPARE THE VEGETABLE FILLING:
2. In a 14-inch sauté pan, over medium heat pour the oil, add the diced onions and cook for 5 minutes. Add the carrot, green beans, red pepper and peas; sauté for 3 to 5 minutes more. Add the cilantro, tomato paste, garlic, Worcestershire, soy sauce, sugar, bouillon cube, salt and pepper and cook for 15 minutes.

PREPARE THE RICE:
3. In a 5- to 7-quart pot over medium high heat pour the oil. Add the rice, salt and color and sauté for 2 minutes. Add the vegetables, mix well and cook together for 3 minutes. Pour the stock and bring to a boil. As soon as you see the rice on the surface, and most of the water has dried out, after about 7 minutes, cover the pot; reduce to minimum heat and cook covered for 20 minutes.

4. Uncover, add the chicken, cilantro and hogao by mixing with 2 large forks carefully to keep the rice fluffy and serve.

TIP: You can use frozen vegetables.

CHICKEN AND STOCK
4 whole chicken breasts, with bones, skin removed
2 medium onions, halved
1 carrot, quartered
1 red bell pepper, quartered
10 sprigs cilantro
6 cloves garlic
1 chicken bouillon cube
1 tablespoon of Sazón Goya with Saffron
¼ teaspoon black pepper

VEGETABLE FILLING FOR THE RICE
2 tablespoons oil
1½ cups diced onion
1½ cups diced carrot
1½ cups diced green beans
1 cup diced red bell pepper
1 cup green peas
¼ cup minced cilantro
2 tablespoons tomato paste
1 tablespoon minced garlic
1 tablespoon Worcestershire sauce
1 tablespoon soy sauce
½ tablespoon sugar
1 chicken bouillon cube
½ teaspoon salt
¼ teaspoon black pepper

RICE
1 tablespoon oil
2 cups rice
2 teaspoons salt
¼ teaspoon color* or turmeric
4 cups chicken stock
¼ cup minced cilantro
½ recipe of Hogao del Pacífico (page 165) or From the Caribbean (page 164)

ARROZ CON ZANAHORIA

Carrot Rice
8 servings

This recipe is another to make children eat vegetables.

2 tablespoons oil
½ cup diced onion
1½ cups grated carrot
2 cups rice
2 teaspoons salt
4 cups vegetable stock

1. In a large pot over medium heat, place the oil. Add the onions and sauté for 2 minutes; add the carrot, rice, and salt, and sauté 2 more minutes.

2. Add the stock and bring to a boil.

3. As soon as you see the rice on the surface, and most of the liquid has evaporated, cover the pot; reduce to minimum heat and cook for 20 minutes.

4. Serve.

ARROZ DE CAMARÓN

Shrimp Rice
8 servings

Typically, this rice is prepared with dried shrimp. Not the tiny variety, but the medium-size, about 1- to 1½-inches long. This makes them easier to peel. The dried shrimp are simmered for 15 minutes, removed from the water, peeled, and set aside to cook with the rice. The shells are blended with the cooking water to make the stock you use to cook the rice. It is a traditional dish for the Holy Week of Easter; that's the time of the year you can find the dry shrimp in the markets. Here I prepared it with fresh shrimp because they are easier to find, but if you come across dried shrimp just follow the recipe and reduce the amount of shrimp by half.

2 pounds fresh shrimp in the shell
1 shrimp or seafood bouillon cube
2½ cups rice
⅓ cup oil
½ cup minced green onion*
1½ tablespoons mashed garlic
½ cup minced red bell pepper
½ cup grated carrot
1 cup peeled, seeded and diced tomato
3 tablespoons minced *aji dulce* (sweet green pepper)**
4 tablespoons minced parsley
3 teaspoons salt
½ teaspoon black pepper
½ teaspoon Tabasco sauce (optional)

1. Wash and peel the shrimp and set aside in the refrigerator. Place the shells in a large pot with 6 cups of water and the bouillon cube; simmer for 15 minutes. Set aside to cool. Puree in a blender for 1½ minute, pass through a very fine sieve. Discard the shells and set the stock aside.

2. Wash the rice and drain thoroughly.

3. In a large pot or *caldero** over medium heat place the oil. Add the green onion and sauté for 2 minutes. Continue with the garlic, red pepper, and carrot, and sauté 3 minutes more. Add the tomatoes, ají dulce, parsley, salt and black pepper, and sauté 10 minutes more. Add the shrimp, and Tabasco if desired; stir, and sauté for 5 minutes. Add the rice and stir.

4. Pour the stock into the vegetable–shrimp mixture and simmer until you see the rice very close to the surface of the liquid.

5. Cover, lower the heat to minimum and cook for 20 minutes.

6. Uncover and serve.

ARROZ DE FRIJOL
DE CABECITA NEGRA

Black-Eyed Peas Rice

10 servings

Here we have the other rice dish we make with beans and coconut. It is very good and can be a one-dish meal by itself.

½ pound dry black-eyed peas
4 cups coconut milk (freshly made, page 107, or canned)
2 cups rice
2 teaspoons salt

1. Place the beans and 1¼ cups of water in a medium pot over medium-low heat. Cover and simmer for 45 minutes, or until the beans have softened and absorbed most of the water; reduce the heat if the water is evaporating too fast. Drain and set aside.

2. In another medium pot place the coconut milk and bring to a simmer. Add the rice, salt and drained beans. Simmer uncovered over medium heat for 5 to 7 minutes or until you see the rice very close to the surface of the liquid.

3. Reduce the heat to low, cover and cook for 20 minutes.

4. Serve.

ARROZ MIXTO

Chicken, Seafood, and Pork Rice
6 to 8 servings

This mixed rice is served as much as *Arroz con Pollo* (page 117) in the coastal zones of Colombia, where there is plenty of seafood year-round. It is a hearty meal that can be prepared with or without *Chorizo* (page 61). Dry beef and pork are sometimes used in its preparation, as well as free-range hens instead of chicken. Nowadays, though, this is the way it is prepared most often.

2 cups white rice
4 cups chicken stock or water
1 teaspoon salt
2 chicken bouillon cubes
5 tablespoons oil
2 teaspoons color* or turmeric
1½ cups fresh peas
1½ cups minced scallion
1 cup diced onion
2 tablespoons minced garlic
2 cups diced carrot, ¼-inch dice
2 cups diced green beans, ¼-inch dice
½ teaspoon ground cumin*
1 whole raw boneless chicken breast, diced (about 2 cups)
2 chorizos, sliced ¼-inch thick (about 1½ cups)
¼ pound diced ham, ¼-inch dice
1½ pounds shrimp, cut in ½-inch chunks if too large
4 tablespoons chopped parsley

1. In a medium pot over medium heat, place the rice, chicken stock, salt, 1 bouillon cube, 2 tablespoons of oil, and 1 teaspoon of color. Bring to a boil, reduce the heat to medium-low and simmer for 10 minutes, or until you see the rice very close to the surface of the water. Add the peas, cover and reduce the heat to low. Cook for 15 minutes and set aside.

2. In a large sauté pan over medium heat, place the remaining 3 tablespoons of oil. Add the scallion, onions and garlic, and sauté for 5 minutes. Add the carrots, green beans, the remaining bouillon cube and 1 teaspoon of color, and the cumin, and cook for 10 minutes more. Next add the chicken and chorizo; stir, cover and cook for 5 minutes. Uncover the pot and add the ham and shrimp; stir and sauté for 5 minutes more.

3. Stir this mixture into the rice, and continue to cook over low heat for 10 minutes.

4. Add the parsley and serve.

SIDE DISHES

This chapter includes some of the best recipes in the world. Our extensive selection of side dishes includes plantains* in many forms, yellow and white potatoes, beans, and yuca or cassava, delicious and high in calories but also very high in fiber and flavor. We eat them twice a day, and even together in the same meal. For example, we might have chicken with potatoes and plantain, or beef with beans and plantain. These are staples around the country, with regional variations. You can see the difference between *antioqueño* beans and red beans from the Caribbean; plantains on the coast are served with grated white farmer's cheese, while in other parts of the country they serve them alone; *patacones* are very thin and crispy on the coast, and small and thicker in the Andean region.

Tostadas or giant plantains are a delicacy from the southern Pacific department of the Valle del Cauca. Yuca balls with sugar and breaded ones are another good example. I only have one of these a day, but I savor it and eat it as if it were fresh truffles or foie gras. For me, nothing compares to the sweetness of a ripe plantain, the tenderness of good yuca, or the saucy consistency of the beans and lentils.

Rice is always served along with the side dishes, which is why it has a whole chapter to itself. Nowadays few people think of a meal with two carbohydrates in it, but in Colombia this is a must. No meal is complete without the side dish and the rice. In the Amazon zones, a lot of stewed yuca is served on the side, and fried green plantains are served with fish. Potatoes come from the Andean zone, but are served all around the country. They are usually baked and in stews or soups in the Andes, and fried in the Coastal regions. *Papas Chorreadas* (page 137) come from the department of Boyacá but were adopted by the rest of the country and are a favorite of all. Yuca is a crop grown everywhere, but it is in the Atlantic zone that we prepare the largest array of products from it. The yuca starch though is best developed and used in the Viejo Caldas departments and around the area.

Enjoy preparing these hearty recipes that can add a touch of internationality to a meal. For example, add some fried plantain strips to a filet mignon and serve them standing over pureed potatoes; or, serve miniature plantain pies at a cocktail party. Dress up a fish filet with very thin and crisp *patacones* and decorate them with some lime slices. Yuca is now sold peeled and ready to fry, so try and prepare some and pass them around at a party with some sour cream; you will see they will be the talk of the party. An outdoor event can also be revived with the sweet and salty *aborrajados*. Try to make them bite-size the first time so people are not afraid to try new things.

ABORRAJADOS

Plantain and Cheese Fritters
8 to 12 fritters

Aborrajados are a battered, fried, cheese-filled sweet plantain delight. After eating these, you will never forget them. Some guava paste can also be placed in the center with the cheese. My first encounter with them was on the golf course of the Club Campestre in Cali. Afterwards, everywhere typical foods were served I ordered them. Some people prepare them by first cutting the plantain into *tajadas* (¼-inch wide, bias cut slices) and then placing the cheese in the center; others prepare it by frying the whole plantain and then slicing it in half lengthwise and making one large *Aborrajado*; others prepare it as you see here.

2 very ripe plantains
2 cups oil for frying
¾ pound white farmer's cheese

1. Cut the ends off the plantains and peel; slice into 1½-inch chunks. Pour the oil into deep, heavy pot, and place over medium-high heat. When the oil is hot (about 350°F), add the plantain pieces and fry for 3 to 4 minutes. Remove the pieces with slotted spoon and drain on paper towels.

DIPPING BATTER
2 eggs
⅓ cup flour
1 tablespoon sugar
1½ teaspoons salt
1 to 2 tablespoons milk (if necessary to thin the batter)

2. Place some plastic wrap on the work surface, and scatter the fried plantains over it. With the cover of a pot or with a mallet, pound each slice to thin it to about ¼-inch thick. If they tear, don't worry.

3. Shred or slice the cheese. The slices of cheese should be about 1 inch wide by ½ inch thick and fit the thinned plantain slices. Put some cheese on half of each of the thinned slices of plantain, and wrap each up to form a ball in the palm of your hand. With the tips of your fingers, press to form a oval shaped ball.

FOR THE BATTER:
4. Mix the eggs, flour, sugar and salt with a wire whisk until smooth in texture, about the consistency of buttermilk. If you feel it is too thick add some milk. Otherwise leave as is.

5. Place the filled plantains in the batter; turn the pieces to cover all over.

6. Increase the temperature of the oil to 375°F. Fry the fritters in batches so that they do not touch each other, for 30 to 45 seconds or until golden brown all around.

7. Drain well as you remove them from the frying oil with a slotted spoon. Place over paper towels to further remove the excess oil. Serve.

ARRACACHA FRITA

Fried Arracacha
4 to 6 servings

Arracacha* is an Andean vegetable like *yuca* or cassava. It is slightly sweet and is colored purple in the center. It is a vegetable the *paisas* (people from the Antioquia and Viejo Caldas regions of Colombia) cultivate and have as a staple.

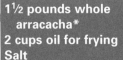

1½ pounds whole arracacha*
2 cups oil for frying
Salt

1. Peel the arracacha and quarter lengthwise. Cut each quarter lengthwise again into ½-inch strips, or into ¼-inch strips if you like more toasted, crispier sticks.

2. Place the arracacha in a medium pot with 6 cups of water. Cover, bring to a boil, and cook until fork tender, about 15 minutes. Drain well and dry with paper towels.

3. Pour the oil into a deep, medium, heavy pot, and place over medium-high heat. When the oil is hot (about 350°F), add the pieces a few at a time, and deep fry for 2 to 3 minutes. Remove the pieces with slotted spoon and drain on paper towels.

4. Immediately sprinkle with salt and serve.

BANANITOS FRITOS

Fried Bananas
8 servings

This recipe is best prepared with what we call *murrapo* bananas or lady's finger bananas. They are small, a bit firmer, and tastier than larger bananas. But regular bananas will work well in this recipe, too. We serve baked, fresh, and fried bananas alongside of many dishes: soups, *sancochos*, meats, and beans. We usually do not serve them as a dessert, but they are so good that you could serve these with ice cream and you would feel very comforted.

1 teaspoon oil
12 lady's finger bananas
   or 8 small bananas,
   peeled
4 tablespoons butter
8 tablespoons light
   brown sugar
1 teaspoon grated lime
   peel
1 tablespoon lime juice
1 tablespoon butter, for
   baking

1. Preheat the oven to 425°F. Lightly coat a large nonstick sauté pan with the oil and place over low medium heat. Add half of the bananas, 2 tablespoons of butter and sprinkle with 4 tablespoons of brown sugar and half the lime peel and juice. Sauté the bananas, turning constantly during 5 minutes; they will cook and the butter and sugar will create a caramel. Lower the heat if your caramel is turning too dark too soon. Repeat with the rest of the bananas.

2. Remove the bananas from the pan and place in a baking pan.

3. Put small pieces of butter over the bananas.

4. Bake for 10 minutes and serve.

BOLITAS DE YUCA APANANDAS

Breaded Yuca Balls
1 dozen 2-inches balls

These yuca balls are eaten alone or as part of a meal. Yuca is very popular in Colombia and, as you can see, I have many recipes for it.

2 pounds peeled yuca*, fresh or frozen
3½ teaspoons salt
2 whole eggs
1 cup bread crumbs
3 cups oil for frying

1. Cut the yuca lengthwise into 1-inch pieces. They will be half-moon-shaped chunks, since yuca is a cylindrical vegetable and is usually cut in long, half-cylinders. Remove the center stem.

2. In a small stockpot place the yuca and 3 teaspoons of salt, and cover completely with water. Simmer over medium heat until the yuca is so soft that you can insert a knife smoothly into it—about 20 minutes for good yuca. It should feel like a potato when done.

3. Remove the yuca from the water. Sprinkle with the remaining ½ teaspoon of salt and mash with a potato masher or pass through a *molino** (corn mill).

4. Form balls of about 3 tablespoons of mashed yuca.

5. Whisk the eggs in a shallow bowl. Place the bread crumbs in another bowl.

6. Dip the balls first in the eggs and then the crumbs.

7. Pour the oil into a deep, medium, heavy pot, and place over medium-high heat. When the oil is hot (about 325°F), add the breaded yuca balls a few at a time and deep fry for 2 to 3 minutes. Remove them with a slotted spoon and drain on paper towels.

8. Drain on paper towels and serve.

BOLITAS DE YUCA CON MELADO

Sweet Yuca Balls
3 dozen 1/2-inch balls

These yuca balls melt in your mouth, with the woodsy sweetness of the *panela** and cinnamon! They are my brother Ed's favorite dish, and one my mother always makes for him when he flies home!

2 pounds peeled yuca*, fresh or frozen
3¼ teaspoons salt
2 cups oil for frying
1 recipe of Melado (page 191)

1. Cut the yuca lengthwise into 1-inch pieces. They will be half-moon-shaped chunks, since yuca is a cylindrical vegetable and is usually cut in long, half -cylinders. Remove the center stem.

2. In a small stockpot place the yuca and 3 teaspoons of salt, and cover completely with water. Simmer over medium heat until the yuca is so soft that you can insert a knife smoothly into it—about 20 minutes for good yuca. It should feel like a potato when done.

3. Remove the yuca from the water. Sprinkle with the remaining ¼ teaspoon of salt and mash with a potato masher or pass through a *molino** (corn mill).

4. Form balls of about 1 tablespoon of mashed yuca.

5. Pour the oil into a deep, medium, heavy pot, and place over medium-high heat. When the oil is hot (about 350°F), add the yuca balls and deep fry for 2 minutes. Remove them with a slotted spoon and drain on paper towels. Let cool for 2 to 3 minutes to set the shape.

6. Place on a serving dish and pour the Melado over them. Enjoy!

CARIMAÑOLAS DE CARNE O QUESO

Beef or Cheese Yuca Turnovers

12 turnovers

Carimañolas are very special to me. They are the dish we ate at home the night my husband told my parents we were getting married. He is from Cali and does not actually like *carimañolas*, but he bravely ate them that night with lots and lots of water. They are very popular throughout the country, but especially in the coastal areas; in other parts, they are called *Pasteles de Yuca*, as you will see on page 141. You can exchange the fillings with other meats and make your own creations; yuca has a neutral flavor so it is very adaptable.

2 pounds peeled yuca*, fresh or frozen
3½ teaspoons salt

MEAT FILLING
3 tablespoons oil
¾ cup minced scallion
¼ cup minced onion
½ tablespoon minced garlic
1 beef bouillon cube
1 teaspoon color* or turmeric
½ teaspoon ground cumin*
½ teaspoon pepper
½ pound ground beef
¾ pound (2 cups) white farmer's Cheese, grated

Ají Antioqueño (page 155), for serving

1. Cut the yuca lengthwise into 1-inch pieces. They will be half-moon-shaped chunks, since yuca is a cylindrical vegetable and is usually cut in long, half-cylinders. Remove the center stem.

2. In a small stockpot place the yuca and 3 teaspoons of salt, and cover completely with water. Simmer over medium heat until the yuca is so soft that you can insert a knife smoothly into it—about 20 minutes for good yuca. It should feel like a potato when done.

3. In the meantime, **PREPARE THE MEAT FILLING:** Heat the oil in a medium sauté pan, over medium heat. Cook the scallion, onion, garlic, bouillon cube, color, cumin, and pepper for 4 minutes. Add the beef, lower the heat and cook for 6 minutes more. Mix well with a wooden spoon to make sure the beef is separated and not in chunks. Set aside to cool.

4. Remove the yuca from the water. Sprinkle with the remaining ½ teaspoon of salt and mash with a potato masher or pass through a *molino*.

5. Form 12 balls of about 3 tablespoons of yuca each. Flatten them to 4 inches rounds. Place 1 tablespoon of beef filling or 2½ tablespoons of grated cheese in the center of each flattened yuca ball. Roll and press the sides to close.

6. Pour the oil into a deep, medium, heavy pot, and place over medium-high heat. When the oil is hot (about 350°F), add the yuca balls and deep fry for 3 to 4 minutes. Remove them with a slotted spoon and drain on paper towels. Let cool for 2 to 3 minutes to set the shape. Serve with Ají Antioqueño (page 155) or just as they are.

FRISOLES ANTIOQUEÑOS

Antioqueño Red Beans
8 servings

These are the famous beans of my mother-in-law's town. They use *cargamanto* beans*, which are brownish spotted beans, and pork. Red kidney beans can also be used. People in Antioquia used to have these beans every night as a side dish to every meal.

1 pound red beans (about 2½ cups)
1 pound piece of pork bone or tail

GUISO
3 tablespoons oil
1½ cups sliced green onions*
1½ cups peeled and diced tomatoes
½ teaspoon ground cumin*
¼ teaspoon salt
2 chicken bouillon cubes
¼ cup minced cilantro

1. Wash the beans with plenty of water, and soak covered with water overnight.

2. Drain the beans and discard the soaking water. Place the beans, the pork bone, and 4 cups of fresh water in a pressure cooker and cook for 30 minutes. You can also cook the beans in a regular pot for 2½ hours, until soft but not cracked or mushy. The beans should be soft but not too soft since they must still cook with the guiso. Uncover the pressure cooker; from now on you will use it as a regular pot for this recipe.

3. While the beans cook, MAKE THE GUISO: place the oil, green onions, tomatoes, cumin, and salt in a medium sauté pan and cook over medium-low heat for 12 to 15 minutes.

4. Add the guiso and the chicken bouillon cube to the beans, and cook over medium-low heat until the beans have softened completely without loosing their shape, about 45 minutes to one hour.

5. Taste for salt. Add the cilantro and cook for 2 minutes more. Serve.

FRÍJOLES ROJOS
DE BARRANQUILLA

Red Beans from Barranquilla
8 servings

> Red beans as made in my hometown of Barranquilla are very good. They are plump, soft on the inside, with a dark red sauce that you could eat alone! The vegetables are processed or blended to a smooth consistency so they blend into the recipe to create a sauce that is silky and very flavorful. Serve them with rice and sweet plantains*; some even add ground beef. Any kind of red beans will do.

1 pound red pinto or kidney beans (about 2½ cups)
¼ of a red bell pepper
1 chicken bouillon cube
1 teaspoon color* or turmeric

1. Wash the beans with plenty of water, and soak covered with water overnight.

2. Drain the beans and discard the soaking water. Place the beans and 4 cups of fresh water, red pepper, bouillon cube, and color in a large pressure cooker and cook for 30 minutes. You can also cook the beans in a regular pot for 2½ hours, until soft but not cracked or mushy. The beans should be soft but not too soft since they must still cook with the guiso. Uncover the pressure cooker and from now on you will use it as a regular pot for this recipe.

GUISO
3 tablespoons oil
1 cup peeled and diced tomatoes
1 onion, halved
¼ cup minced cilantro
6 seeded ají dulce* (sweet green peppers)
7 cloves garlic
4 whole scallions
1 celery stalk
¼ of a red bell pepper
1 teaspoon salt

3. While the beans cook, **MAKE THE GUISO**: place the oil, tomatoes, onion, cilantro, ají dulce, garlic, scallion, celery, red pepper, and salt in a food processor and process for 1 minute. Remove and place in a medium sauté pan and cook over medium-low heat for 12 to 15 minutes.

4. Add the guiso to the beans, and cook over medium-low heat until the beans have softened without loosing their shape, about 45 minutes to one hour.

5. Taste for salt and serve.

LENTEJAS DE ELVIRA

Elvira's Lentils
8 servings

I am a big lentil lover, and so are my three children. Beans and lentils are the one food we all eat. Here is the recipe from my mother's house-keeper of over twenty years. The lentils are prepared with a very tasty guiso sauce, which gives the soft flavored lentils a hearty flavor and a thick, brown, velvety sauce. In other parts of the country such as Nariño, they are prepared with ¼-inch cubed potatoes, and still served with rice and plantains.

1 pound dry lentils (about
   2 cups)
¼ of a red bell pepper
1 vegetable bouillon cube
1 teaspoon color* or
   turmeric

GUISO
3 tablespoons oil
1 cup peeled and diced
   tomatoes
1 onion, halved
4 cloves garlic
4 whole scallions
2 seeded ají dulce*
   (sweet green pepper)
1 celery stalk, roughly
   cut up
¼ of a red bell pepper
¼ of a green bell pepper
2 teaspoons salt

1. Wash the lentils with plenty of water and place in a medium pot with 4 cups of water, add the ¼ red pepper, bouillon cube, and the color; cook for 25 minutes over medium-low heat. The lentils should be soft but not mushy since they must still cook with the guiso.

2. While the lentils cook, MAKE THE GUISO: place the oil, tomatoes, onion, garlic, scallions, ají dulce, celery, the red and green pepper pieces, and the salt in a food processor and process for 1 minute. Remove and place in a medium sauté pan and cook over medium-low heat for 12 to 15 minutes.

3. Add the guiso to the lentils, and cook over medium-low heat until the lentils have softened completely without loosing their shape, about 45 minutes to one hour.

4. Taste for salt and serve.

MONEDITAS DE PLÁTANO
Y PLATANITOS

Plantain Coins and Chips

8 servings

Plantain* coins and chips are best when cut with a mandoline slicer; the thinner the better, as they will toast evenly and yield a completely crisp product. One plantain goes a long way if you cut them like that. These chips and coins can be used to decorate many dishes. In Colombia, we buy the chips in white paper bags on the streets. When I was a little girl, we used to buy them at the entrance to movie theaters and schools. We still get them there, and the ones sold on the streets are the best, because they are always thin and crispy.

1 large green plantain*
2 cups oil for frying
Salt to taste

1. Cut the ends off the plantain and peel. Cut in ⅛-inch thick rounds if making coins, and ⅛-inch thick by 3- to 4-inches-long strips if making chips.

2. Pour the oil into a deep, medium, heavy pot, and place over medium-high heat. When the oil is hot (about 350°F), add the plaintain pieces one by one, so they don't stick to each other, and deep fry for 1 to 2 minutes or until golden. Remove them with a slotted spoon and drain on paper towels.

3. Add salt immediately and serve.

PAPA ABORRAJADA

Batter-Fried Potatoes
8 servings

Batter-dipped, fried potatoes are very common in the colder Andean region of Colombia. Serve them with *Ají de Aguacate* (page 156).

3 pounds (about 18) small potatoes
1½ tablespoons salt
1 chicken bouillon cube

1. Wash the potatoes thoroughly. Cut in half lengthwise.

2. In a large pot place 8 cups of water, salt and the bouillon cube. Bring to a boil. Add the potatoes, cover and simmer for 20 to 30 minutes or until the potatoes are tender when pricked with a fork. Drain the potatoes and discard the water. Let cool for 10 minutes.

DIPPING BATTER
1¼ cups flour
½ teaspoon salt
½ teaspoon color* or turmeric
¼ teaspoon ground cumin*
1 egg

FOR THE BATTER:
3. Place the flour, salt, color, cumin, egg, and 1 cup water in a bowl and mix with a wire whisk or fork until the mixture is smooth and free of lumps.

3 cups oil for frying

4. Pour the oil into a deep, heavy pot, place over medium-high heat, and bring to a temperature of 350°F.

5. Dip the potato pieces one by one into the batter, and drop carefully into the oil.

6. Deep fry for 3 to 4 minutes or until golden all around.

7. Drain over paper towels.

8. Serve with Hogao del Pacífico (page 165) or Ají Valluno (page 162).

PAPA SALADA

Salted Potatoes
4-6 servings

A very common, daily preparation in the colder cities of Colombia, this is prepared at home with small to medium size (about 1½ to 2½ inches long) round or oval red potatoes; the color is part red and part yellow. Like the yellow potatoes, they have with many indentations or grooves. Use yellow potatoes or small baking potatoes if red are not available.

1 pound (about 10) very small red potatoes
1½ tablespoons salt

1. Wash the potatoes well. Do not peel or cut.

2. Place the potatoes in a small pot with water to barely cover them.

3. Add all the salt, cover, and turn the heat to medium.

4. Cook covered until all the water has evaporated, about 30 to 45 minutes. Be careful to take it off the heat when the water has evaporated but before the potatoes have burnt.

5. Uncover and swirl the potatoes around in the pot. The salt will adhere to the potatoes' skin.

6. Serve.

PAPAS CHORREADAS

Potatoes in Scallion Sauce
8 servings

These potatoes are typical from the Andean center of the country, prepared with a sauce that is creamy and delicious. On the coast, where you cannot find the thicker green onions*, we prepare it with scallions and onions.

1½ pounds potatoes
1½ tablespoons salt
2 tablespoons oil
2 cups cut green onions*, sliced in half lengthwise, then into pieces 2½ inches long
2 cloves garlic, mashed
1½ cups diced tomatoes
½ cube chicken bouillon
½ teaspoon ground cumin
⅛ teaspoon pepper
½ cup milk
½ cup heavy cream or half-and-half
1 cup shredded white farmer's cheese* or mozzarella, shredded (6 ounces)

1. Wash the potatoes and peel only partially. (Unevenly, about half of each potato.)

2. In a medium pot place the potatoes and 1 tablespoon of the salt. Cover with water completely. Bring to a boil and cook until the potatoes feel soft when you prick them with a knife, about 15 to 20 minutes. Drain and set aside.

3. While the potatoes cook, heat the oil in a large sauté pan over medium-low heat and sauté the green onions until translucent and very soft, about 8 minutes; add the garlic, stir, and cook 1 minute. Add the tomatoes, bouillon cube, cumin, the remaining ½ tablespoon of salt, and pepper. Stir and cook 5 minutes more. Add the milk and cream or half-and-half (your choice) and cook 2 minutes. Finally, add the cheese, mix well, and cook covered for 3 to 4 minutes or until the cheese has melted.

4. Place the cooked potatoes in the sauce and serve.

PAPAS RELLENAS

Stuffed Potatoes
4 to 6 servings

These stuffed potatoes are a meal in itself and more. They are basically potatoes mashed but not completely smooth, which are stuffed with an egg, rice, and meat filling before being coated in a batter and fried. They are very typical of colder zones and the Pacific areas.

1½ tablespoons salt
2 eggs, at room temperature
3 pounds (about 10) medium potatoes

1. In a large pot place 8 cups of water, the salt, and the eggs. Bring to a boil.

2. Wash and quarter the potatoes (with or without skin). Add to the eggs, cover and simmer for 15 to 20 minutes or until the potatoes are tender when pricked with a fork. Drain the potatoes and eggs. Discard the water. Mash the potatoes with a fork or potato masher; they should chunky. Peel and dice the eggs. Set both aside for assembly later.

RICE FILLING
⅔ cup rice
1 chicken bouillon cube
1 tablespoon oil
½ teaspoon salt
½ teaspoon color* or turmeric

3. While the eggs and potatoes cook, **PREPARE THE RICE**: In a small pot place the rice, 1¼ cups water, bouillon cube, oil, salt, and color. Bring to a boil, reduce the heat and simmer for 10 minutes on medium-low heat, or until you see the rice very close to the surface of the water. Cover and decrease the heat to low. Cook for 15 minutes. Set aside.

4. **PREPARE THE MEAT FILLING:** In a medium sauté pan, over medium heat, place the oil, scallions, tomatoes, garlic, bouillon cube, color, and cumin; sauté for 5 minutes. Add the beef, decrease the heat to low and cook for 10 minutes, breaking up the meat to remove chunks. Remove from the heat, add the rice, diced eggs, and set aside.

5. Place all the dipping batter ingredients in a medium bowl and mix with a wire whisk or fork until the mixture is smooth and free of lumps.

6. Form half-cupfuls of mashed potatoes into balls. Flatten to ½ inch thickness. Add 2 tablespoons of filling to the center and place them in the palm of your hand. Close your hand and tightly press. Roll with both your hands to make even spheres.

7. Pour the oil into a deep, medium, heavy pot, and place over medium-high heat to bring to a temperature of 350°F.

8. Dip the potatoes one by one into the batter, and drop carefully into the oil.

9. Deep fry for 3 to 4 minutes or until golden all over.

10. Drain over paper towels.

11. Serve with Hogao del Pacífico.

BEEF FILLING
4 tablespoons oil
¾ cup minced scallion
½ cup peeled diced
    tomatoes
1 tablespoon mashed
    garlic
1 beef bouillon cube
¾ teaspoon color* or
    turmeric
¼ teaspoon ground
    cumin*
¾ pound ground beef

DIPPING BATTER
1¼ cups flour
1 cup water
1 egg
½ teaspoon salt
½ teaspoon color* or
    turmeric
¼ teaspoon ground
    cumin*

4 cups oil for frying
Hogao del Pacífico (page
    165), for serving

PAPITA AMARILLA ASADA

Baked Yellow Potatoes
4 servings

Yellow potatoes are to me definitely the tastiest of all potatoes; they are used to thicken many soups. They are small, in general from ½ to 1½ inches in diameter, and are therefore very quick and easy to cook. Originally from the Andes regions, these were brought to us by the Incas. You can use Yukon gold potatoes instead, but the taste is not quite the same; in Latin markets you can find them as Peruvian yellow potatoes or Colombian yellow or criolla potatoes. Here they are baked, but we also deep fry them; they are sold like plantain chips in white paper bags on the streets all over the country, but especially in the central to southern part.

1 pound (about 8) small yellow potatoes
2 teaspoons butter
½ teaspoon salt

1. Thoroughly wash and clean the potatoes; do not peel. Preheat the oven to 350°F.

2. Place the potatoes in a baking pan and rub the butter all over them. Sprinkle with the salt.

3. Bake for 30 to 45 minutes or until tender.

4. Serve.

PASTEL DE YUCA CON GUISO

Yuca Pie with Guiso Filling
24 turnovers

These are similar to the *Carimañolas* (page 130), but prepared in the way of the people in the Andean region of Colombia. They are served with *ajíes* (see Salsas and Sauces chapter, page 153) and served as appetizers at outdoor parties.

MEAT FILLING
½ pound pork, cut in
   ½-inch dice
½ pound beef skirt, cut in
   ½-inch dice
¼ teaspoon salt
¼ teaspoon pepper
¼ teaspoon ground
   cumin*
¼ teaspoon color* or
   turmeric
1 small onion, halved
2 cloves garlic
½ beef bouillon cube

YUCA
4 pounds peeled yuca*,
   fresh or frozen
2½ tablespoons salt

1. Combine the pork and beef with salt, pepper, cumin, and color. Set aside for 10 minutes.

2. In a pressure cooker place 1½ cups of water, onion, garlic, bouillon cube and the seasoned meats. Cook over medium-low heat for 30 minutes. Release the pressure and uncover. If using a regular pot, cook for 2 to 3 hours, or until the beef and pork are tender.

3. While the meats cook, cook the yuca and prepare the hogao.

4. Cut the yuca lengthwise into 1-inch pieces. They will be half-moon-shaped chunks, since yuca is a cylindrical vegetable and is usually cut in long, half-cylinders. Remove the center stem.

5. In a small stockpot place the yuca and 2 tablespoons of salt, and cover completely with water. Simmer over medium heat until the yuca is so soft that you can insert a knife smoothly into it—about 20 minutes for good yuca. It should feel like a potato when done.

6. While the yuca cooks, **PREPARE THE HOGAO OR GUISO:** Heat the oil in a large sauté pan over medium heat, Add the green onions, tomatoes, garlic, salt, cumin, and color and cook for 15 to 20 minutes or until the onion flavor has completely blended in. Add the cilantro and remove from the heat. Set aside.

CONTINUED

7. Remove the yuca from the water. Sprinkle with the remaining ½ tablespoon of salt and mash with a potato masher or pass through a *molino**.

8. Remove the meats from the liquid and set aside the cooking liquid. Chop the meats as small as you can. Add to the hogao.

9. Add the potatoes to the meat meat liquid, cover, and cook for 20 minutes. The potatoes will have overcooked and some of them will look mashed. That is they way it is supposed to be. Combine them with the hogao and meat mixture.

10. Form 24 balls of about 3 tablespoons of yuca. Flatten them to 4 inches rounds. Add 1½ to 2 tablespoons of meat mixture to the center of each flattened yuca circle. Roll and press the sides to close.

11. Pour the oil into a deep, medium, heavy pot, and place over medium-high heat. When the oil is hot (about 350°F), add the yuca balls and deep fry for 3 to 4 minutes. Remove them with a slotted spoon and drain on paper towels. Let cool for 2 to 3 minutes to set the shape.

12. Serve.

HOGAO OR GUISO
1 tablespoon oil
1 cup chopped green
  onions*
¾ cup peeled and diced
  tomatoes
1½ tablespoons minced
  garlic
¼ teaspoon salt
¼ teaspoon ground
  cumin*
¼ teaspoon color* or
  turmeric
2 tablespoons minced
  cilantro

POTATOES
1 cup peeled, diced russet
  potatoes, ½-inch dice
1½ cups peeled, diced
  yellow potatoes,
  ½-inch dice

PATACONES CON AJO Y LIMÓN

Fried Plantain Rounds With Garlic and Lime

8 to 10 patacones

The very popular *patacón* is served every time you order fish in a typical Colombian restaurant. At homes around the country, this dish is eaten very often. This delicacy is sometimes used as a dipper or chip dip. Serve them with lime juice and hot sauce to heighten the experience! The thinner you make them, the better they taste.

2 green plantains*
2 cloves garlic, mashed
1 teaspoon salt
2 cups oil
2 limes, quartered

1. Cut the ends off the plantains and peel. Cut in 1½-inch chunks.

2. In a shallow bowl, pour 1 cup water, the garlic and the salt, and mix a little with a fork. Set aside.

3. Pour the oil into a deep, medium, heavy pot, and place over medium-high heat. When the oil is hot (about 350°F), add the plantain pieces a few at a time, and fry 6 to 8 minutes. (If the oil doesn't cover the pieces, fry for 4 minutes, turn and leave 4 more minutes). Remove the plantains from the oil with a slotted spoon.

4. On the work surface, place a piece of plastic wrap, put the pieces of plantain on it, and cover with another piece of plastic. With a heavy pot, press well on the pieces of plantain, until they become very thin (¼ inch) and even.

5. Dip each thin slice in the garlic water for a couple of seconds, and fry again in the same oil at 350°F for 2 to 3 minutes on each side. Remove them with a slotted spoon and drain on paper towels.

6. Add more salt if desired and serve with lime wedges.

PLÁTANO ASADO

Baked plantains* are a good side dish that can be prepared one or two days ahead of time. Keep them refrigerated in sealed bags or foil, and reheated by placing them in a 375°F preheated oven, wrapped in foil for 15 minutes or until they reach serving temperature. Plantains are eaten in every home in the country almost every day of the week.

2 very ripe plantains*
2 teaspoons butter, softened
2 teaspoons sugar
¼ pound white farmer's cheese* (optional)
¼ pound guava paste (optional)

1. The plantains for this dish have to be very ripe, the peel almost black, but still have to be firm to the touch. When you press them gently, they should not feel mushy inside; if they are, the taste will be rancid and overripe. If you buy green plantains and wait for them to ripen it might take a week or so. Do not refrigerate them or they will not ripen well. It is better to buy plantains fully ripe or only a couple of days before, as this ensures you they haven't been refrigerated and will ripen fully without getting mushy.

2. Preheat the oven to 350°F. Cut the ends off the plantains and peel; leave whole.

3. Place in a baking dish. Spread the butter all over the plantains. Cover tightly with foil.

4. Bake for 20 to 30 minutes. When you remove the foil, the plantains should look golden, and feel cooked through the center.

FOR SIMPLE BAKED PLANTAINS:
5. Sprinkle the sugar all over the plantains and bake uncovered for 5 more minutes or until the sugar has melted and they look lightly browned.

FOR PLANTAINS WITH CHEESE:
5. Slice the plantains lengthwise but do not go all the way though. Cut the cheese into ½ inch thick strips. Arrange the cheese in the slits of the plantains and sprinkle with the sugar. Bake uncovered until the cheese warms up and melts, about 8 minutes.

FOR PLANTAINS WITH CHEESE AND GUAVA:
5. Slice the plantains lengthwise but do not go all the way though. Cut the cheese and guava paste into ½ inch thick strips. Arrange the cheese and the guava paste in the slits of the plantains and sprinkle with the sugar. Bake uncovered until the cheese and guava paste warm up and cheese melts, about 8 to 10 minutes.

PLÁTANOS EN TENTACIÓN O CALADOS

Temptation Plantains

6 servings

I don't know whether to call this a side dish or a dessert. In my hometown, we serve them as a part of the meal; in other towns they are served at the end of the meal as dessert. Both are perfect!

2 very ripe plantains*
⅔ cup panela* or dark brown sugar
12 whole cloves
2 cinnamon sticks

1. The plantains for this dish have to be very ripe, the peel almost black, but still have to be firm to the touch. When you press them gently, they should not feel mushy inside; if they are, the taste will be rancid and overripe. If you buy green plantains and wait for them to ripen it might take a week or so. Do not refrigerate them or they will not ripen well. It is better to buy plantains fully ripe or only a couple of days before, as this ensures you they haven't been refrigerated and will ripen fully without getting mushy.

2. Cut the ends off the plantains and peel. Cut each into 4 chunks, about 1½ inches thick.

3. In a small heavy saucepan place the plaintain chunks, 2 cups of water, the panela, cloves, and cinnamon sticks.

4. Cook over medium heat until the plantains are very soft, the water has reduced, and a caramel-colored syrup has formed, about 15 minutes for brown sugar and 35 minutes for panela.

5. Serve hot or refrigerate to serve cold.

ROSCAS DE YUCA CON AZÚCAR

Sweet Yuca Rings
1 dozen 2-inch rings

Roscas de yuca bring memories of my childhood, all of us sitting around the table with one thing in common: we all loved the *roscas*; the rest of the meal we couldn't agree on. *Roscas* are very light and sweet, and the sugar on the outside is like music to a child's heart.

2 pounds peeled yuca*, fresh or frozen
1¼ tablespoons salt
2 cups oil for frying
1 cup sugar

1. Cut the yuca lengthwise into 1-inch pieces. They will be half-moon-shaped chunks, since yuca is a cylindrical vegetable and is usually cut in long, half-cylinders. Remove the center stem.

2. In a small stockpot place the yuca and 1 tablespoon of salt, and cover completely with water. Simmer over medium heat until the yuca is so soft that you can insert a knife smoothly into it—about 20 minutes for good yuca. It should feel like a potato when done.

3. Drain the yuca and discard the water. Sprinkle with the remaining ¼ teaspoon of salt and mash with a potato masher or pass through a *molino** (corn mill).

4. Form 4 x ⅓ inch-long logs of about 2 tablespoon of yuca.

5. Pour the oil into a deep, medium, heavy pot, and place over medium-high heat. When the oil is hot (about 325°F), add the yuca rings and deep fry for 2 minutes. Remove them with a slotted spoon and drain on paper towels. Let cool for 2 to 3 minutes to set the shape.

6. Place on a serving dish and sprinkle with the sugar while warm. Serve and enjoy!

TAJADAS DE PLÁTANOS

Fried Sweet Plantain Strips with Cheese and Sugar

16-20 strips

If I may quote the Colombian writer, Plinio Apuleyo Mendoza, in his sensational story about my hometown, *Volver a Barranquilla*:

> *En la casa de la familia más rica y antigua de la cuidad, se come todo los días tajadas de plátano con arroz como en el ultimo tugurio de Carrizal.*

He clearly explains that every day in Barranquilla, both the oldest, richest families and those in the farthest, poorest huts eat *Tajadas de Plátano* and rice; we all have a very close relationship with plantains* imbedded in our soul.

2 very ripe plantains*
2 cups oil for frying
10 ounces white farmer's cheese,* grated (1¼ cups)
3 tablespoons sugar

1. The plantains for this dish have to be very ripe, the peel almost black, but still have to be firm to the touch. When you press them gently, they should not feel mushy inside; if they are, the taste will be rancid and overripe. If you buy green plantains and wait for them to ripen it might take a week or so. Do not refrigerate them or they will not ripen well. It is better to buy plantains fully ripe or only a couple of days before, as this ensures you they haven't been refrigerated and will ripen fully without getting mushy.

2. Cut the ends off the plantains and peel. Cut on the bias into ¼-inch-thick slices.

3. Pour the oil into a deep, medium, heavy pot, and place over medium-high heat. When the oil is hot (about 350°F), add the plantain pieces and fry 2 to 3 minutes. (If the oil doesn't cover the pieces, fry for 1 to 2 minutes on each side.)

4. Remove the plantains from the oil with a slotted spoon and drain over paper towels.

5. Combine the cheese and the sugar. Put half a tablespoon on each slice and serve.

6. Another option is to roll and close with a toothpick and serve as hors d'oeuvres.

TORTA DE PLÁTANO

Plantain Pie
8 servings

Torta de Plátano is prepared in several ways. One of them consists of cutting the plantains* into thin strips instead of squares and layering them with the cheese and guava paste; another is blending all the ingredients together and then adding the mixture to the plantain strips; and this one, which is easier to prepare. Use different types of molds like tart pans or mini-muffin pans for different occasions.

4 very ripe plantains*
2 cups oil for frying
4 eggs
½ cup milk
4 tablespoons butter
2 teaspoon sugar
2 teaspoon salt
½ teaspoon vanilla extract
½ teaspoon ground cinnamon (optional)
1 pound (about ⅔ cup) guava paste, diced
½ pound (1¼ cups) grated white farmer's cheese*, plus extra for topping**
Butter and flour, for the baking pan

1. The plantains for this dish have to be very ripe, the peel almost black, but still have to be firm to the touch. When you press them gently, they should not feel mushy inside; if they are, the taste will be rancid and overripe. If you buy green plantains and wait for them to ripen it might take a week or so. Do not refrigerate them or they will not ripen well. It is better to buy plantains fully ripe or only a couple of days before, as this ensures you they haven't been refrigerated and will ripen fully without getting mushy.

2. Preheat the oven to 350°F. Cut the ends off the plantains and peel. Cut into ¼-inch dice.

3. Pour the oil into a deep, medium, heavy pot, and place over medium-high heat. When the oil is hot (about 350°F), add the plantain cubes and fry for 2 to 2½ minutes. Since they are small keep your eye on the frying pan all the time and swirl them in the oil with the slotted spoon. Remove the plantains from the oil with the slotted spoon and drain over paper towels; set aside.

4. In a small mixing bowl, combine the eggs, milk, butter, sugar, salt, vanilla, and cinnamon if using.

5. In a medium bowl mix the fried plantain cubes with the guava paste and the cheese.

6. Fold the egg mixture into the plantain mixture and pour into a greased and floured 8-inch square baking pan. Sprinkle extra cheese on top.

7. Bake 30 to 40 minutes until browned and bubbly.

TOSTADAS

Giant Fried Plantain
8 tostadas

If you ever fly to Colombia or come across a Colombian restaurant, please try these. Then you will run to make them. The plantains* for this recipe should be completely green. When you peel green plantains they should have a slightly orange color; if they are very pale and yellow they are not of the optimum quality for these large *tostadas*! The secret to keeping them from breaking when pounded is that they must be completely cooked in the middle. You can even add together several plantains to make huge ones—you would just need a giant frying pan.

8 green plantains*
2 quarts of oil for frying
Salt, for serving
Ajíes, for serving

1. If you have your plantains refrigerated, or live in a very cold climate, place the plantains in warm water for 2 hours to bring them back to room temperature.

2. Cut the ends off the plantains and peel. Leave whole.

3. Heat the oil in a very large and wide frying pan or *caldero** over medium heat. When it is hot (about 275°F), add the whole plantains and fry for 20 to 30 minutes, or until the whole plantain is cooked through but not browned. The oil must cover the plantains.

4. Remove the plantains from the oil with a slotted spoon. On the work surface, place each plantain between 2 pieces of plastic wrap or damp towels, and pound gently until the whole plantain is about ⅛-inch thick. If it breaks don't worry, play with it and add a piece from the sides of the same plantain. You can even add two pieces, one whole and another half a plantain if you want to make an even larger one.

5. Increase the heat of the oil to 350°F. Carefully peel the pressed plantain from the plastic or cloth and drop it into the hot oil. Fry it for 6 to 8 minutes or until very crisp.

6. Remove the tostada carefully from the oil with a pair of slotted spoon and drain over paper towels.

7. Lightly salt, and serve with a variety of ajíes from the Salsa and Sauces chapter (page 153).

YUCA FRITA

Fried Yuca
6 to 8 servings

These fried *yuca** sticks are served in many of the restaurants that serve braised meats, *chorizos*, and *empanadas*. They make great party snacks to serve along with sausages and salsa (see Salsas and Sauces, page 153).

1 pound peeled yuca*,
  fresh or frozen
1 tablespoon salt
2 cups oil for frying
Salt, for serving

1. If using fresh yuca, quarter it lengthwise. (Frozen yuca is already cut into chunks.) Cut each piece of yuca lengthwise into ½-inch sticks, or into ¼-inch sticks if you like more toasted, crispier sticks.

2. Place the yuca in a medium pot with 6 cups of water. Cover, bring to a boil and cook until fork tender, about 20 minutes. Drain well and dry with paper towels.

3. Pour the oil into a deep, medium, heavy pot, and place over medium-high heat. When the oil is hot (about 325°F), add the yuca sticks and deep fry for 5 to 7 minutes or until lightly golden on all sides.

4. Remove the pieces with slotted spoon and drain on paper towels. Sprinkle lightly with salt and serve.

YUCA GUISADA

Stewed Yuca
6 servings

Yuca Guisada is served more in homes than in restaurants. Like potatoes, it is served with soups and meats alongside white rice and salad.

2 pounds peeled yuca*, fresh or frozen
2 tablespoons salt
1 chicken bouillon cube

1. If using fresh yuca, quarter it lengthwise. Cut each piece of yuca lengthwise again and then cut into 2-inch chunks.

2. Place the yuca in a medium pot with 6 cups of water, the salt and bouillon cube. Cover, bring to a boil and cook until fork tender, about 30 to 35 minutes. Prick with a knife and it should go all the way in very easily; it will look almost undone on the edges. Set aside.

3. FOR THE GUISO: In a large sauté pan over medium heat, place the oil, onion, tomato, garlic, cilantro, bouillon cube, color and pepper; cook for 12 minutes. Add the chicken stock, cook for 5 minutes more.

GUISO
4 tablespoons oil
1½ cups thinly sliced onion
1 cup thinly sliced tomato
1 tablespoon mashed garlic
1 tablespoon minced cilantro
1 chicken bouillon cube
1 teaspoon color* or saffron powder
½ teaspoon pepper
¾ cup chicken stock

4. Drain the yuca and add it to the guiso pan; gently mix it all together. Cover and cook over low heat for 5 minutes.

5. Serve.

SALSAS AND SAUCES

In Colombia, we spice up our dishes with many pungent flavors, some of them coming from various kinds of onions, others from cumin* seeds, curry or coloring seeds like achiote and saffron threads, which all give food life and flair. These salsas or sauces accompany many of the meats, poultry, seafoods, and side dishes in the book, and can do the same for your everyday foods. For example, I once served my husband a filet mignon with the tomato sauce I had prepared for the Oyster Cocktail (page 95): a tangy tomato sauce full of color and spice, only I omitted the oyster liquid. He absolutely loved it and had no idea what it was until I told him. You can elevate everyday meals with these and other sauces and salsas throughout the book. They keep perfectly well for a week or more in the fridge, and are very easy to prepare.

The recipes throughout this chapter and the rest of the book call for both scallions and green onions. That is because in the Carribbean zone we have scallions, and in the Andean zone green onions. The difference is that the green onions are about half-an-inch thick and about sixteen inches long, whereas the scallions are about one-eighth-of-an-inch thick and twelve inches long. They are very close in flavor and can be used one in place of the other. Also, the hot peppers we have in Colombia are very small: one inch long (at the most) by one-third-of-an-inch thick; you can use any hot pepper you like in place of them. The *ají dulce**, a small sweet pepper, is mainly found on the coast and widely used there; if you cannot find them, replace with the same amount of regular red or green bell pepper. Another ingredient is *color**, which you can replace with turmeric in some recipes and Sazón Goya with Saffron in others. *Color* is an ingredient that originally came from the achiote seed and gives foods a yellow orange tint. An indigenous shrub of the Andean region produces these tiny red seeds, which were used for body painting in pre-Colombian times. Later, it was used almost exclusively for cooking, and now it is being relegated to favor the more processed powdered product, *color*.

I have so much fun preparing different kinds of salsas that I would like to write many more of my own creation, but would lose some of the authenticity of the book if too many were added. The yellow gooseberry salsa is not a traditional recipe, but a delicious one that I created, and one you can serve with *empanadas*, *tostadas*, salmon, and other seafood too.

AJÍ ANTIOQUEÑO

Hot Antioqueño Salsa
1½ to 2 cups

This spicy salsa is a traditional sauce that is kept in most *antioqueño* refrigerators year-round. They use it to flavor dishes from beans to meats, and many times just saltine crackers will do. It is a very strong sauce that goes very well with the high working capacity of the people of this region. You can change the variety of peppers and use milder ones when you first try this recipe.

1. In a blender puree the habanero with the vinegar, lime juice, salt, and ⅓ cup of water for 1 minute.

2. Pour into a nonreactive bowl.

3. Add cilantro, tomatoes, green onions, onions, sugar, pepper, and oil and mix well.

4. Add the Tabasco, if using (this will make a very hot sauce even hotter!), and mix well.

5. Refrigerate 8 hours to improve flavor. This is a mixture of ingredients that will blend with each other and become one with special character and aroma if left to set for this time period or overnight. It will keep refrigerated for about a week.

2 teaspoons minced, seeded red habanero* pepper (about 1)
⅓ cup white vinegar
2 tablespoons lime juice
1 tablespoon salt
⅓ cup chopped cilantro
½ cup chopped tomatoes
½ cup chopped green onions*
½ cup diced white onions
1½ teaspoons sugar
½ teaspoon pepper
4 tablespoons sunflower seed oil or corn oil
1 tablespoon Tabasco sauce (optional)

Serve with Fried Green Plantains (page 143), soups, sancochos, or meats.

AJÍ DE AGUACATE

Avocado Salsa
2½ to 3 cups

Ají de Aguacate is a delicious salsa to serve as a dip for crackers. It is mostly served at family and weekend gatherings in the Andean zones of Colombia. You can prepare it up tp twelve hours ahead of time, keeping the pit in the mixture to keep it from browning; remember to remove it before serving.

⅓ cup (about 6) seeded ají dulce* (sweet red pepper)
1 teaspoon minced, seeded red habanero* pepper (optional)
¼ cup white vinegar
2 tablespoons lemon juice
½ teaspoon salt
½ teaspoon pepper
2 hard-boiled eggs, peeled and chopped fine
1½ cups mashed or diced avocado (about 1); reserve the pit
1 cup chopped tomatoes
¾ cup finely diced onion
⅓ cup chopped green onions*
⅓ cup chopped cilantro

1. In a blender puree ají dulce and habanero (if you like it hot!) with ⅓ cup of water, the vinegar, lemon juice, salt, and pepper for 1 minute. Pour in a nonreactive bowl.

2. Add the eggs, avocado, tomatoes, onion, green onions, and cilantro, and mix. Place the avocado pit in the mixture to prevent the avocado from browning (oxidizing) while in the refrigerator. Cover and refrigerate until ready to use.

Serve with *Tostadas* (page 149), soups and *sancochos*, or meats.

AJÍ DE AGUACATE LICUADO

Colombian Guacamole
1½ cups

This sauce is our Colombian version of the Mexican guacamole, only much milder and without tomatoes. It is great with *Empanadas Vallunas* (page 24), *Tostadas* (page 149), and meats and poultry. The secret to keeping it fresh for two or three days is to keep the pit in the sauce; this prevents it from turning brown, so you can use the leftovers the next day. It is a delicious ají to serve with roasted meats and barbecued specialty sausages such as our *Chorizos* (page 61).

1 avocado
4 tablespoons oil
3 tablespoons lime juice
2 tablespoons minced scallion or green onion*
2 tablespoons minced cilantro
1 teaspoon minced, seeded red habanero* pepper
1 teaspoon salt
¼ teaspoon pepper

1. Slice the avocado in two, lengthwise; remove the peel and the pit (save the pit for later on). Chop or dice and place in a nonreactive container.

2. Place oil, lime juice, scallion or green onion, cilantro, habanero, salt, and pepper in the blender and mix until smooth.

3. Add the puree to the avocado in the nonreactive container. Mix gently but thoroughly. Add the pit to prevent the mixture from turning black or oxidizing. Cover and refrigerate until ready to use.

AJÍ DE AJO

Sauce, seasoning, or *ají*: call it what you want. This is a great sauce to serve with meats, *Tostadas* (page 149), or even pasta or potatoes. Keep it on hand in the refrigerator, and use it to season meats. It will give an extra bite to foods.

**¾ cup (about 16 to 20) cloves garlic
¾ cup olive oil
½ cup mayonnaise
1 teaspoon salt
¼ teaspoon pepper
3 tablespoons cilantro leaves**

1. Bring some water to a boil in a small saucepan. Drop in the garlic. Cook for 5 minutes, drain, and cool.

2. In a blender puree the garlic, oil, mayonnaise, salt and pepper until smooth, about 30 seconds.

3. Add the cilantro and blend 10 seconds more.

4. Serve or keep refrigerated. This ají will keep for up to a month if well refrigerated; just make sure to only put clean spoons in it when using!

AJÍ DE MANÍ

Peanut Salsa
1¼ cups

I got this great recipe when I visited the restaurant of Claudia Mejía, Tentenpié, in the city of Cali for a whole week. It is originally from the Popayán area, a zone in the south Pacific of Colombia where peanuts are indigenous. Peanuts are said to come from the zones ranging from Brazil to Paraguay, from where they spread throughout the continent all the way to the southern and central zones of Colombia. It is prepared with fresh peanuts, sun dried for two days, then hand roasted and ground in a *molino**. I have made some changes to prepare it at home. It is traditionally served with *Tamales de Pipián* (page 84) and is surprisingly hot. You will love it and can serve it also with poultry and as a dipping sauce for crudités. This sauce will keep for up to two weeks refrigerated.

⅓ cup minced green
    onions*
1 tablespoons lard or oil
½ cup unsalted roasted
    peanuts
¼ cup minced red onion
3 tablespoons minced
    cilantro
2 cloves garlic
1 teaspoons color* or
    turmeric
½ beef bouillon cube
¼ teaspoon salt
¼ teaspoon pepper
¼ teaspoon ground
    cumin*
1 teaspoon minced,
    seeded red habanero*
    pepper

1. In a medium sauté pan over medium-low heat, cook the green onions in the fat until translucent, about 4 minutes. Remove from the heat and set aside.

2. In a blender pulse the peanuts, onion, 1 tablespoon of the cilantro, the garlic, color, bouillon cube, salt, pepper, and cumin with 1¼ cups of water for 30 seconds, to make for a sauce with some mouth feel and texture. If you prefer, blend it to a smooth sauce. It will also be fine; it is just a matter of preference.

3. Pour the puree from the blender into the sauté pan with the green onions. Return to the heat, low heat this time, and simmer for 15 minutes.

4. Remove from the heat and add the habanero and remaining 2 tablespoons of cilantro.

5. Set aside to cool.

6. Refrigerate covered until ready to use.

AJÍ DE TOMATE DE ARBOL

Tree Tomato Salsa

1¼ cups

Here is a very versatile salsa! I keep it in the refrigerator for up to two weeks and add it to salads, hearts of palm, and even use it to marinate chicken and seafood. Just mix a tablespoon of this salsa, a teaspoon of honey or brown sugar, and a teaspoon of oil, and you will have a great marinade for salmon.

½ pound (about 3)
tomates de arbol*
(tree tomatoes)
½ cup minced green
onions
½ cup minced cilantro
3 teaspoons lime juice
1½ teaspoons white
vinegar
1 teaspoons sugar
½ teaspoon salt
¼ teaspoon pepper
¼ teaspoon hot sauce, or
to taste

1. Peel and puree the tree tomatoes in a blender.

2. Place in a nonreactive bowl; add the green onions, cilantro, lime juice, vinegar, sugar, salt, pepper, hot sauce, and 3 tablespoons of water.

3. Refrigerate overnight if desired as this improves the flavors.

Serve with *Empanadas* (page 23), *Patacones* (page 143), soups, and seafood.

AJÍ DE UCHUVAS

Yellow Gooseberry Salsa
1¼ cups

Yellow gooseberries are one of my favorite fruits. This is probably the only recipe that is not traditional, but it is just wonderful. Try it—it keeps refrigerated for over a week, and can be used with white seafood, asparagus, and other vegetables.

½ pound (1 cup) uchuvas*
(yellow gooseberries)
5 tablespoons minced
green onions*
4 tablespoons minced
cilantro
2 tablespoons lime juice
2 teaspoons sugar
1 teaspoon salt
½ teaspoon pepper
½ teaspoon hot sauce, or
to taste

1. In a blender puree the yellow gooseberries.

2. Place in a nonreactive bowl; add the green onions, cilantro, lime juice, sugar, salt, pepper, and hot sauce.

3. Refrigerate covered overnight, if possible, as this improves the flavors.

Serve with *Empanadas* (page 23), *Patacones* (page 143), soups, and seafood.

AJÍ VALLUNO

Valluno Sauce
1½ cups

My favorite *ají*! This is a mild, very cilantro-intensive sauce. I add it to salads, shrimp, and oysters, and use it the traditional way with *Patacones* (page 143) and *Empanaditas Vallunas* (page 24). Add as many peppers as you like to take it from mild to hot. Keep it in your fridge for up to ten days; the cilantro starts turning brown afterwards.

⅓ cup lime juice
⅓ cup white vinegar
1 teaspoon minced,
  seeded red habanero*
  pepper, or more to taste
1 cup minced green
  onions*
1 cup chopped cilantro
½ cup peeled and diced
  tomatoes
½ tablespoon olive oil
½ teaspoon salt

1. Blend the lime juice, vinegar, ⅓ cup water and habanero. Pour into a nonreactive bowl.

2. Add the green onions, cilantro, tomatoes, olive oil, and salt, and mix well.

3. Set aside for at least 1 hour before serving, for the flavors to blend.

CHIMICHURRI

Herb Sauce
1 cup

This sauce is served mainly on the side with *Carne Asada* (page 57), and can also be used with roasted poultry and barbecued foods. It has an aroma that will take you to a garden of fresh herbs and flowers; it is just fantastic!

3 cloves garlic
1½ cups minced parsley
1 cup minced cilantro leaves
⅓ cup minced green onions*, green part included
1 tablespoon red wine vinegar
2 teaspoons lime juice
1 teaspoon salt
¼ teaspoon pepper
¾ cup oil

1. In the dry bowl of a food processor place the garlic and process until all the garlic pieces are stuck to the sides of the bowl.

2. Add the parsley, cilantro and green onions and process 15 seconds. Stop, scrape the bowl and process again for 15 to 20 seconds.

3. Add the vinegar, lime juice, salt, and pepper, and process 10 seconds more.

4. Add the oil, mix for 2 seconds, and pour into a nonreactive covered container or jar. Keep refrigerated for up to a week or use immediately.

HOGAO DEL CARIBE O GUISO

Tomato and Onion Seasoning Sauce
1½ cups

In Colombia, we use this sauce to flavor many of our typical dishes. It is sometimes called *hogao*, mainly by people from the Andean regions, and *guiso* by the rest. You can use it as a finished sauce for potatoes, yuca* or cassava, and meats and poultry as well as an ingredient during preparation. It differs from the *Hogao del Pacífico* (page 165) mainly in the kind of onion used; this one uses scallions and the other green onions. Also, this one uses *ají dulce* (sweet green peppers) and has other small variations; but you can use them interchangeably. This is a sweeter sauce with a less oily consistency. You can keep it refrigerated in jars for up to two weeks.

4 tablespoons olive oil
1½ cups diced onion
1 cup peeled and diced tomatoes, seeds included
4 cloves garlic, mashed
2 tablespoons minced ají dulce* (sweet green pepper)
2 bay leaves
1½ tablespoons chopped cilantro
1 tablespoon chopped scallion
1 tablespoon Worcestershire sauce
2 tablespoons red wine vinegar (optional)
1 teaspoon salt
½ teaspoon sugar
¼ teaspoon pepper

1. In a large sauté pan, heat the oil over medium heat. Add the onions and cook for 2 to 3 minutes.

2. Add the tomatoes, garlic, sweet peppers, bay leaves, cilantro, scallion, Worcestershire, vinegar (if using), salt, sugar, and pepper, and cook for 6 minutes more.

3. Remove bay leaves.

4. You should have a very soft and moist consistency, almost like a sauce. If the heat is high, and your sauce looks dry like a *sofrito*, then add some beef stock or water, about ½ cup.

Serve the sauce with meats, chicken, potatoes, and yuca. It gives a zest of flavor to many foods.

HOGAO DEL PACÍFICO

Tomato and Green Onion Seasoning Sauce
1½ cups

Here is a second kind of *hogao*, which comes from the Pacific region and is used both as an ingredient and a sauce. Here, as in many Pacific region recipes, you find that the onion used is the green onion, a thick and larger type of scallion; also, cumin* is more present. This is an oilier sauce with a more pungent taste and smell. You can keep it refrigerated in jars for up to two weeks.

3 tablespoons olive oil
1½ cups sliced green onions*
1 cup peeled and diced tomatoes, seeds included
4 cloves garlic, mashed
½ chicken bouillon cube
½ teaspoon salt
½ teaspoon color* or Sazón Goya with Saffron
½ teaspoon ground cumin* (optional)
¼ teaspoon pepper
3 tablespoons chopped cilantro

1. In a large sauté pan, heat the oil over medium heat. Add the green onions, tomatoes, garlic, bouillon cube, salt, color, cumin (if using), and pepper, and cook for 5 minutes.

2. Add the cilantro, reduce the heat to low, and cook for 20 minutes more.

3. You will have a very soft and moist consistency, almost like a sauce.

Add this recipe to meats, chicken, potatoes, and yuca.

PASTA DE AJO

Garlic Paste
¼ cup

This paste is used in many of the soups and stocks prepared in the Pacific regions of our country. It is very useful when you have many dishes to prepare. You could use a teaspoon of paste to replace one garlic clove in other dishes; but the tastes differ somewhat. You can keep it refrigerated for up to a week. If you want to keep it longer, first drop the garlic in boiling water for ten seconds and then process the ingredients; you can then keep it refrigerated for up to a month.

2 large heads of garlic (7 ounces), cloves separated and peeled
2 tablespoons oil
1 teaspoon salt

1. Process all the ingredients in the food processor until a paste is formed. You can also make this in the blender, but have patience because you have to turn on the blender for 15 seconds, scrape down, and repeat about 5 times.

SWEETS

Do we Colombians have a sweet tooth! Maybe the fact that we are such a large sugarcane grower and that we have so many fruits has had an influence in our passion for sweets. I love all desserts, especially when properly prepared with the best ingredients, no matter how many calories they have. My own personal theory is that it is better to have a bite of a great dessert than a huge slice of a "light" one. I was trained in my mother's bakery since I was a little girl, and started decorating birthday cakes when I was thirteen. Together with my mother, I trained at Lenôtre in Paris, the American Institute of Baking, and many other places; she used to take me so I would help her with her bags. My mother is a sensational baker and taster.

We love to eat sweets; at ten in the morning, we usually go out for our first sweet snack, and then at four thirty in the afternoon for the second. Sweets are very important on our menus; that little something at the end of the feast we call lunch or dinner is always there to close the great moment.

In each department of Colombia are specialty desserts for different occasions. On the coast, vendors set up in parks so people can purchase their *dulces de Semana Santa* (Easter Holy Week) prepared in the true traditional ways. During the Christmas holidays, the same happens, with the *Torta de Pastores* (page 198) in Buga; *Torta de Coco* (page 197), *Manjar Blanco* (page 169) and *Hojaldras* (page 26) in Cali; *Natilla* (page 192), *Dulce de Moras* (page 182) in Bogotá; and *hojaldras* and *natilla* in Medellín. These are usually fruit purees that are sweetened and cooked to a paste—the one commonly seen outside of the country being guava paste. During the Christmas holidays, we also give away many of these delicacies to our friends and family. There is a lot of dessert baking and giving during the whole month before Christmas. For the "Virgin's Novena," from December 15 to 24, we meet in family and friends' houses to pray to the Virgin Mary and then, at the end, we share the typical sweets of each town. On the Pacific Coast, *Cocadas* (pages 175-177) and desserts with a fruit called *arbol del pan* are the favorites.

We tend to eat sweets all the time, in small sizes but very often. At the beach, together with fresh fruit vendors we find *cocada* and candied fruit vendors that offer the best quality of all. Pastry shops and bakeries are found in every single town in the country. In some towns, handmade spun candy is still produced, and sold in paper wrappers on the streets. People are very proud to be the ones to prepare special desserts; every household has its own recipe that attracts friends and family over to chat and eat. Younger generations are starting to get into the cooking mood, which was starting to get lost in the humdrum of large city living and lack of time. In general, we are a country that loves to eat, and most of all enjoy the moments related to foods and especially desserts.

Various recipes use raw unpasteurized milk. In the United States, regulations on the sale of non-pasteurized (raw) cow's milk vary from state to state. It is legal for licensed dairies to sell raw milk in California, but it is illegal in Wisconsin and many other states as the National Dairy Council wrote me. The easiest way to find it is to contact a local dairy farm or supplier.

AREQUIPE, DULCE DE LECHE, O MANJAR BLANCO

Colombian Caramel Dessert
6 cups

Arequipe is originally from the Andean zone, *Dulce de Leche* from the Caribbean Coastal area, and *Manjar Blanco* a relative of the two that comes from the small towns of el Valle del Cauca. They are all our Colombian caramel sauce, *manjar blanco* being the thickest and *dulce de leche* and *arequipe* the lighter. They are all cooked in copper pots or *pailas* for different amounts of time; *manjar blanco* the longest. *Manjar blancos* are typically sold in *totumos*, which are the outer most shell of the fruit of the totumo tree; *arequipes* and *dulce de leche* are commercially sold in plastic or glass containers. They keep forever you could say; the only problem being that they harden and form a crust. This dessert is just absolutely scrumptious. The original recipes all include rice; it is strained out and people never knew it was there! When I was small, what we used to do was place a closed can of condensed milk into a pressure cooker and cook it for twenty minutes. Then... voilà!... *arequipe*. Add it to candied fruit, to *Cuajada* (page 178), to ice cream, or just eat it by the spoonful as I do—after ten at night!

¼ cup rice
3 quarts whole milk
3 cups sugar

1. Combine the rice and 2 cups of water in a bowl, and set aside for 2 days.

2. Drain and rinse the rice well and discard the water; blend the rice with one 1 cup of milk, strain (discarding the liquid) and place into a medium pot.

3. Add the remaining milk and the sugar in to the pot and bring to a boil. Decrease the heat to medium and simmer for 2 hours. Decrease the heat to low if you see little brown bits coming up to the surface, or when the mixture has turned caramel color. Cook for 1 hour more.

4. To know when it is ready, spread some of the mixture onto a plate and wait 5 minutes; when cool it should be thick as a pudding.

5. Keep it refrigerated up to a week. Cover with plastic wrap to prevent crust formation.

ARROZ CON LECHE

Sweet Rice Pudding
1 dozen 6-ounce servings

Arroz con Leche is served all over the country as a dessert, especially during the holidays. You will find it in many restaurants in the country but especially in the Valle del Cauca. This is one of those dishes you can gobble up a tablespoon at a time!

1½ cups rice, washed
2 cups sugar
2 cinnamon sticks
1 teaspoon salt
6 whole cloves
3 cups whole milk
1 cup (13.5- or 14-ounce can) sweetened condensed milk
1cup heavy cream
½ cup raisins

1. Combine rice and 6 cups of water in a bowl. Set aside at room temperature for 1 hour. Do not drain.

2. In a large heavy pot or *caldero**, over medium heat place the rice, the soaking water, ¼ cup of sugar, cinnamon, salt, and cloves. Cover, decrease the heat to medium-low and simmer for 1 hour and 10 minutes.

3. Uncover, add the remaining 1¾ cups of sugar, the milk, condensed milk, and cream. Stir with a wooden spoon. Cover and simmer on low for 5 minutes.

4. Turn off the heat, stir in the raisins, and cover. Let stand for 10 minutes.

5. Uncover, let cool for 1 hour and refrigerate in a nonmetallic container. Cover with plastic wrap or parchment paper placed directly on the pudding so it doesn't form a crust.

6. Serve cold in custard or ice cream cups.

BOCADILLO CON QUESO

Guava Paste and Cheese
12 servings

Bocadillo originally came from the town of Velez in the department of Santander, a town in Colombia famous from its *bocadillo* wrapped in dry plantain leaves and packaged in wooden boxes called *bocadillo veleño*. In Colombia, especially in the coastal areas, we eat many sweet things with cheese: bananas and cheese, pineapple with cheese, and all of the fruits in syrups with cheese; in the Pacific and Andean zones, they eat sweets with *Cuajada* (page 178). It's a great mix, a great snack that can take you for hours without feeling hungry.

1 pound white farmer's cheese*
1 pound guava paste

1. Slice the cheese into 2 by 1 by ½-inch rectangles.

2. Cut the guava paste into 2 by 1 by ¼-inch rectangles.

3. Place the cheese over the guava paste.

4. Serve.

BOLAS DE TAMARINDO

Tamarind Balls
2 dozen 1½-inch balls

Tamarind Balls are a Caribbean coastal delicacy. They are prepared with the tamarind pulp that has all the seeds in it. You can find the pulp in Latin or Asian food stores, unprocessed, which means that it has seeds and no extra sugar or water added, only the shells removed. It will look like a brown, odd shaped ball wrapped in paper or plastic. People eat the balls with the seeds in it, as you would grapes. This sweet and tart concoction keeps you asking for more.

1 pound tamarind pulp, unsweetened
2 cups sugar

1. Make sure your pulp has no water or sugar added; just the tamarind pulp with its seeds.

2. Place the pulp in a bowl, and break up with your hands. Add the sugar ½ cup at a time. Mix with your hands to incorporate the sugar into the tamarind. When the pulp has absorbed the sugar add the next ½ cup, until all the sugar has been absorbed.

3. Form into balls and serve.

BORRACHO

Drunken Cake
16 to 20 servings

Borracho is a very simple dessert to prepare. It can be prepared with various bases: pound cake, vanilla cake, sponge cake, or ladyfingers. Just prepare the syrup, sauce and assemble it.

RUM SYRUP
¾ cup sugar
½ cup dark rum
1½ cups pitted prunes

1. In a small pot mix the sugar and ¾ cup of water, and bring to a boil. Remove from the heat and let cool for 10 minutes. Add the rum and pitted prunes and set aside. (This can be left overnight for stronger flavored prunes.)

CRÈME ANGLAISE
2 cups milk
½ cup sugar
4 egg yolks
1 tablespoon flour
Pinch of salt
1 teaspoon vanilla extract

2. In a blender mix the milk, sugar, yolks, flour, salt and vanilla. Place in a medium, heavy pot, and cook over medium-low heat for 8 to 10 minutes, stirring constantly. Remove from the heat, cool, and cover with parchment paper placed directly on the sauce so it doesn't form a crust; set aside.

One round 8 to 10 inch by
4-inch tall vanilla,
sponge, or pound cake

3. Cut the cake into two layers; place the bottom cake into a ceramic or glass platter that has at least 1-inch-high sides. With a brush, soak the cake with ⅓ to ½ of the rum syrup. (Keep the prunes in the syrup.) Pour half of the Crème Anglaise over the soaked cake half, and add most of the prunes over the sauce (keep some for decoration).

4. Cover with the other cake half. Soak again with the remaining syrup. You might have some syrup left, depending how dense the cake is; just try to soak it as much as you can without making it soggy. Pour the rest of the Crème Anglaise over it and decorate with the remaining prunes.

5. Refrigerate and serve cold.

CASCOS DE GUAYABA

Guava Halves in Syrup
6 to 8 servings

Casquitos de Guayaba originated in my grandmother's home department of Tolima. They are a delicious way to fill your house with the most satisfying sweet and delicious aroma in the world. Fresh guavas have a great fragrance that is extracted and dispersed when cooked slowly for long periods of time. Guavas are either pear-shaped or apple-shapped. Use the pear-shaped ones that run about two inches long by one wide and are very deep orange-pink color. The apple-shaped variety is very hard and has a white colored pulp inside. Fresh guavas are sometimes available in the southern states closest to the Mexican peninsula; also look for them in specialty supermarkets. Frozen guavas can only be used for juice as they soften and get mushy when thawed.

2 pounds fresh guavas
3 cups sugar

1. Peel the guavas, cut in half and remove the seeds with a spoon.

2. In a medium, heavy pot place the sugar and 4 cups of water. Bring to a boil and cook covered over medium heat for 5 to 7 minutes.

3. Add the guavas and simmer covered for 20 minutes.

4. Remove the cover, decrease the heat to medium-low and cook for 1½ hours more.

5. Cool and keep refrigerated.

6. Serve cold alone or with white farmer's cheese* or ice cream.

COCADAS BLANCAS

White Cocadas

8 large 3-inch cocadas or 16 small 2-inch cocadas

This is the best way to use coconuts. Keep these in airtight tins or containers and serve as dessert. They keep perfectly for one or two weeks if tightly sealed.

2 coconuts
¾ cup sugar

1. Pick two large coconuts with plenty of water inside; drain, open, and peel off the brown skin from the coconut meat. Shred the coconut (page 107) to yield 3¾ cups shredded coconut and 2½ cups coconut water.

2. Mix the coconut water and sugar in a medium, heavy pot over medium heat. Simmer for 10 minutes to thicken and create a light syrup.

3. Add the coconut, decrease the heat to low and cook stirring constantly for 15 to 18 minutes. The heat has to be very low to prevent the cocadas from turning brown, which is actually okay otherwise, but for this recipe they should stay white!

4. Drop spoonfuls of the size you desire in oil coated pans or over parchment covered pans.

5. Cool completely.

COCADAS CON PANELA
O PANELITAS DE COCO *Coconut Panela Balls*
12 large 3-inch balls, 24 smaller 2-inch balls, or 4 dozen 1-inch balls

Originally from the Pacific zones of the Valle del Cauca and Antioquia, both *Cocadas con Panela* and *Panelitas* can be prepared in the same manner. All you have to do is shred the coconut finer for the *panelitas* than for the cocadas and form into tablespoon-size balls. These *cocadas* keep fresh for up to a month if stored tightly in tin cans.

1 coconut
2 cups (1pound) grated panela*

1. Pick a large coconut that has water inside; drain, open, and shred the coconut (page 107) to yield 1¼ cups of coconut water and 3 cups shredded or finely grated coconut.

2. Place the coconut water, panela and ½ cup of water in a medium, heavy pot. Bring to a boil and simmer for 8 to 10 minutes.

3. Add the coconut and cook over medium heat, stirring constantly, until the liquid has evaporated or been completely absorbed, about 20 minutes.

4. Drop spoonfuls of coconut onto a buttered foiled baking pan.

5. Let cool completely, about 2 hours.

6. Serve, or keep in an airtight container.

COCADAS COSTEÑAS

Caribbean Cocadas
12 large 2-inch cocadas

These *cocadas* and the white ones are sold on the streets and at the beach by ladies who carry them in large aluminum platters on their heads, with such balance and poise that they seem to walk on air. The platters are filled with a great variety of sweet and traditional fare, and the ladies will bring it down to you on the beach, as they display them all for you to choose. These *cocadas* keep fresh for up to a month if stored tightly in tin cans.

1 coconut
2 cups sugar
1 cinnamon stick
1 tablespoon butter

1. Pick a large coconut that has water inside; open, drain, and shred the coconut (page 107) to yield 3 cups shredded coconut and ⅔ cup coconut water.

2. In a medium, heavy pot place the coconut, coconut water, sugar, and cinnamon; cook over high heat for 15 to 20 minutes, stirring continuously. The appearance must be brown, but be careful not to let it burn.

3. Add butter and mix again.

4. Drop spoonfuls of coconut onto a buttered foil-covered baking pan.

5. Let cool completely, about 2 hours.

6. Serve, or keep in an airtight container.

CUAJADA

Fresh Milk Cheese
5 cheese balls

> *Cuajada* is a cheese prepared with fresh, raw, non-pasteurized milk. It is soft, not very salty and goes perfectly with many candied or fresh fruits. It is served at many outdoors events in the Andean and colder regions of Colombia. People on farms prepare it weekly, and eat it with *Melado* (page 191) after lunch or dinner.

5¼ quarts fresh raw (non-pasteurized) milk
½ rennet tablet or cuajo
1 tablespoon salt

5 plastic sieves lined with cheesecloth

1. Place the milk in a large container that can be placed near heat. Take ½ cup of the milk and warm it to 110°F, just warm enough like what you would give a baby in a bottle; mash the half rennet tablet and dissolve it in the warm milk. Pour it back into the container of milk. Add the salt.

2. Place in a warm spot or near a flame, but not directly over or under it, for 3 hours. It will set.

3. Make six cuts, forming a star in the semi-solid milk. Mix with a fork to break the curd completely. Set aside for 1½ to 2 hours more.

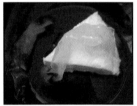

4. Divide the curd into 5 portions and place each one in a cheesecloth-lined sieve. Place the sieves over draining pots or bowls. Set aside for 4 hours to drain out the whey.

5. Discard the whey. Place the cheeses in plastic bags and refrigerate.

CUAJADA CON MELADO

Fresh Milk Cheese with Melado
10 to 12 servings

1. Cut each cuajada into 6 pieces and place in dessert dishes.

2. Pour the melado over each piece.

3. Serve with mint leaves or orange tree leaves to decorate.

2 balls of cuajada*
1 recipe of Melado (page 191)
Mint or orange leaves, for decorating

DULCE DE BREVAS

Figs in Syrup
1½ cups

Brevas grow in the Andean region. This *dulce* is said to be from Cundinamarca, and also from the Huila and Tolima departments. These figs are delicious with *Arequipe* (page 169), with *Cuajada* (page 178), or with ice cream.

1 pound figs
1 teaspoon salt
1¾ cups sugar
1 tablespoon lime juice

1. Wash the figs well to remove the hairy crust. Make a cross cut on the top of each fig.

2. In a medium, heavy pot place the figs, 4 cups of water, and the salt. Bring to a boil, drain the figs, and discard the water.

3. Return the figs to the pot and add 4 cups fresh water. Simmer over low heat for 45 minutes.

4. Add the sugar and continue to simmer over low heat for 1½ hours more. The figs should have softened and the syrup will be light. Add the lime juice, mix, and remove from the heat.

5. Cool, refrigerate, and serve.

DULCE DE GROSELLAS

Yellow Currants in Syrup
1½ cups

Dulce de Grosellas is traditionally from Santander, but it is prepared in the Valle del Cauca very much. *Grosellas** (yellow currants) are small and greenish yellow in color, and have a pit that is not usually removed before preparing this dish. So be careful and discard it as you eat.

**2 cups (½ pound)
grosellas***
1½ cups sugar
**1 teaspoon lime juice
(optional)**

1. Wash the grosellas well to remove dirt. Make a cross cut on each one.

2. In a medium, heavy pot place the grosellas, sugar and 1 cup of water. Simmer over medium-low heat for one hour. The syrup will turn pink and so will the fruit.

3. If you desire, add the lime juice and mix; remove from the heat.

4. Cool, refrigerate, and serve. It will keep up to two weeks.

DULCE DE MAMEY

Mamey in Syrup
3 cups

Mamey* is a brown fruit with a large pit and a fibrous orange pulp; another similar fruit is *zapote*. This is a dessert from the coffee-growing zones of Colombia called El Viejo Caldas. This recipe comes from Claudia Mejía of Tentenpié Restaurant in Cali. *Mamey* is available from March until October in Puerto Rico, and specialty markets carry it throughout the United States.

One (2 pound) mamey*
1½ cups sugar

1. Peel the mamey to remove the thick crust. Cut the fruit in half and slice into ¼-inch thin, short pieces until all you have left it the pit. You should have about 2½ cups of sliced fruit.

2. In a medium, heavy pot mix the sugar and ½ cup of water. Cook over medium heat until syrupy about 10 to 12 minutes.

3. Add the mamey pieces and simmer for 3 to 5 minutes more. The fruit should feel al dente.

4. Cool, refrigerate, and serve. It will keep up to two weeks.

DULCE DE MORAS

Raspberries in Syrup
6 cups

Traditionally from the Andean zones, this delicious dessert can be served with *Cuajada* (page 178) or ice cream, or as a topping on desserts or sponge cake. This recipe comes from Claudia Mejía of Tentenpié Restaurant in Cali.

6 cups whole raspberries, rinsed
4 cups sugar
1 tablespoon lime juice

1. Place the raspberries in a nonreactive container. Add the sugar and set aside overnight.

2. In a medium, heavy pot place the berries over high heat. Bring to a boil, reduce the heat and simmer for 15 minutes. Do not move or mix too much, so the berries keep their shape. Skim to remove the foamy gunk from the top.

3. Add the lime juice and simmer for 2 to 3 minutes more.

4. Remove from the heat. Cool, refrigerate, and serve. It will keep up to two weeks.

DULCE DE
PAPAYA VERDE

Green Papaya Chutney
1 cup

The following papaya desserts from the Huila, Tolima, and Cundinamarca departments are very good. In Colombia, we have both the native large papaya as well as the small Hawaiian ones. We are a very large consumer of both varieties. They are great with *Cuajada* (page 178) or ice cream. The papaya must be completely green for the first, meaning yellowish on the inside with absolutely no red. Even if papayas are not your favorite foods, this will become one of them.

1 (1-pound) green
Hawaiian papaya
1 cup sugar
1 tablespoon lime juice
(optional)

1. Peel the papaya, cut lengthwise and remove the pits. Cut into ⅛-inch-thick strips.

2. Mix the sugar with 1 cup of water in a small, heavy pot over medium heat. Bring to a boil and cook for 10 minutes.

3. Add the papaya strips and cook for 10 minutes more. They will change to a bright yellow color and will be shiny and translucent. If you cut them thicker then they will take longer.

4. Add the lime juice if using and remove from the heat.

5. Cool, refrigerate, and serve. It will keep up to two weeks.

DULCE DE PAPAYUELA

Candied Papaya Jelly
1 cup

1. Peel the papaya, cut lengthwise and remove the pits. Cut into ⅛-inch-thick strips.

2. Mix the sugar with 1 cup of water in a small, heavy pot over medium heat. Bring to a boil and cook for 10 minutes.

1 (1-pound) ripe Hawaiian papaya
½ cup sugar
1 tablespoon lime juice (optional)

3. Add the papaya strips and cook for 10 minutes more. If you cut them thicker then they will take longer.

4. Add the lime juice if using and remove from the heat.

5. Cool, refrigerate, and serve. It will keep up to two weeks.

DULCE DE QUESO

Sweet Cheese Curd
10 to 12 servings

This traditional dessert is like a grandmother's dessert, but is not served very often due to the length of time it takes to prepare. I think it can be prepared easily in a slow cooker with a removable ceramic liner. This recipe comes from Claudia Mejía of Tentenpié Restaurant in Cali.

2¼ quarts fresh, raw, non-pasteurized milk
⅛ rennet tablet or cuajo
1½ cups sugar

1. Remove the ceramic bowl from the slow cooker. Pour the milk into the slow-cooker bowl. Remove ½ cup of the milk and warm it to 110°F (just as warm as what you would give a baby in a bottle); mash and dissolve the piece of rennet tablet in the warm milk. Pour it back into the milk in the slow-cooker bowl.

2. Place the slow-cooker bowl in a warm spot or near a flame, but not directly over it, for 1 hour. It will set.

3. Once set, take a knife and make 6 cuts, forming a star into the semi-solid milk.

4. Without disturbing the curd, sprinkle the sugar over it.

5. Place the bowl back in the slow cooker, cover, and cook on low for a total of 8 hours. After the first 1 or 2 hours, pass a knife through the cuts you made before adding the sugar. This will separate the curd into triangular pieces. After 3 or 4 hours, run the knife through the cuts again; at this point, the curds will look odd-shaped. Turn them upside down in the container. Uncover and continue cooking for the 4 hours more, for a total of 8 hours. The mixture will have turned into a sort of crème anglaise with soft and chewy cheese inside.

6. Serve warm or cold.

DULCE DE UCHUVAS

Gooseberry Jam
3 Cups

From the region of Antioquia, this is one of my favorites of all *dulces*. *Uchuvas** (yellow gooseberries) are a very versatile fruit. This can be used for desserts, sauces, fish, and salads; as a dessert, it is especially good over white farmer's cheese* or ice cream.

¾ cup sugar
2½ cups husked and
   washed uchuvas*
1 tablespoon lime juice

1. In a small, heavy pot mix the sugar and ½ cup of water over medium heat. Simmer for 15 minutes.

2. Add the washed fruit and simmer for 5 minutes more.

3. Add the lime juice, mix, remove from the heat, and set aside to cool.

4. Refrigerate and serve cold.

ENYUCADO

Enyucado is traditionally cooked embedded in hot coals; it makes for a more moist cake. Do not refrigerate, or it will get very hard.

4½ cups (about 2 coconuts) finely shredded fresh coconut (page 107)

2 cups (¾ pound) finely shredded white farmer's cheese*

2¾ cups sugar

4 tablespoons melted butter

2 teaspoons whole aniseed

7 cups (about 4 pounds) finely shredded peeled yuca* or cassava

1. Preheat the oven to 350°F. Set aside 1 cup of coconut, 1 cup of cheese, ¾ cup of sugar, 2 tablespoons of melted butter and ¼ teaspoon of aniseed in a small bowl. Mix with a fork.

2. Place the remaining aniseed into a coffee mill and grind to a powder.

3. In a large bowl, place the yuca, the ground aniseed, and the remaining coconut, cheese, sugar, and melted butter. Mix with your hands or with 2 forks.

4. Place in a buttered 10 by 14-inch baking pan. Sprinkle with the reserved mixture from the first step.

5. Bake for 45 minutes or until lightly browned. Let cool and cut into brownie-like squares to serve.

ENYUCADO CON PANELA

Cassava Cake with Panela
16 to 20 servings

This is made the same way as the preceding recipe, only *panela** replaces the sugar. In this recipe, *panela* can be substituted with the same amount of dark brown sugar.

1 pound grated panela*
4½ cups (about 2 coconuts) finely shredded fresh coconut (page 107)
2 cups (1 pound) finely shredded white farmer's cheese*
4 tablespoons melted butter
2 teaspoons whole aniseed
7 cups (about 4 pounds) finely shredded peeled yuca* or cassava

1. In a small pot over medium heat melt the panela in ½ cup of water. Cool.

2. Preheat the oven to 350°F. Place 1 cup of coconut, 1 cup of cheese, ¼ of the melted panella, 2 tablespoons of melted butter and ¼ teaspoon of aniseed in a small bowl. Mix with a fork and set aside.

3. Place the remaining aniseed into a coffee mill and grind to a powder.

4. In a medium bowl place the yuca, the ground aniseed, and the remaining coconut, cheese, panela, and butter. Mix with your hands or with 2 forks.

5. Place in a buttered 10 by 14-inch baking pan. Sprinkle with the reserved mixture from the second step.

6. Bake for 45 minutes or until lightly browned. Let cool and cut into brownie-like squares to serve.

ESPONJADO DE LULO

Lulo Pudding
12 to 16 servings

Esponjados are very popular desserts in Colombia. We prepare them with *lulos**, limes, *curubas** or passion fruit.

2 cups (about 14) peeled lulos*
½ cup honey
1 cup (13.5- or 14-ounce can) sweetened condensed milk
2 tablespoons unflavored gelatin
1 cup heavy whipping cream, very cold
2 egg whites
¼ cup sugar
1 lulo* cut in wedges, for decoration

1. Place the peeled lulos, honey, ¼ cup of water and the condensed milk into the blender. Blend for 30 seconds.

2. Place ½ cup of water into a very small pot and add the gelatin. Place over very low heat and stir about 30 seconds to dissolve (do not simmer). Remove from the heat, pour into the blender, and mix 5 seconds.

3. Pour the cold cream in the bowl of a mixer and beat on high for 2 minutes. Mix a tablespoon of whipped cream to the lulo mixture. Carefully pour the puree from the blender into the bowl of whipped cream. Gently fold the mixtures together.

4. Beat the egg whites in a very clean and dry bowl over high speed for 30 seconds; add the sugar and beat for 2 to 3 minutes more, until the whites are shiny but not dry. Combine just as you did with the cream, first a spoonful into the cream mixture and then fold the whole into the rest of the whites.

5. Pour into a serving dish. Refrigerate until set, preferably overnight.

6. Decorate with lulo wedges and serve cold.

FLAN DE COCO

Coconut Pudding
12 to 16 servings

Flan or custards are prepared all over the country with different ingredients. *Flan de Leche* is the most common, which is plain milk custard; *Flan de Piña* (pineapple flan) is also popular, as are prune and many other fruit flans. This one is very common in the coastal areas of both the Pacific and the Atlantic.

½ cup sugar
1½ cup flaked sweetened coconut
8 eggs
1 cup (13.5- or 14-ounce can) sweetened condensed milk
1 cup heavy whipping cream, very cold
1 tablespoon vanilla extract

1. Prepare a caramel for the bottom of the pan: Place the sugar and 1 cup of water in a small, heavy pot over high heat. Once it starts to boil decrease the heat to medium and cook for 7 to 10 minutes or until light golden in color. Pour immediately into a 9-inch round Pyrex mold or cake pan. Swirl to cover the bottom of the mold. Be careful, as the caramel is very hot. Set aside.

2. Preheat the oven to 350°F. In a food processor, chop the coconut for 30 seconds to reduce its size.

3. Place the eggs, condensed milk, cream, and vanilla in a blender and mix for 1 to 2 minutes. Finally add the coconut and mix 10 seconds.

4. Gently pour the flan mixture into the caramelized mold.

5. Place the mold into a larger mold or baking dish and pour in water to a depth of 1 inch.

6. Bake for 1 hour.

7. Remove from the oven and from the outer pan containing the water.

8. Pass the pointed end of a knife around the sides of the pudding to help release it. Set aside for at least 10 minutes or until you can comfortably touch the glass mold with your hands and not get burnt. Place your serving dish upside down over the glass mold and quickly flip the whole thing over. Remove the glass mold.

9. Serve at room temperature or chill and serve cold.

MELADO

Melado is a sugarcane syrup originally from the Valle del Cauca Department, where most of the sugarcane in the country is grown and cut year-round. *Melado* is used there for many desserts and as an ingredient in various other non-sweet recipes like the *Arepas de Choclo* (page 11).

½ pound grated panela*
1 cinnamon stick
¼ teaspoon lime juice
(optional)
Grated peel of one lime
(optional)

1. Place the panela, cinnamon, lime peel, if using, and 1½ cups of water in a small saucepan. Simmer to dissolve the panela completely.

2. Increase the heat and bring to a boil for about 5 minutes or until it thickens slightly. Test the thickness of the syrup by placing a drop of it on a cool dish and making sure it is thick but runs smoothly when cool.

3. Add the lime juice if desired.

4. Set aside to cool.

NATILLA

Raw Sugar Pudding
8 to 12 servings

Natilla is the traditional dessert for the Christmas holidays, the Novenas to the Virgin Mary and the Christmas Eve dinners. It is served in most of the country, although it is thought to have originated in Antioquia. It is a thick custard that is later sliced into one- or two-inch squares or slices and sweetened with *panela*, which in this recipe could be substituted for dark brown sugar; you would use one cup, firmly packed.

4 cups whole milk
½ pound panela*, grated or 1 cup firmly pressed dark brown sugar
2 sticks cinnamon
¼ teaspoon baking soda
⅛ teaspoon salt
1 cup cornstarch
1 tablespoon butter
Ground cinnamon, for garnishing

1. In a medium, heavy pot over very low heat place 3 cups of the milk, the panela, cinnamon, baking soda, and salt. Simmer, stirring once in a while, for 10 to 15 minutes or until the panela has completely dissolved. Do not let the mixture boil.

2. In a small bowl, stir the remaining 1 cup of milk and the cornstarch until completely dissolved; stir it into the panela mixture on the stove top.

3. Raise the heat to medium and stir continuously, scraping the bottom of the pot, until the mixture has thickened and you can see the bottom of the pot when you stir. This should take about 5 to 7 minutes.

4. Remove the pot from the heat, add the butter, mix well and remove the cinnamon sticks.

5. Pour into an 8-inch square or round Pyrex mold or serving dish. You can spray the mold with oil spray and it will unmold very easily if you prefer to serve it on a platter.

6. Sprinkle with ground cinnamon.

7. Let cool and set; serve.

POLVOROSAS

Sugar Cookies
2 dozen 2-inch cookies

These cookies are served to children all around the country since they are very small. They are simple to make but the tricks are to use clarified butter and to beat them for a very short time after adding the flour.

½ pound clarified butter
¾ cup powdered sugar, plus extra garnishing (optional)
1 teaspoon vanilla extract
2¼ cups flour

1. Preheat the oven to 350°F. In the bowl of a mixer place the butter and beat at medium speed for 2 minutes.

2. Add ½ cup of the powdered sugar and vanilla and continue mixing for 6 to 8 minutes.

3. Decrease the speed to low, add the flour and beat only to incorporate, no more than 1 minute.

4. Form into 2-tablespoonful balls, flatten and place on a buttered baking sheet.

5. Bake for 25 to 30 minutes or until lightly golden.

6. Set aside to cool.

7. Dust with the remaining ¼ cup of powdered sugar if desired, and serve or save in covered tins for a week.

PASTEL DE DULCE DE COCO

Coconut Pie
16 to 20 servings

This is the most famous dessert from the city of Cartagena de Indias, our colonial walled city on the Caribbean coast. They are very famous for it and many other coconut recipes, such as *Cazuela de Mariscos* (page 90) and *Sancocho de Pescado al Coco* (page 46).

FILLING
4 cups grated fresh
   coconut (2 coconuts)
   (page 107)
2½ cups sugar
1 cup milk
2 tablespoons flour

PIE PASTRY
4 cups flour
2 teaspoons sugar
1 teaspoon salt
1 cup (½ pound, 2 sticks)
   butter, cut into 16
   pieces and frozen

1. In a medium, heavy pot or *caldero** place the coconut and sugar with 4 cups of water. Cook over medium heat for 45 minutes, stirring occasionally.

2. In a medium bowl combine the milk and flour; pour into the pot and continue cooking for 12 to 15 minutes more.

3. Remove from the heat and set aside to cool.

4. While the filling is cooking, **MAKE THE PASTRY:** Place the flour, sugar, and salt in the bowl of a food processor and mix for 10 seconds. Add the butter and process 15 seconds more. Add ¼ cup of water and process for 45 seconds or until the dough forms a ball and leaves the side of the bowl.

5. Wrap the dough in plastic and refrigerate for 45 minutes.

6. Preheat the oven to 350°F. Remove the dough from the refrigerator and divide in two. Roll each dough half into a 14-inch circle. Place one of the circles in the bottom of a 10-inch tart pan. Fill with the cool coconut mixture and cover with the second dough circle. Press the two doughs together and make a design on the edges. Cut some holes in the top crust to let the air out while baking.

7. Bake for 1 hour and 10 minutes or until light golden brown.

8. Cool before serving, or serve warm.

POSTRE DE LECHE CORTADA

Milk Curd Pudding
16 half-cup servings

This *Postre de Leche Cortada* recipe is the quick version of the *Postre de Natas*, a dessert that is a bit long and tedious, as you have to heat the milk and remove the *nata* or skin and set it aside little by little. It is originally from the country's capital. This one is prepared differently, as the milk and eggs are "curdled" first; in the original *postre de natas* the milk is cooked so the *natas* (papery curd) is skimmed off the top and kept aside to mix it back into the dessert. The idea here is to get the curd, so don't panic when you get it.

4 cups whole milk
1 cup (13.5- or 14-ounce can) sweetened condensed milk
3 tablespoons sugar
2 cinnamon sticks
1 cup raisins, plus extra for garnishing
6 eggs, beaten
1 teaspoon vanilla extract

1. In a medium, heavy pot place the milk, condensed milk, sugar, cinnamon, and ½ cup of the raisins. Cook for 7 minutes or until it begins to boil.

2. Decrease the heat to low and while the milk is simmering, add the eggs. Stir continuously as you add the eggs. Keep cooking over low heat for 4 minutes; add the other ½ cup of raisins and the vanilla and cook for 2 minutes more.

3. Pour into ramekins, decorate with more raisins and refrigerate until set, about 1 to 2 hours for individual ramekins.

4. Serve cold.

SORBET DE FEIJOA

Feijoa Sorbet
1 quart

Feijoas* are small guavas. Found mostly in Antioquia, they are a true delicacy. My first encounter with them was when my children were very young and we would go to Rio Negro to their grandparent's farm, called El Remanso. There, people would pick them off the trees and eat them all the time; they call them *guayavitas*.

20 feijoa* guavas
¾ cup sugar
1 teaspoon lime juice

1. Peel all but 2 of the feijoas, and quarter all of them.

2. In a small saucepan mix the sugar and ¼ cup of water. Place over medium-high heat to melt the sugar, but do not boil.

3. In a blender or food processor place all the feijoas, the sugar syrup and the lime juice. Process or blend until smooth.

4. Freeze in an ice-cream machine, or pour into a pan and freeze in the freezer to serve as an ice.

TORTA DE COCO

Christmas Coconut Pudding
12 to 16 servings

Torta de Coco is a traditional Christmas cake from the Valle del Cauca department. It is very rich and tasty, and keeps very well (up to a week). It tastes better every day.

**1 recipe of Cocadas Blancas (page 175), partially prepared
1 cup raisins
1 cup Moscatel, sweet wine
4 cups sponge cake crumbs
4 eggs
1 teaspoon vanilla extract
½ teaspoon coconut extract
½ teaspoon ground cinnamon
¼ teaspoon salt**

1. Preheat the oven to 300°F. Prepare the recipe for Cocadas Blancas (page 175), but remove them from the heat 10 minutes after adding the coconut. Set aside to cool.

2. In a small pot, place the raisins and wine. Simmer over medium heat for 3 minutes. Remove from the heat and set aside.

3. In a large bowl combine the cocadas mixture, the raisins, and the cake crumbs, and mix with a fork.

4. In the bowl of a mixer place the eggs, vanilla, coconut extract, cinnamon, and salt, and mix for 3 minutes on medium speed. Add the cocadas and crumb mixture and mix gently by hand.

5. Pour into a buttered 8 by 12-inch baking dish.

6. Bake for 35 to 40 minutes or until set.

7. Cool and serve.

TORTA DE PASTORES

Christmas Pudding
12 to 16 servings

Torta de Pastores is another Christmas holiday favorite of the Valle del Cauca. When I lived in Cali, I used to sell many cakes for people to make this dessert. I got this recipe from my daughter's very much loved physical education teacher at our school there, Patricia Varela. She is a very good cook, who also taught me to make the *Torta de Coco* (page 197) in this chapter.

1 cup raisins
½ cup Moscatel wine
6 ounces (1cup) white farmer's cheese*
5 eggs, separated
4 tablespoons butter, softened
1 teaspoon ground cinnamon
1 teaspoon vanilla extract
4 cups sponge cake crumbs
½ recipe (4 cups) of Arroz con Leche (page 170)
Pinch of salt

1. In a small bowl place the raisins and wine and set aside for 1 hour, or place in a small pot and cook over low heat for 3 to 5 minutes. Set aside.

2. Preheat the oven to 300°F. In a food processor, process the cheese to a fine grain.

3. Place the egg yolks, butter, cinnamon, and vanilla in the bowl of a mixer and mix on low for 2 minutes. Add the crumbs, raisins, cheese, and arroz con leche.

4. Place the egg whites in the clean and dry bowl of a mixer. Add a pinch of salt and a teaspoon of water. Beat on high speed for 2 minutes or until soft and airy.

5. Add some of the egg white mixture to the yolk mixture; gently fold all the yolk mixture into the rest of the whites.

6. Carefully pour the batter into 2 buttered and floured 8-inch baking pans or a rectangular Pyrex mold or baking pan.

7. Bake in a preheated 300°F oven for 25 to 30 minutes or until set. Let cool about 10 minutes before unmolding.

TORTA NEGRA

Dark Rum Cake
24 to 30 servings

In many parts of Colombia, especially in the south Pacific, children's parties are celebrated with *Torta Negra*. The alcohol in the cake evaporates during baking and even the youngest children learn to eat it, and enjoy being served this for their celebrations. In the northern coastal areas, we serve it during the Christmas holidays and for New Year. This *Torta Negra* is so good that I like it better before it goes into the oven!

DAY 1

1. In small pot place the prunes and 2 cups of water and cook for 20 minutes or until the prunes are very soft and mushy. Drain the prunes and set the water aside in the refrigetator.

2. In a large, nonreactive bowl place the drained prunes, candied fruit, rum, wine, ½ cup of the marmalade, coffee, cinnamon, nutmeg, and allspice; set aside overnight or as long as 2 weeks. (The longer they sit the better the cake and the more alcohol will be evaporated. I always keep mine for 2 to 3 weeks.)

DAY 2

3. Preheat the oven to 350°F. In the bowl of a mixer place the butter and 1¾ cups of the sugar and beat on medium for 10 to 15 minutes or until you have a creamy mixture and the sugar has dissolved completely into the butter.

4. In the meantime, prepare the dry ingredients: in a bowl mix the flour, baking powder, and salt; sift 3 times and set aside.

¾ pound pitted prunes
1 pound candied fruit
½ cup dark rum
½ cup Moscatel or Port wine
1 cup orange marmalade
½ tablespoon instant coffee
1 teaspoon ground cinnamon
½ teaspoon ground nutmeg
½ teaspoon ground allspice
2 cups (1 pound, 4 sticks) butter, softened
2¼ cups sugar
3 cups flour
1 tablespoon baking powder
½ teaspoon salt
4 eggs, separated
½ tablespoon vanilla extract
2 tablespoon burnt sugar (see Note below)

5. Add the egg yolks to the butter and sugar one at a time, mixing after each addition. Add the vanilla and mix just to blend in. Stop the mixer, add all the flour mixture and turn on minimum speed; mix for one minute, scraping down the sides of the bowl. Add the burnt sugar and mix one minute more. Remove bowl from the machine, fold in all the macerated fruit by hand, and set aside.

CONTINUED

6. In the bowl of a mixer, making sure it is very clean and completely free of grease or fat, place the egg whites. Mix on high speed for 30 seconds and when foamy add the remaining ½ cup white sugar. Mix for 2 minutes more or until it looks shiny but not dry.

7. Fold the whites into the cake mixture.

8. Butter and flour a 10-inch round by 3-inch deep cake pan. If you wish you can cover the bottom of the pan with parchment paper. Gently pour in the batter.

9. Bake for 1½ to 2 hours.

10. Let the cake cool for 10 minutes before unmolding.

11. In a small pot mix ½ cup of the prune cooking liquid, the remaining ½ cup of orange marmalade and ¼ cup of rum, and cook over low heat only to blend the ingredients and dissolve the jam. Brush on the cake, cool completely and serve.

NOTE: Burnt sugar is a liquid coloring available in some specialty stores and in Latino and Caribbean markets.

TRES LECHES

Three Milks Dessert
8 to 10 servings

> *Tres Leches* is a very traditional and delicious cake all around Colombia and the neighboring Latin American countries. Now there is even a newer version called *Cuatro Leches* (Four Milks) in fancier restaurants and homes, which has evaporated or powdered milk added too. But this traditional one is wonderful.

CAKE
2 cups flour
2 teaspoons baking powder
½ teaspoon salt
4 tablespoons butter, plus extra for preparing the pan
1 cup milk
4 whole eggs
1½ cups sugar

THREE MILKS SAUCE
2 cups boiling water
1 cup powdered milk
1 (13.5- or 14-ounce) can of sweetened condensed milk
1 (10-ounce) can of cream or 1 cup of heavy cream
1 teaspoon vanilla extract

FROSTING
6 tablespoons sugar
¼ teaspoon cream of tartar
1 egg white
½ teaspoon vanilla extract

1. Preheat the oven to 350°F. Sift together the flour, baking powder, and salt. Set aside.

2. In a small saucepan melt the butter in the milk, and set aside to cool.

3. Beat the eggs in a mixer on high speed for 8 to10 minutes, until they look very light and fluffy. Add the sugar and keep beating for 2 minutes more. Reduce the speed to minimum, add the sifted mixture, and last the melted butter and milk, and mix for 2 minutes or until well blended.

4. Butter a 4 by 10-inch round cake pan; pour the mixture into the pan.

5. Bake for 45 to 50 minutes.

6. Set aside to cool for 15 minutes. Leave the cake in the pan.

7. While the cake is cooling, make the sauce: In a medium bowl, mix the boiling water and milk powder; mix well. Add the condensed milk, cream, and vanilla, and whisk to a smooth texture.

8. Pour over the warm cake; with a fork make some holes into the cake so it absorbs all the sauce.

9. Set the cake aside to let cool while you prepare the frosting.

CONTINUED

10. In a small pot over medium heat place 3 tablespoons of water, the sugar, and cream of tartar; bring to a boil and simmer over medium-low heat for 5 minutes.

11. Beat the egg white in the bowl of a mixer until foamy, about 30 seconds. Pour the hot sugar mixture slowly into the egg white and beat for 5 minutes. Add the vanilla and mix 1 more minute.

12. Frost and decorate the dessert with this meringue.

13. Refrigerate and serve cold.

DRINKS

Our drinks are either piping hot or very cold. We love iced or frappé juices, hot chocolate concoctions, fiery alcoholic beverages, and blends of different fruits, all in a wide variety of tastes and textures. We delight in the wonderful foods with which nature has blessed our country. The beautiful colors of all of these fruits reassure us that we capture a whole rainbow of essential vitamins and minerals.

It is now easy to find most of our fruits in American markets, especially in large cities; you can buy them, peel them, blend them, and enjoy a real treat of 100 percent fruit full of life, flavor and sun. Some you might not find around the corner, but as you read the recipes, you can go back in time with me and savor the moments that once were. Refresh yourself with the smell, color, and memories as you read through this chapter.

In Colombia, we eat fruit every day: as juices during the three main meals of the day and as snacks in mornings and afternoons. I eat a banana every mid-morning; I buy a handful of bananas every two days and a pineapple that gets cut as soon as it arrives and placed in a plastic container; next evening all are gone. Even on weekend outings, fruits are eaten by adults and children as they are sold all over towns and beaches cut up into pieces so that they can be eaten as finger foods. My kids enjoy green mangos with salt and lime juice like the best dessert. At the beach, that is what they munch on. In their grandmother's farm, they would wake up early in the mornings and watch the cows being milked by hand; soon after, they would walk about the fruit trees and bushes and pick the best *feijoas* and yellow gooseberries in the land to eat. It was all a game of who got the best and the most fruit.

We have many fruits that are now beginning to appear in world markets. From the Andean zones, we have *lulos, pithayas, carambolos, mamey, curubas, feijoas, granadillas, uchuvas,* and more. From the Caribbean and Pacific zones, we have bananas, coconuts, papayas, mangoes of many varieties, tamarind, *mamoncillos, guavas, corozos, ciruela, chontaduro* and so many colorful fruit that allow for a variety of juices and snacks that bring color and joy to our menus. We decorate our kitchens and dining rooms as well as our farm houses with wooden or ceramic plates full of these colorful and deep scented produce. Centerpieces with fruit and flowers are given on special occasions like when babies are born or people arrive from far away and we want to fill their moments with some joy.

Some of the recipes in this chapter and many throughout the book call for *panela**. *Panela* is a product that comes from sugarcane; it is very sweet and reddish brown in color. Sold in round or squared blocks that weigh half or one pound, it has only recently appeared in stores packaged and wrapped. You can purchase it shredded too. It has no additives or chemicals and is therefore thought to be healthier. The flavor is very aromatic and could be replaced with dark brown sugar.

CANELAZO

Hot Firewater Tea
16 servings, 2 ounce each

Warm up on a very cold evening with this romantic drink!

2 cups (about ½ pound) panela*, shredded
2 cinnamon sticks
8 whole cloves
Pinch of salt
1 cup Aguardiente* or any aniseed flavored liqueur
1 tablespoon lime juice

1. In a medium pot, over medium heat, place 2 cups of water, the panela, cinnamon, cloves, and salt. Simmer for 10 minutes to extract the flavors of the spices.

2. Remove from the heat and add the Aguardiente and lime juice. Put back on the stove and reduce the heat to very low. Cook for 2 to 3 minutes just to bring the heat back up, but the mixture should not boil.

3. Serve hot in very small portions.

CHAMPÚS

Corn, Pineapple, and Lulo Drink
16 servings, 6 ounces each

This popular drink of the Valle del Cauca is served cold with a lot of ice. It is very traditional and is sold from carts on the streets and in popular specialty places. If you cannot find orange leaves, just omit them.

2½ cups (1 pound) dried corn kernels*, washed and picked clean
½ pound panela*
3 cinnamon sticks
5 leaves from orange tree
8 whole cloves
1 cup peeled, mashed lulos* (about 6 lulos)
1¼ cups sugar (or more if desired)
3 cups diced pineapple (1 whole pineapple)

DAY 1

1. Wash the dry corn kernels with plenty of water. Soak for 24 hours in a bowl with enough water to cover. This will rehydrate the corn a little.

DAY 2

2. In a small pot, place 4 cups of water, the panela, cinnamon, orange leaves, and cloves. Simmer for 20 minutes and set aside. Just before using in Step 5, strain and discard the solids.

3. Drain the corn and discard the soaking water. Place the corn in a medium pot or pressure cooker, and add 8 cups of water. If using a regular pot, cover and simmer over medium-low heat for 2½ hours; keep adding water, 1 cup at a time, if it dries out. If using a pressure cooker, cover and cook under pressure on medium heat for about 1 hour.

4. The corn should be very soft; if not, return the pot to the stove and cook 20 minutes more.

5. Uncover and let cool. You should have about 8 cups of corn. Take 2 cups of the corn and in a blender or food processor, process for 30 seconds with the

strained panela mixture. Place the whole corn and corn puree in a large, nonreactive bottle or pitcher.

6. In a blender or food processor puree the lulos, sugar and ½ cup of water, and add to the corn and panela mixture.

8. Refrigerate and cool completely.

9. Serve cold with ice.

CHICHA DE MAÍZ

Fermented Corn Drink
12 servings, 8 ounces each

Be careful—this is tasty but wild. *Chicha* is actually a drink that ferments into an alcoholic beverage, which is what actually conserves it. It can become stronger but the taste then is not so sweet. There is always about half a cup that is kept to ferment the next chicha, and in that case the pineapple is not needed. *Maiz peto* is what we call the corn that is dried and sold in bags at the market.

2½ cups (1 pound) white or yellow dry processed corn kernels* (maiz peto)
Skin of one pineapple
½ pound panela*

DAY 1
1. Wash the dry corn kernels with plenty of water. Soak for 24 hours in a bowl with enough water to cover. This will rehydrate the corn a little.

DAY 2
2. Drain the corn and discard the soaking water. Place the corn in a medium pot or pressure cooker, and add 6 cups of water and the skin of a whole pineapple. (The pineapple will act as a starter, if you have old chicha you can disregard the pineapple and add 1 cup of fermented chicha.) If using a regular pot, cover and simmer over medium-low heat for 2½ hours; keep adding water, 1 cup at a time, if it dries out. If using a pressure cooker, cover and cook under pressure on medium heat for about 1 hour. The corn should be very soft; if not, return the pot to the stove and cook 20 minutes more.

3. Uncover, and let cool, you will have about 8 cups of corn. Take half of the corn and in a blender or food processor, process for 30 seconds.

4. Place both corns, processed and whole, together with the pineapple skin in a very large nonreactive stockpot. Add 5 gallons of water and the panela. (If you have a large clay pot, this is the ideal container to keep the chicha in while it ferments.)

DAY 3
5. Let rest for the next 2 to 3 days at room temperature; if you live in a very hot climate leave out overnight and then refrigerate for 2 days.

DAY 5
6. Pass through a fine sieve and serve.

CHOCOLATE CALIENTE

Hot Chocolate
4 servings

Hot chocolate, together with coffee and milk, is the standard beverage for breakfast in Colombia. It is a delicious, energizing beverage, and needless to say we produce some of the greatest chocolate in the world. Cacao beans are indigenous to the country and are grown mainly in the Santanderes, Arauca and Tolima departments. The chocolate used is plain dark chocolate; ours comes in sweetened and unsweetened varieties, and they are both hard in consistency. It comes divided into rectangles that you break into one-ounce pieces that will each make one cup of the beverage.

4 ounces sweetened table chocolate
4 cups milk or 2 cups water and 2 cups milk
2 tablespoons sugar

1. Place the chocolate, milk, and sugar in a pot over medium heat. Bring to a simmer (but do not let it boil) for about 5 to 7 minutes, or until the chocolate is very soft.

2. Remove from the heat and with a wire whisk stir rapidly and continuously until the chocolate forms a lather or foam.

3. Serve.

JUGO DE BOROJÓ

Borojó Juice
8 to 10 servings, 6 ounces each

Borojó* is a tropical fruit native to the Pacific regions of Colombia; it is green when young and brownish when ripe. From the look of the fruit you would never expect this drink to taste so good! Plus it is really an aphrodisiac.

Kola Granulada is a sugar-based nutritional supplement of eleven vitamins, iron and calcium, that is sold in Colombia; I do not usually add it to any of my drinks, but the original recipe does. Whether you add it or not, it does not greatly change the flavor.

½ pound borojó*
¾ cup sweetened condensed milk
1 cup whole milk
2 tablespoons Kola Granulada (optional)
2 tablespoons cognac or brandy
2 cups crushed ice

1. Remove the peel from the borojó with your hands. Place the fruit in a bowl with 1½ cups of water and mash it with your hands, removing the seeds. Mix well with a fork to make sure you have removed all the seeds. Measure; you should have a total of 2¾ cups of liquid and fruit. Add more water if necessary.

2. Place the mashed fruit in a blender together with ½ cup of water, the condensed milk, whole milk, Kola, and cognac; blend to a smooth consistency. Refrigerate until ready to serve.

3. Add 2 cups of ice and blend for 5 to 10 seconds. Serve immediately.

JUGO DE COROZO

Corozo Juice
4 servings

Corozo* is a tiny dark red fruit. It comes from a wild palm and we love it. As a kid, we would eat it with salt—alone it is very sour. We drink the juice weekly at home; it is very refreshing, and even sweetened is still somewhat tart.

2 cups corozo*
6 tablespoons sugar
2 cups ice

1. In a medium pot over medium heat cook the corozo in 4 cups of water for 8 to 10 minutes, or until you see the water has turned a deep, red wine color.

2. Remove from the heat, strain and keep the liquid; discard the fruit.

3. Add the sugar to the fruit juice. Mix until the sugar is dissolved.

4. Cool, add the ice and serve immediately.

JUGO O SORBETE
DE CURUBA

Curuba Juice or Milk Shake
2 servings

This is a juice that I prefer with milk; it makes me feel like having a healthful and delicious milk shake. When making with milk, it is called *sorbete* instead of *jugo*. It has an astringent flavor, which I think complements many meals just beautifully.

2 curubas* (about ⅓ cup)
3 tablespoons sugar
1 cup crushed ice

1. Cut the curubas in half and remove the pulp with a spoon. Place the pulp in a blender with ½ cup of water and the sugar. Blend and pass through a sieve.

2. Return the liquid to the blender; add the ice, blend, and serve immediately.

NOTE: To prepare the sorbete or milk shake, replace the water with ½ cup of milk.

JUGO DE LULO

*Lulos** are my youngest daughter Daniela's favorite fruit. Their taste is somewhat acid and therefore great for juices as well as desserts and chutneys.

**1 large lulo* (about
²⁄₃ cup) or 2 small lulos***
3½ tablespoons sugar
1 cup crushed ice

1. Peel and quarter the lulos. Place in a blender with ½ cup of water and the sugar. Blend.

2. Add the ice, blend, and serve immediately.

JUGO O SORBĘTE
DE MARACUYÁ

Passion Fruit Juice or Milk Shake

2 servings

*Maracuyá** (passion fruit) is nowadays very popular around the world. Try it with milk and you will discover a whole new way to its flavor; in that case, the name changes from *jugo* to *sorbete*. I use it for sauces for seafood, and jellies and desserts like passion fruit cheesecake.

1 large passion fruit*
(6 to 7 ounces yield
about ⅓ cup of pulp)
3 tablespoons sugar
1 cup crushed ice

1. Cut the passion fruit in half and remove pulp with a spoon. Place the pulp in a blender with ½ cup of water and the sugar. Blend 10 seconds, pulsing on and off in order to keep the seeds as whole as possible. Strain through a sieve and discard the seeds.

2. Return the puree to the blender, add the ice, blend, and serve immediately.

NOTE: To prepare the *sorbete* or milk shake, replace the water with ½ cup of milk.

JUGO DE NÍSPERO EN LECHE

Níspero Juice in Milk
4 servings

*Nísperos** are our Colombian version of the kiwi, because they are about the same color on the outside and of similar texture, but brownish red on the inside; the flavor is somewhat different and maybe the yellow kiwi resembles them more than the green. They are great to eat alone or prepared as follows.

4 nísperos*
(about 1⅓ cups)
1 cup milk
1 tablespoon sugar
1 cup crushed ice

1. Cut the nísperos in half, remove the 2 large seeds and scoop the pulp out with a spoon.

2. Blend the pulp with the rest of the ingredients.

3. Serve immediately in tall glasses.

JUGO DE PAPAYA CON LIMÓN

Papaya Juice with Lime
2 servings

Papayas are becoming a more popular fruit every day now. With the arrival of smaller Hawaiian papayas to America, it is now easier to buy and use the fruit because its smaller size makes it more practical. In Colombia, our native papayas are the large ones believed to have come from Mexico. You can use either for this recipe; they work great with lime juice. They create a delicious juice that is beautiful in color and flavor.

2 cups peeled, seeded, diced papaya (two 1-pound Hawaiian papayas or ¼ of a large 6-pound papaya)
2 tablespoons lime juice
2 tablespoons sugar
1 to 2 cups crushed ice

1. Place the diced papaya in a blender with the lime juice, sugar, and 1 cup of ice.

2. Blend until smooth and serve immediately.

3. Add the second cup of ice if you want a lighter smoothie, or serve over crushed ice.

JUGO DE PAPAYA
CON NARANJA

Papaya Juice with Orange
2 servings

This is the best way to give kids papaya. Try it; intensely sweet but textured and with more body, this juice is a must.

1. Place the diced papaya in a blender with the orange juice, sugar, and 1 cup of ice.

2. Blend until smooth and serve immediately.

3. Add the second cup of ice if you want a lighter smoothie, or serve over crushed ice.

2 cups peeled, seeded, diced papaya (two 1-pound Hawaiian papayas or ¼ of a large 6-pound papaya)
1 cup orange juice
1 tablespoon sugar
1 to 2 cups crushed ice

JUGO DE PAPAYA, BANANO Y MARACUYA

Papaya, Banana, and Passion Fruit Juice

2 to 4 servings

Another way to make "frosties" for kids! Teach them how to place all the fruit into the blender and let them have fun with fruit.

2 large passion fruits*
(12 to 14 ounces yield
about ⅔ cup of pulp)
1½ cups peeled, seeded,
diced papaya
(2 1-pound Hawaiian
papayas or ¼ of a large
6-pound papaya)
1 small banana, peeled
and sliced
(about ½ cup)
3 tablespoons sugar
1 to 2 cups crushed ice

1. Cut the passion fruit in 2 and remove pulp with a spoon. Place all the fruits in a blender and blend pulsing on and off for 5 to 10 seconds in order to keep the seeds as whole as possible. Strain through a sieve; discard the pits.

2. Return the puree to the blender and add the sugar and 1 cup of ice. Blend until smooth and serve immediately.

3. Add the second cup of ice if you want a lighter smoothie, or serve over crushed ice.

JUGO DE PATILLA

Watermelon Juice

2 servings

> Many people enjoy eating watermelon at the beach. Try the juice; it will make you want to buy them all year round.

3 to 4 pounds watermelon pieces, rind included (about 3 cups)
1 cup crushed ice
2 tablespoons sugar
2 teaspoons lime juice

1. Remove all the seeds and rind from the watermelon pieces.

2. Place the watermelon, ice, sugar, and lime juice in a blender and puree to a smooth consistency, about 20 to 30 seconds.

3. Serve immediately.

JUGO DE PIÑA, PAPAYA, TOMATE DE ARBOL Y BANANO

Pineapple, Papaya, Tree Tomato, and Banana Juice
2 to 4 servings

This is another mixed fruit juice that can really be enjoyed by both children and adults. With the mix of colors and flavors, you prepare a variety of delicious nutrients for a healthful meal. Tree tomatoes are sold in specialty and Latin American grocery stores.

1 cup peeled, diced pineapple
1 cup peeled, seeded, diced papaya (a 1-pound Hawaiian or ¼ of a medium 4- pound papaya)
1 tree tomato*, peeled and diced (about ¼ to ⅓ cup)
1 small banana, peeled and sliced (about ½ cup)
2 tablespoons sugar
1 to 2 cups crushed ice

1. Place all the fruits in a blender with the sugar and 1 cup of ice. Puree until smooth and serve immediately.

2. Add the second cup of ice if you want a lighter smoothie, or serve over crushed ice.

JUGO DE PIÑA Y TOMATE DE ARBOL

Pineapple and Tree Tomato Juice

2 to 4 servings

Sweet pineapples and tart tree tomatoes* complement each other in this juice. The color of the latter brings out a festive environment. Great for parties served in decorative tall glasses with pieces of fruit to decorate, or in small pineapples where the fruit has been scooped out to make the juice. Tree tomatoes are sold in specialty and Latin American grocery stores.

1. Place the fruits in a blender with the sugar and 1 cup of ice. Puree until smooth and serve immediately.

2. Add the second cup of ice if you want a lighter smoothie, or serve over crushed ice.

2 cups peeled, diced pineapple
1 tree tomato*, peeled and diced (about ¼ to ⅓ cup)
3 tablespoons sugar
1 to 2 cups crushed ice

JUGO DE TAMARINDO
Tamarind Juice

8 servings plus 3 cups of pulp to freeze

Tamarind is an acquired flavor. Its lemony taste is pungent, a bit acid, very aromatic, and all around great. Tamarind pulp must be unsweetened and with no water added. It generally comes with seeds and looks like a dark brown thick paste. Look for it in Asian and Latin American grocery stores.

With the leftover pulp, you can prepare sauces for lobster, prawns, pork, or cornish hens; desserts such as tamarind mousse, tamarind squares; or just make more juice later on.

1 pound unsweetened tamarind pulp, with seeds

PURE CONCENTRATED JUICE

1. Place the tamarind pulp and 4 cups of water in a nonreactive pot. Bring to a boil and set aside. Let cool completely, and refrigerate overnight.

2. Mix with a wire whisk or your hands to separate the fruit from the seeds.

3. Strain through a sieve. Help yourself by using a wooden spoon to press.

4. This will yield about 4 cups of pure concentrated juice; 1 cup you can use right away and the other 3 you can freeze in Ziploc bags or ice cube trays for later use.

TAMARIND JUICE DRINK

Blend the juice, ice, and sugar with 1 cup of water; serve immediately.

1 cup pure concentrated tamarind juice
1 cup crushed ice
4 tablespoons sugar

JUGO DE TOMATE DE ÁRBOL

Tree Tomato Juice

2 servings

Tomates de árbol* (tree tomatoes) are a yellowish red fruit, used mainly for the production of juice. Tree tomatoes are sold in specialty and Latin American grocery stores.

2 tree tomatoes*
(about ½ to ⅔ cup)
4 tablespoons sugar
1 cup crushed ice

1. Peel and quarter the tree tomatoes. Blend with the sugar and 1 cup of water. Strain through a sieve.

2. Return the juice to the blender, add the ice, and puree to a smooth consistency.

3. Serve immediately.

KUMIS

Sour Milk
12 servings, 6 ounces each

Kumis is traditionally made with fresh, raw, non-pasteurized milk. A fermenting agent or bacillus acidophilus is added and the milk is left to stand for two to three days. Then sugar or *panela** is added with a pinch of cinnamon. Here I have a recipe that uses the same proportions but has lime juice added to ease the preparation at home with pasteurized milk.

2 quarts whole milk
2½ tablespoons lime juice
2 cups sugar
1 teaspoon cinnamon

1. Combine the milk and lime juice in a large bowl or nonreactive container.

2. Set aside in the warmest place in your kitchen overnight, covered with a damp towel.

3. Transfer to a blender and mix with the sugar and cinnamon. You may have to do this in batches.

4. Refrigerate until cold; keep refrigerated for another day to thicken. If you live in a cool climate you can leave it at room temperature for 3 days.

5. Serve cold or at room temperature.

LULADA

Lulo Cooler
2 to 4 servings

If you ever come across lots of *lulos**, buy them all and prepare *Lulada*. My favorite drink from the region of the Valle del Cauca, it is absolutely delicious. Since it has so much ice, you have to eat it with a spoon. This forces you to enjoy each and every spoonful of this delicacy.

3 to 5 lulos* (about 1½ cups)
6 tablespoons sugar
1 tablespoon lime juice
2½ cups crushed ice

1. Peel and quarter the lulos. Mash them with a fork or process for 2 seconds. Place the mashed pulp in a nonreactive container.

2. Add the sugar and let stand until the sugar has been absorbed and the lulos have given up some liquid, about 1 to 2 hours. Refrigerate until ready to use.

3. Add lime juice to the refrigerated mixture and stir well.

4. Fill tall glasses with crushed ice and divide the lulo mixture among them. Serve immediately.

MAZAMORRA CON LECHE Y PANELA

Mazamorra with Milk and Panela

8 to 10 servings, 6 ounces each

This is definitely an acquired taste. Somewhat bland, the corn is softened with the milk and sweetened with the *panela**. It is a semi-solid drink that is full of energy and that people in the agricultural areas love.

1 cup dried corn kernels*
3 tablespoons yellow corn masa flour*
1 cup (¼ pound) shredded panela*, for serving
1 to 2 cups milk, for serving

1. Wash the corn well with plenty of water. Add 5 cups of water and set aside to soak overnight. This will soften and rehydrate the corn.

2. In medium pot or pressure cooker, place the corn and add 5 cups of water. If using a regular pot simmer over medium-low heat for 2 hours; keep adding water, 1 cup at a time, if it dries out. If using a pressure cooker, simmer over medium heat for about 45 minutes. Turn the heat off, let it rest for 5 minutes, release the pressure and uncover.

3. Add another 5 cups of water and keep cooking over low heat, until the corn has almost lost its shape and the water has thickened, for about 2 hours in the regular pot (stirring every once in a while),and 45 minutes in the pressure cooker. Turn the heat off, let rest for 5 minutes, release the pressure and uncover.

4. Add the corn masa flour and cook for 20 minutes more, uncovered, whichever pot you are using.

5. Serve hot or cold, with panela and milk on the side.

6. Each person adds about 2 tablespoons of milk and enough panela to sweeten their mazamorra.

LIGHTER SECRETS OF COLOMBIAN COOKING

In the years since *Secrets of Colombian Cooking* was first published, I have received many requests from readers for low-fat or low-calorie versions of some favorite recipes. I'm very pleased in this new edition to bring the lighter side of the Colombian table to my readers. In this chapter I revised and adjusted some of my favorite home recipes to make them more nutritious, lower in fat, and still full of flavor.

These delicious recipes come from all the diverse regions of Colombia—the tropical rainforest, the seafood-rich oceans and rivers, as well as the mountainous Andean region. The versatile recipes make the most of fresh, locally grown fruits and vegetables, along with lean meats and seafood. Perfect for entertaining, these offerings are colorful and nutritious—all with the unique tastes of the Latin Americas!

Colombians utilize many low-fat ways of cooking. A lot of Colombian foods were originally cooked either in clay pots over coals, or under the earth with hot coals covering them. Plantain leaves wrapped many of our most delicious dishes, and still do in my kitchen. Marinating foods in seasoning overnight and cooking them for a longer time at a low temperature is another authentic Colombian method used long before the pressure cooker came along. We have some very tasty dishes that are slow cooked with plenty of herbs. Ribs immersed in beer and then slow-cooked are a delicious example of this long-lived tradition. The double-frying and sugar-coating techniques used to cook plantains has been eliminated, with single-frying and baking the plantains in their own peel having great advantages in flavor, calorie content, texture, and energy content.

Squash is one of our low-calorie indigenous foods, and it now has become very popular among other international cuisines as well. It can be used on its own or as part of slow-cooked soups and stews. Mangoes, pineapple, plums, ají, curry, and lime are all low-calorie ingredients used to intensify the flavors of foods. Delicious yellow potatoes are often served with their skins to retain their many minerals.

And fruit is what Colombians eat most! We enjoy fruit for breakfast, with lunch, as an afternoon snack (such as peeled mango with lime and salt), and pureed into juice to serve alongside lunch and dinner and especially after coming home from a hot, long day of work. Here you'll find recipes for making delicious fruit smoothies and desserts incorporating those favorite fruits—perfect low-fat delights.

I hope you enjoy this journey through the lighter side of Colombian cooking!

ENSALADA PLAYERA A LA MARACUYA

Green Salad with Sliced Tomatoes and Passion Fruit Vinaigrette

4 servings

In my home, passion fruit is one of our favorite fruits to make into drinks, and in the last decade ice creams and desserts. Here is a twist on the use of this deliciously tart and aromatic fruit. I have added it to the most popular salad of the country—lettuce and tomatoes with a vinaigrette.

½ onion, thinly sliced
1 tablespoon pure, unsweetened passion fruit juice
½ teaspoon salt
¼ teaspoon ground black pepper
2 tablespoons oil
2 tablespoons thick or Greek yogurt
4 large salad tomatoes, sliced ¼ inch thick
4 cups lettuce leaves

1. In a bowl, combine the onion, passion fruit juice, ¼ teaspoon salt, and a pinch of ground black pepper. Allow to sit for 10 minutes or more for the onion to lose some of its bitterness.

2. Add the oil and yogurt to the onion mixture and stir to combine.

3. Sprinkle the tomato slices with the remaining salt and pepper, and add to the onion mixture. Place over lettuce leaves and serve.

TIP: To extract juice from the passion fruit, cut the fruit in half and squeeze onto a spoon. Press the seeds through a sieve with your hands to extract all the flavors.

ENSALADA DE TOMATE
VERDE

Green Tomatoes with Green Yogurt Vinaigrette

4 servings

Green tomatoes are served mostly in the inner part of Colombia. This vinaigrette is the traditional recipe, just made lighter with Greek yogurt. It goes great with the crunchiness of the tomatoes.

⅓ cup thick or Greek yogurt
2 tablespoons minced cilantro
2 tablespoons white wine vinegar
1 tablespoon honey
½ teaspoon salt
¼ teaspoon ground black pepper
2 tablespoons olive oil
4 large green salad tomatoes, thinly sliced

1. In a bowl place the yogurt, cilantro, vinegar, honey, salt, and pepper. Slowly drizzle in the olive oil and whisk to mix well.

2. Place tomato slices on a shallow dish, pour on dressing, allow to sit for 10 minutes and serve.

ENSALADA DE MAIZ Y QUINOA

Quinoa Corn and Red Bean Salad with Pineapple Ají Vinaigrette

4 Servings

This Andean grain is very popular again after centuries of being only an indigenous food. Here I have prepared quinoa with some of the ingredients that typically grow in the same area, and seasoned it with a sensational fresh and lightly spicy vinaigrette.

½ cup quinoa
½ teaspoon salt
¼ cup fresh pineapple juice with pulp
2 tablespoons white vinegar
2 tablespoons minced fresh cilantro
4 tablespoons canola oil
¼ teaspoon hot sauce (ají sauce)
¼ teaspoon ground black pepper
1 cup seeded and diced roma tomatoes
1 cup cooked red beans
⅔ cup cooked corn kernels
⅓ cup toasted cashews, chopped
4 lettuce leaves

1. Place 1½ cups water in a saucepan over medium-high heat. Pour in the quinoa and ¼ teaspoon of the salt. Bring to a boil, cover, reduce heat to low and simmer until the quinoa looks lighter (which happens when it opens and is fully cooked), approximately 10 minutes.

2. Transfer the quinoa to a sieve and discard the water. Rinse under cold running water and drain thoroughly. Transfer quinoa to a large bowl.

3. Combine pineapple juice, vinegar, cilantro, canola oil, hot sauce, pepper, and remaining ¼ teaspoon of salt. Add to quinoa along with the tomatoes, beans, corn, and cashews. Toss to coat all the ingredients well. Serve over lettuce leaves.

CHIMICHURRI LIGERO

Light Herb Sauce
Makes 1 cup

Chimichurri traditionally is made with a lot of oil and eaten with grilled steak. Here you will find a light version that can also be used as a dipping sauce for chicken wings and even carrot sticks. It is delicious on its own while retaining the classic flavors of Chimichurri.

1. Grate or press garlic. Transfer to a food processor. Add parsley, cilantro, scallions, vinegar, hot sauce (if using), salt, and pepper and process to a fine mince, about 2 minutes.

2. Remove from processor and transfer to a glass container. Whisk in yogurt and then oil. Set aside in refrigerator for 1 hour or even overnight.

1 clove garlic
1¾ cups parsley leaves
1½ cups cilantro leaves
3 whole scallions
1 tablespoon vinegar
¼ teaspoon hot sauce or ají pepper sauce (optional)
1 teaspoon salt
¼ teaspoon ground black pepper
½ cup plain low-fat yogurt
2 tablespoons oil (canola or similar)

ARROZ CON POLLO-INTEGRAL

Chicken and Brown Rice
6 to 8 servings

This Arroz con Pollo, one of our signature dishes in Colombia, is prepared with fiber-rich brown rice. The dish is still full of flavor, and your family will hardly notice the substitution of brown rice. Try it, and give yourself the pleasure of eating Arroz con Pollo without any guilt.

CHICKEN AND STOCK
2 whole chicken breasts
   with bone (4 halves)
1 medium onion, grated
1 carrot, grated
1 red pepper, grated
10 cilantro sprigs
2 bay leaves
¼ teaspoon ground black
   pepper

1. **TO COOK THE CHICKEN AND PREPARE THE STOCK:** Place the chicken breasts, 10 cups of water, onion, carrot, red pepper, cilantro, bay leaves, and black pepper into a large 5 to 7-quart pot and bring to a boil. Cover and cook 2 minutes; turn the heat off and allow the breasts to sit in the hot liquid for 25 minutes, covered. Remove the breasts from the pot, bone them, set the breast meat aside to cool. Place the bones back into the pot and simmer, uncovered, to reduce the liquid to 4 to 5 cups. Strain the stock, discarding solids. Cut the breast meat into ½-inch chunks or strips.

RICE
1 tablespoon oil (canola
   or similar)
1 onion, chopped
1 12-ounce bag frozen
   mixed vegetables
   (carrot, green beans)
½ cup sweet peas, cooked
2 tablespoons
   Worcestershire sauce
1 tablespoon minced
   garlic
1 packet Adobo Goya
   with saffron
2½ teaspoons salt
1 tablespoon sugar
¼ teaspoon ground black
   pepper
2 cups brown rice
1 cup tomato soup (not
   condensed)
¼ cup minced cilantro

2. **TO PREPARE THE RICE:** Put oil in a pot or caldero over medium-high heat. Add the onion, mixed vegetables, peas, Worcestershire sauce, garlic, Adobo Goya with saffron, salt, sugar, and black pepper and cook for 2 minutes.

3. Add the rice and toss to coat. Add the tomato soup and 4 cups of the strained chicken stock. Bring to a boil over medium-high heat. As soon as you see the rice rising close to the surface of the liquids, cover the pot and reduce heat to low and cook for 45 minutes.

4. Remove the cover, add the chicken and cilantro. Cover and allow to sit for 2 minutes and then serve.

DORADO EN HOJA
DE PLÁTANO

Mahi-Mahi in Plantain Leaves

4 to 6 servings

Mahi-Mahi (also known as dolphinfish although it is not related at all to dolphins) is a Pacific Ocean variety that is easily available in Colombia's coastal towns. The large whole fish are usually cooked in plantain leaves since this is the easiest way to handle them in the sandy places where it is seasoned with simple ingredients and then cooked to peak flavor over wood.

1. Prepare grill.

2. Make slanted cuts 1 to 2 inches apart on the fish's sides, going halfway down to the bone.

3. Place scallions, lemongrass, garlic, salt, pepper, and olive oil in a bowl and mix. Add lime slices and mix to coat them. Remove the lime slices and set aside.

4. Spread the remaining seasoned oil all over the fish, especially in cuts you just made. Place lime slices into the cavity of the fish and into the cuts as well.

1 (3 to 4 pound) whole fresh mahi-mahi (dolphinfish) or dorado, cleaned, scaled, and gutted
3 scallions, minced
3 lemongrass stalks, minced
2 garlic cloves, grated
½ tablespoon kosher salt
1 teaspoon coarsely ground black pepper
2 tablespoons olive oil
6 limes, thinly sliced
2 plantain leaves

5. Cover the fish with plantain leaves, one on top and one on bottom. Place over hot coals, cover, and cook for 25 to 30 minutes.

PESCADO AL COCO CON LIMONCILLO

Coconut-scented Snapper with Lemongrass

6 to 8 servings

Lemongrass is often found in dishes from Colombia's Pacific southwest. In the rest of the country we basically use it to infuse water with extra flavor and to make teas. Red snapper is native to both coasts and available nowadays all over the country. This is a lighter version of traditional Colombian fish in coconut milk.

1 teaspoon mashed garlic
1 ¼ teaspoons salt
1 tablespoon plus
   1 teaspoon canola oil
6 to 8 red snapper filets
   (about 2 to 3 pounds
   total)
½ cup minced scallions
1 tablespoon minced
   lemongrass plus
   1 teaspoon grated
   lemongrass
¼ teaspoon ají sauce or
   hot sauce
¼ teaspoon ground black
   pepper
1 to 2 tablespoons flour
   or finely ground oats
½ cup coconut milk,
   freshly made (see page
   107) or canned
1 cup fish stock
¼ cup lime juice
1 tablespoon minced
   cilantro

1. Combine the garlic, 1 teaspoon of the salt and 1 teaspoon of canola oil and rub mixture over the snapper filets. Refrigerate for 10 minutes.

2. In a deep sauté pan, place remaining 1 tablespoon oil, scallions, minced lemongrass, ají sauce, ¼ teaspoon salt, and pepper. Cook over medium-low heat, covered, for 3 minutes.

3. Remove the fish filets from the refrigerator and sprinkle them with flour or finely ground oats on both sides.

4. Remove the cover from the pan and increase the heat to medium-high. Add the fish filets and cook for 2 minutes on each side. Pour the coconut milk, fish stock, and lime juice over the fish. Cover the pan and reduce the heat to medium-low. Cook for 10 to 15 minutes or until fish is cooked through and flaky.

6. Uncover the pan and remove the fish from the pan. Place on a serving platter. Add cilantro and grated lemongrass to the pan sauce and pour over fish. Serve.

VARIATION: Instead of cooking the fish on top of the stove, bake the filets at 450°F for 10 minutes on each side or broil for 6 minutes on each side.

CAMARONES CON FLOR DE JAMAICA

Shrimp with Hibiscus Sauce
4 servings

Hibiscus is commonly known in Colombia as *"flor de Jamaica"* (Jamaican flower), so it must have been brought from Jamaica by the Spaniards. In Colombia, we use it mostly to prepare fresh juice, the same way the Corozo Juice (page 210) is prepared. In this recipe, the antioxidant properties and vitamins of the juice are added to the sautéed shrimp.

2 pounds jumbo shrimp, cleaned, peeled, and deveined
1 tablespoon plus 1 teaspoon minced cilantro
½ teaspoon salt
¼ teaspoon ground black pepper
1 tablespoon olive oil
1 cup hibiscus juice (*see below*)
¼ cup honey
2 tablespoons Worcestershire sauce
1 teaspoon fresh green peppercorns or ½ teaspoon ground black pepper
Oil spray for baking pan

1. Place shrimp in a bowl. Sprinkle with 1 tablespoon cilantro, ¼ teaspoon salt, pepper, and olive oil. Toss and set aside in the refrigerator while you prepare the sauce.

2. Place hibiscus juice, honey, Worcestershire sauce, peppercorns, and ¼ teaspoon salt in a small pot over medium heat. Cook until reduced by half.

3. Place shrimp in an oiled baking pan (make sure they do not touch one another). Broil for 5 minutes on one side, turn and broil for 2 minutes on the other side. Remove from the pan and place in a serving bowl.

4. Stir 1 teaspoon cilantro into the hibiscus mixture and pour into the pan where the shrimp were cooked. Stir, scraping up any browned bits in the pan. Pour over the shrimp and toss. Serve hot.

HIBISCUS JUICE

Put 1 pound hibiscus flowers and enough water to cover them in a large pot. Place over high heat and bring to a boil. Reduce the heat to medium-low and simmer for 25 minutes. One pound can yield 2½ to 3 cups of strong juice concentrate. (To prepare the juice for drinking, only simmer it for 10 minutes and you will have a tart juice; about 5 cups total.)

LANGOSTINOS AL AJÍ

Prawns with Squash and Picadillo
4 servings

Originally a cocktail (hors d'oeuvre) recipe, this is lightened up and flavored with squash, one of the foods used by the native Indian tribes.

1. **PREPARE PICADILLO AHEAD OF TIME:** In a nonreactive bowl, combine scallion, cilantro, tomato, lime juice, salt, and pepper. Add oil and hot pepper to taste. Refrigerate until ready to serve (this is best if made day before).

2. Preheat the oven to 350°F.

3. **PREPARE THE SQUASH SAUCE:** Place squash, onion, garlic, oil, salt, turmeric, and pepper in a bowl and toss. Transfer to a baking dish. Bake for 30 minutes or until the vegetables are very tender. Remove from the oven, allow to cool a bit, and transfer to a blender. Add the stock and blend until smooth. Taste for salt and add more if necessary. Add ají or hot sauce (adjusting amount to taste).

4. Sprinkle prawns with some salt and pepper. Add 1 teaspoon of oil to the pan and add prawns. Place over medium heat and cook prawns for 2 minutes per side. Remove pan from the heat and add the squash sauce and yogurt. Mix well, scraping up any bits from the pan. Serve hot with picadillo on the side.

1½ pounds prawns, shelled and deveined
Salt and pepper
1 teaspoon oil
6 tablespoons Greek yogurt

PICADILLO
¼ cup minced scallion
¼ cup minced cilantro
¼ cup minced, peeled, and seeded tomato
1 tablespoon lime juice
¼ teaspoon salt
⅛ teaspoon ground black pepper
1 teaspoon oil
1 pinch minced habanero pepper or ají pepper, seeded, or hot sauce

SQUASH SAUCE
1 pound small squash pumpkin, peeled and diced (about 2 cups)
1 large onion, diced
1 clove garlic, grated
1 teaspoon oil
1 teaspoon salt
1 teaspoon turmeric
¼ teaspoon ground white pepper
½ cup vegetable or fish stock
¼ teaspoon ají sauce or hot sauce

LOMO AL TRAPO

Wrapped Barbecued Beef
6 to 8 servings

Lomo al trapo is prepared as a festive food on farms all over the country but especially in higher altitudes. Here I prepare it in a different—and in my opinion, much more aromatic—way. I've even made this recipe on board a boat while at sea using a coal-heated barbecue, which is the best way to flavor beef filet and cook it medium to a perfect taste.

1 all-cotton kitchen towel (not very thick)
1 cup coarse salt
16 sprigs fresh thyme
1 head garlic, separated into cloves and peeled
1 tablespoon black peppercorns
1 whole beef filet, about 2½ pounds
kitchen twine

1. Prepare charcoal grill and have coals hot before assembling the beef in the towel.

2. Place kitchen towel on the counter and spread half of the salt over one end in an area the size of the roast. Arrange half of the thyme, garlic cloves, and peppercorns over the salt. Place the whole filet on the towel over the salt. Put remaining thyme, garlic cloves, and peppercorns on top and then add the rest of the salt, covering all of the filet.

3. Wrap the filet in the towel and tie with kitchen twine.

4. Place over hot coals, about 2 inches from the heat. Cover and bake 7 minutes; turn the filet (the towel will be burnt), cover and cook 7 more minutes. Remove the filet from the heat and set aside for 10 minutes.

5. Cut the towel with scissors (it will be hard and burnt like a thin cast). Slice the beef and serve. Discard towel and all the ingredients in it.

LOMO ASADO CON SALSA AGRIDULCE

Slow-Cooked Roast Beef with Mango Sauce
6 to 8 servings

Roast beef is a weekly tradition in Colombian homes. This is a simple way to cook this dish without the stove top and the mango sauce is a delicious accompaniment.

1 cup cilantro, packed
3 whole scallions
2 tablespoons dark brown sugar
6 garlic cloves, minced
2 bay leaves
½ teaspoon ground black pepper
½ teaspoon ají sauce or hot pepper (optional)
1 (3-pound) rolled rump, eye of round, or top round beef roast with bones
2 teaspoons kosher salt
¾ cup beef broth

MANGO SAUCE
1½ cups diced sweet mango
4 tablespoons chopped cilantro
1 tablespoon white wine vinegar
1 tablespoon honey
¼ teaspoon salt
⅛ teaspoon ground black pepper
2½ tablespoons olive oil

1. Process cilantro, scallions, brown sugar, garlic, bay leaves, pepper, and ají or hot pepper, if using, to make a paste. Rub beef with mixture and refrigerate overnight.

2. **PREPARE MANGO SAUCE:** In a blender, purée mango, cilantro, vinegar, honey, salt, and pepper. Gradually add olive oil in a stream until blended. Set aside.

3. Srinkle beef with salt. Sear meat fat side down for 5 minutes, turn and sear 2 minutes on other sides. Transfer to a baking pan and keep the searing pan and juices for the sauce. Pour broth into the baking pan. Cook in a preheated 225°F oven for 2 to 3 hours, or until thermometer inserted in center of roast reads 130°F.

4. To finish the mango sauce, transfer it to the searing pan, place it back over medium heat and stir, scraping the bottom of the pan. Cook for 2 minutes and set aside until the roast is ready.

5. When the roast reaches the desired temperature, remove from the oven and the pan, cover with foil, and let rest for 30 minutes to 1 hour.

6. Remove the pan drippings from the baking pan. Skim off all the fat and add drippings to the mango sauce. Reheat the sauce and boil for 3 to 5 minutes.

7. Slice the beef and serve with the sauce. (Any leftover meat is delicious thinly sliced for sandwiches.)

POSTA NEGRA CON CIRUELAS PASAS

Blackened Beef with Dried Plum Sauce

8 servings

Blackened beef (*Posta Negra*, page 80) is a delicious dish and one that originated in Cartagena de Indias, our lovely walled city in the Caribbean. Here I make it lighter by accompanying it with a prune sauce that is more typically used in Colombia with pork. It is a delicious way to blacken the beef and flavor the sauce without all the sugar from the ingredients (brown sugar and cola) in the original recipe.

⅔ cup grated onion
3 tablespoons prepared mustard
3 cloves garlic
¼ teaspoon ground black pepper
3-pound beef roast (rolled rump, eye of round, or top round)
1 cup seeded prunes
¼ cup red wine
3 tablespoons Worcestershire sauce
2½ teaspoons salt
2 bay leaves

1. Process onion, mustard, garlic, and pepper to a puree. Place the beef in a nonreactive container. Rub the onion mixture all over the beef and refrigerate 1 to 3 days. (The longer you marinate it, the more tender the beef will be.)

2. Cook the prunes in 2 cups of water over low heat for 10 minutes, or let the prunes sit in a bowl in the warm water on the countertop overnight. Drain and purée the prunes in blender.

3. Thirty minutes before cooking, remove the meat from the refrigerator and set aside to reach room temperature.

4. Place a medium or large pressure cooker over medium-high heat and add the beef fat side down. Brown for 7 minutes; turn and brown the other side of the beef for 2 more minutes. Add prune mixture, the wine, Worcestershire sauce, salt, and bay, leaves. Cover and cook under pressure on medium heat for 25 minutes. (If using a regular pot, cook for 2 to 3 hours.)

5. Remove the pot from the heat; release the pressure, let stand for 10 minutes and then open. Simmer over low heat for 1 hour with the cover ajar (this step is the same if using a regular pot).

7. Remove the meat from the pot, let it stand for 10 minutes, and then slice. Skim the fat from the sauce in the pot. Serve over the sliced beef or on the side.

POLLO ASADO CON AJÍ DE MANÍ

Spicy Chicken with Ají de Maní
6 servings

> *Ají de maní* is a delicious, spicy peanut sauce native to the southern Pacific zone where most of the peanuts are grown. Here we use it to flavor chicken without the tamale masa, making it a light and tasty dish. The original recipe for this sauce is very hot, so I have decreased the amount of habanero by half.

12 chicken thighs, skinned
6 cloves garlic (4 grated and 2 whole)
2¼ teaspoons salt
½ teaspoon ground cumin*
½ teaspoon minced, seeded red habanero* pepper
1 tablespoon canola oil
1 cup thinly sliced onions
½ cup unsalted roasted peanuts
¼ cup minced red onion
3 tablespoons minced cilantro
1 teaspoon color* or turmeric
1½ cups chicken stock
½ teaspoon ground black pepper
Cooked white rice, for serving

1. In a large, nonreactive bowl place the chicken thighs, 4 cloves grated garlic, 1 teaspoon of the salt, ¼ teaspoon cumin, and ¼ teaspoon habanero. Mix well and set aside for 30 minutes or in refrigerator overnight.

2. In a large pot over medium heat, warm the tablespoon oil and cook the sliced onions, covered, for 4 minutes. Uncover, mix and remove the onions from the pan and set aside. Add chicken thighs to the pot, skin side down, and cook for 3 to 4 minutes to sear.

3. In the meantime, purée peanuts, red onion, cilantro, 2 cloves garlic, color or turmeric, stock, pepper, remaining 1¼ teaspoon salt, ¼ teaspoon cumin, and ¼ teaspoon habanero.

4. Discard the excess fat from the pot, add the onions back in and pour in the blended peanut mixture. Cover, lower the heat to medium-low, and cook for 40 minutes.

5. Serve over white rice.

POLLO SUDADO AL CURRY

Chicken with Guiso and Curry Pot
6 servings

In the northern zone of Colombia, there is a large community of immigrants from the Middle East who brought some of their delicious foods with them. This curry pot is something that can be served with brown rice to imitate our *guiso* sauce chicken, which is always served with a cup of white rice.

12 chicken thighs, skinned
1 onion, grated
3 cloves garlic, grated
1 tablespoon curry powder
2 bay leaves
3 teaspoons salt
¼ teaspoon ground black pepper
1 tablespoon canola oil
2 cup sliced onion
2 cups peeled and diced tomatoes
4 tablespoons cilantro leaves
2 tablespoons raisins
2 teaspoons Worcestershire sauce
3 cups chicken stock
1½ pounds potatoes, cut in half
Cooked brown rice, for serving

1. In a large, nonreactive bowl place the chicken thighs, grated onion, grated garlic, curry powder, bay leaves, 1 teaspoon of the salt, and the pepper. Mix well and set aside for 30 minutes or in the refrigerator overnight.

2. In a large pot over medium heat, warm the oil and sauté the sliced onions for 4 minutes. Puree the tomatoes, cilantro, raisins, Worcestershire sauce, and remaining 2 teaspoons of salt in a blender and transfer to the pan. Cook for 4 minutes more.

3. Add the seasoned chicken and stock. Cover and cook for 30 minutes.

4. Add the potatoes and cover and cook until the potatoes are tender, about 20 minutes more.

5. Serve over brown rice.

PAVO RELLENO DE CERDO, CARNE Y HONGOS

Roasted Herbed Turkey with Mushroom and Meat Stuffing

12 to 14 servings

This recipe for roasted turkey is a delicious option at the holidays or any other special occasion, with enough Colombian flavor to whet anyone's appetite and at the same time offer a healthy meal to guests. It is very simple to prepare because all the work is done the day before you roast it. The bird does not have to be basted, so you can enjoy time with your guests.

1 (14-pound) whole turkey
1 cup plain yogurt, plus more for gravy
1 cup mixed fresh herbs (culantro/cimarrón, cilantro, and/or parsley)
2 teaspoons salt
½ teaspoon ground black pepper
1 bunch each parsley, scallions, and cilantro
1 head garlic, peeled
1½ cups chicken stock
½ cup white wine
Cornstarch

ONE DAY BEFORE COOKING

1. Defrost turkey if needed and wash it well inside and out with plenty of water.

2. Place 1 cup yogurt, herbs, 1 teaspoon salt, and pepper in food processor and process for 30 seconds. Rub the mixture under the turkey's skin and on the outside.

3. Coarsely chop or process parsley, scallions, and cilantro with garlic cloves and 1 teaspoon of salt and some pepper. Spread into the bird's cavity. Set the turkey in the refrigerator, covered, for 1 day.

DAY OF COOKING

4. MAKE THE MUSHROOM AND MEAT STUFFING: Blend or process yogurt, mustard, olive oil, port wine, capers, olives, green peppercorns, and coarse salt. In a bowl combine the beef, pork, mushrooms, onions, red pepper, and almonds with the yogurt mixture. Place in a Ziploc bag and refrigerate until ready to cook.

MUSHROOM AND MEAT STUFFING

½ cup plain yogurt
¼ cup Dijon mustard
3 tablespoons olive oil
3 tablespoons port wine
2 tablespoons tiny capers
2 tablespoons chopped green olives
1 tablespoon fresh green peppercorns, ground
2 teaspoons coarse salt
1 pound lean ground beef
1 pound lean ground pork

5. Remove turkey from the refrigerator 1 to 2 hours before roasting to reach room temperature. Preheat the oven to 325°F. If cooking the stuffing in the turkey, place the cold meat mixture inside the turkey belly and front at this point. Truss the turkey, tying the legs last. Place it on a rack in a roasting pan. Pour the stock and wine into the bottom of the pan.

1 pound whole button or cremini mushrooms
2 large onions, cut in eighths
2 red bell peppers, cut in eighths
½ cup almonds

6. Roast for approximately 18 minutes per pound. Once the breasts start to brown lightly, place foil over them and continue to cook. The turkey is done when you pinch the thickest part of the thigh and the liquid runs clear and not pink. The internal temperature at the thigh of the bird should be 160º to 180° F. Let rest 30 minutes before carving and serving.

7. If you are not cooking the stuffing in the turkey, transfer it with all the sauce to a large baking pan and roast for 40 to 45 minutes.

8. While the turkey is resting, make the gravy: Remove all the fat from the juices in the roasting pan. Measure the liquid and place it in a saucepan. For each cup of liquid, add ½ teaspoon cornstarch mixed with 1 tablespoon yogurt. Cook to thicken, stirring occasionally, about 5 to 10 minutes. Taste and season with salt and pepper and serve with turkey and stuffing.

CAÑÓN DE CERDO CON AJÍ DE PIÑA

Pork Loin with Pineapple-Lime Salsa
6 to 8 servings

The Spanish word *cañón* means "*cannon*" in English and in the Andean zone of Colombia the pork loin is referred to by this name because of its cannon-like shape. Here we prepare it with an ají sauce in order to lighten it up. The original recipe calls for a raw sugar or panela sauce.

1 (2½-pound) boneless pork loin
1½ tablespoons fresh thyme leaves, minced
½ teaspoon grated ginger root

1. Remove pork from the refrigerator and rub with ginger and thyme. Set aside for about 30 minutes to reach room temperature.

2. **PREPARE SALSA:** In a nonreactive container mix all salsa ingredients except oil. Set aside for 20 minutes, then add the oil, if using. Set aside until ready to serve.

3. **PREPARE GLAZE:** Mix all glaze ingredients and rub them over the pork. Place pork in a foil-lined baking dish. Cover with sauce. Refrigerate for 20 minutes.

4. Preheat the oven to 325ºF.

5. Roast the pork in the preheated oven for 45 minutes to 1 hour or until it reaches an internal temperature of 160ºF. Remove from the oven, place pork on a serving platter, cover, and set aside for 10 minutes.

6. Use a spatula to carefully stir and scrape up all the pan juices (trying not to tear the aluminum foil). Pour over the pork and serve with salsa.

PINEAPPLE-LIME SALSA
1½ cups diced fresh pineapple
½ cup minced red onion
1 tablespoon minced cilantro
¼ cup lime juice
½ teaspoon hot pepper or ají sauce
½ teaspoon salt
¼ teaspoon black pepper
2 tablespoons olive oil (optional)

GLAZE
½ cup diced fresh pineapple
2 tablespoons honey
1 tablespoon grated lime peel
1 tablespoon fresh lime juice
1 teaspoon salt
¼ teaspoon ground black pepper

JAMÓN A LA PIÑA
Ham with Fresh Pineapple
20 to 25 servings

During the Christmas holidays in Colombia, we typically serve pork dishes. Tamales of all sorts are filled with pork. When serving fresh pork, we prefer the whole hind leg (with bone) and bake it for hours at low temperatures. This yields a very crispy skin and a juicy meat that separates from the bone. The fat can be used to baste the meat while it cooks, and then be removed before eating it if desired. The fresh pineapple compliments the pork perfectly.

1 fresh ham or leg of pork (about 12 pounds; see step 1)
1 cup grated onion
1 cup Dijon mustard
8 cloves garlic, minced
2 tablespoons fresh thyme leaves
4 teaspoons salt
1 teaspoon ground black pepper
4 bay leaves, crushed

PINEAPPLE SAUCE
2 (20-ounce) cans pineapple slices in juice
1 cup brown sugar
½ cup cilantro leaves, packed
4 garlic cloves
4 bay leaves, ground
1 tablespoon grated lime peel
½ tablespoon fresh thyme leaves
½ teaspoon dark sesame oil
1 teaspoon ground cloves
1 teaspoon ground allspice
½ teaspoon ground black pepper
flour for the sauce

1. Buy the whole leg of pork with the bone, fat, and skin included. Ask your butcher to make crisscross cuts, 1 inch apart, on the skin.

2. Place the pork in a large nonreactive container; add the onion, mustard, garlic, thyme, 3 teaspoons of the salt, pepper, and crushed bay leaves and rub all over the pork leg. Cover and refrigerate until the next day.

3. Remove the pork from the refrigerator and let it come to room temperature, about 1 to 2 hours. Rub with the remaining teaspoon of salt. (If you bought the pork already boned, tie it with twine to hold it together while cooking. A leg with the bone will hold together on its own.)

4. Preheat the oven to 325°F. Place the leg on a rack in a roasting pan. Pour the leftover marinating juices in the bottom of the pan together with 1 cup of water. Roast pork for 20 minutes.

5. Meanwhile prepare the pineapple sauce: Purée all the sauce ingredients except flour in a blender. Transfer to a pot and place over medium heat. Bring to a boil, reduce the heat and simmer for 5 minutes, stirring occasionally so it doesn't burn. Set aside until needed.

CONTINUED

6. After the pork has roasted for 20 minutes, pour the pineapple sauce over the pork and loosely cover with foil. Continue to roast for 20 minutes per pound, about 4 hours. During cooking, check that the liquids on the bottom of the pan have not started to burn or evaporate and add extra ½ cups of water or stock as needed.

7. Remove the pork leg when the internal temperature is 160°F to 180°F. Let it rest for 30 minutes before carving.

9. To prepare the serving sauce, remove fat from pan drippings. Measure the remaining juices into a small pot and add 1½ teaspoons of flour per cup of liquid. Stir well and cook until thickened.

10. Serve pork slices with the pan juices and enjoy!

COSTILLITAS EN CERVEZA

Beer-Drunken Beef Ribs

4 to 6 servings

Most of the country's cattle is grown in the southeastern plains of Colombia, Los Llanos Orientales, where they cook whole racks of ribs over teepee-style fires. I have taken the main seasoning procedure and ingredients typically used to give pork ribs a great flavor and used them here to do the same for beef ribs.

2 3-to 4-pound racks baby back ribs
2 10-ounce cans of beer

RUB
¼ cup mustard
¼ cup grated onion
¼ cup brown sugar
3 garlic cloves, grated
3 tablespoons minced cilantro
1 teaspoon salt
¼ teaspoon ground cumin
¼ teaspoon ground black pepper
¼ teaspoon curry powder
1 small hot pepper or 10 drops Tabasco sauce

1. Place all rub ingredients in a small bowl and mix. Rub all over the ribs and refrigerate at least 10 to 20 minutes, or preferably overnight.

2. Place ribs in baking pans, pour beer over them, and cook in preheated 225°F oven for 3 to 4 hours or until the meat falls off the bones when pricked.

3. Remove from the oven and serve.

ARAÑITAS

Spiders—Fried Green Plantain Fritters
8 to 10 fritters

This is a traditional dish from the northern part of Colombia. Its name translates as "spiders." They are crispy and delicious green plantain fritters formed by grating the green plantains and making patties. Although regularly served with a sour cream called *Suerno Costeño* and *chicharrones* (pig skin fritters), you can serve them on their own or with Greek yogurt and avocado ají or any other picadillo or salsa.

2 green plantains*
2 cups oil
Salt

1. Cut the ends off the plantains and peel. Grate them on the large hole side of a grater.

2. Pour the oil into a deep, medium, heavy pot, and place over medium-high heat. When the oil is hot (about 350°F) form heaping tablespoons of the grated plantains into balls and flatten between the palms of your hands. Transfer them carefully into the hot oil, making a few at a time depending on the size of your pan. Deep-fry for 3 to 5 minutes or until lightly golden and crisp. Remove from the oil with a slotted spoon, salt lightly, and drain on paper towels. Serve hot with suggested accompaniments.

SUGGESTED ACCOMPANIMENTS:
Guacamole
Greek yogurt
Picadillo
Tomato salsa
Shredded Chicken or Beef
Grated cheese
Sour cream

PLÁTANO ASADO

Skin-Roasted Sweet Plantains
6 servings

Sweet plantains are naturally sweet and very high in fiber. This recipe calls for baking them in their own skin without adding any butter or extra sugar as is traditionally done when they are baked in a pan. The plantains release a fantastic aroma that tells you when they are ready. They are very easy to cook, so much so that we often prepare them aboard our boat on the grill.

2 very ripe plantains* (see Note)

1. Prepare a barbecue with cover and hot coals or preheat the oven to 350ºF.

2. Leave the plantains whole with skins on. Place on foil if using an oven; place on the grill directly over the coals if using a barbecue.

3. Bake or grill with cover on for 30 to 40 minutes or until the skin ruptures and some of the plantain comes out of the skin and lightly browns.

4. Remove the plantains from their skins and serve whole or in 2-inch chunks.

NOTE: The plantains for this dish have to be very ripe with the peel almost black but still firm to the touch. When you press them gently, they should not feel mushy inside; if they are, the taste will be rancid and overripe. If you buy green plantains you will need to wait for them to ripen which might take a week or so. Do not refrigerate them or they will not ripen properly. It is better to buy plantains fully ripe or close to ripe, as this ensures you they haven't been refrigerated and will ripen without getting mushy.

TORTA DE PLÁTANO ASADO

Baked Plantain Pie
8 servings

This baked plantain pie is lighter than the original one (see page 148) as it relies more on the sweetness of the plantains. When you go to the market, buy plantains that are almost black and firm, but yield when you touch them. They will be the sweetest.

4 very ripe plantains,
  baked or grilled (see
  page 249)
2 eggs
½ cup milk
1 tablespoon butter,
  softened
¼ cup sugar
1 teaspoon salt
½ teaspoon vanilla
  extract
1 cup guava jam
¼ teaspoon cinnamon
½ pound low-fat white
  farmer's cheese, diced
  (1 ¼ cups)
Non-stick cooking spray
  for the baking pan

1. Preheat oven to 350°F. Cool the grilled or baked plantains and remove the skins. Cut into ¼-inch dice.

2. In a small mixing bowl, combine the eggs, milk, butter, sugar, salt, vanilla, guava jam, and cinnamon, if using.

3. In another medium bowl mix the cooked plantain cubes with the cheese.

4. Spray an 8-inch square baling pan with cooking spray. Fold the egg mixture into the plantain mixture and pour into the prepared pan.

5. Bake 30 to 40 minutes until browned and bubbly. Cut into 2-inch squares and serve.

PLATANITOS AL HORNO *Baked Plantain Chips*

8 servings

This recipe illustrates how most Colombian restaurants make their long, decorative, very thin plantain chips. If you want to keep the plantains crispy in a humid environment, turn off the oven and let them sit there on the serving platter or on a baking dish until ready to serve. At this point they can all be piled into a bowl or on top of each other.

1 large green plantain*
2 tablespoons oil or oil spray
Salt to taste

1. Cut the ends off the plantain and peel. Cut in ⅛-inch-thick rounds if making coins, or ⅛-inch-thick by 3-to-4-inch-long strips if making chips. Preheat the oven to 350°F.

2. Spray or brush the plantain chips with oil and place them on an oiled baking pan, arranging the plantain chip pieces one by one in a single layer so they don't touch each other. Bake for 15 to 20 minutes or until lightly golden and somewhat curved. Sprinkle with salt to taste. Remove from the baking pan and serve immediately.

YUCA CON QUESO

*Cooked Yuca with
Yogurt and Cheese*
6 servings

Yuca is another one of Colombia's native foods. Many people mistakenly think they are just another white carbohydrate, but in fact they are very high in fiber. Made with yogurt and cheese to add protein, make this dish a staple that will remind you of home.

2 pounds peeled yuca*
(fresh or frozen)
1 tablespoon plus
1¼ teaspoons salt
2 bay leaves
2 tablespoons melted
butter
1 cup Greek yogurt
6 ounces low-fat white
farmer s cheese, grated

1. If using fresh yuca, quarter it lengthwise. Cut each piece of yuca lengthwise again and then cut into 3 x 2-inch chunks.

2. Place the yuca in a medium pot with 6 cups of water, 1 tablespoon of salt and the bay leaves. Cover, bring to a boil and cook until fork tender, about 45 to 50 minutes. To check for tenderness, prick a piece with a knife and it should go all the way in very easily; it will look almost undone on the edges. Set aside.

3. In a small bowl mix melted butter, yogurt, and ¼ teaspoon salt. Set aside.

4. Drain the yuca and sprinkle with the remaining 1 teaspoon of salt. Add the yogurt mixture and gently mix it all together. Sprinkle with cheese and serve.

PAPAS AMARILLAS AL HORNO

Baked Yellow Potatoes
4 to 6 servings

Yellow potatoes have so much taste on their own that it is great to eat them baked with just a dash of salt. This is the best way to learn the difference between each variety of the hundreds of them in Colombia. Yellow potatoes are also called Peruvian Yellow Potatoes as they are indigenous to all the Andean region.

1 pound (about 10) very
   small yellow potatoes
2 teaspoons salt
1 tablespoon oil or
   cooking oil spray

1. Wash the potatoes well. Do not peel or cut. Place them in a small pot with water to cover them plus 1 inch. Add 1 teaspoon salt, cover, and turn the heat to medium-high.

2. Cook covered until the water comes to a boil. Uncover and cook about 5 to 10 minutes or until potatoes are tender but not overcooked.

3. Preheat the oven to 425ºF.

4. Drain the water from the potatoes. Spray them with olive oil and sprinkle with remaining 1 teaspoon salt. Transfer to a baking pan.

5. Bake for 5 to 7 minutes or until lightly golden. Serve immediately.

PAPITA AMARILLA CHORREADA

Yellow Potatoes with Yogurt and Roasted Garlic Sauce

8 servings

Saucy yellow potatoes, a must in any Andean home, are lightened up here with the use of yogurt instead of cream. The addition of the cherry tomatoes also adds lots of flavor and nutrients. Also use your favorite cheese, but go with the part-skim variety.

2 cups cut green onions*, sliced in half lengthwise, then into 2½-inch-long pieces
1½ cups quartered cherry tomatoes
1 tablespoons oil
½ head garlic, whole and unpeeled
¼ teaspoon curry powder
⅛ teaspoon ground cumin
⅛ teaspoon plus ¼ teaspoon ground black pepper
1 tablespoon plus ½ teaspoon salt
1½ pounds yellow potatoes
½ cup whole milk
½ cup plain yogurt
½ cup vegetable stock
½ teaspoon cornstarch
6 ounces white farmer's cheese* or part skim mozzarella, shredded (1 cup)

1. Preheat the oven to 350ºF. Toss together the green onions, tomatoes, oil, garlic, curry powder, cumin, ⅛ teaspoon pepper, and ½ teaspoon salt on a large piece of foil. Fold to cover tightly and bake for 30 to 40 minutes or until garlic is soft and buttery.

2. Wash the potatoes and remove about half of the peel from each potato. Place the potatoes in a medium pot with the 1 tablespoon of salt and water to cover. Bring to a boil and cook until the potatoes feel almost done through the center, about 10 to 12 minutes. Drain and set aside, covered.

3. Open the foil around the vegetables, remove the garlic cloves from their natural casing and mash them. Transfer the tomato mixture to a large sauté pan, add the mashed garlic, and mix well.

4. Add the milk, yogurt, stock, cornstarch, and ¼ teaspoon pepper to the tomato-garlic mixture and bring to a boil, simmer 2 minutes. Add the potatoes and cheese; mix well, and cook covered for 2 to 3 minutes or until the cheese has melted.

5. Place in a serving dish and serve hot.

PITHAYA CON QUESILLO
Sweet Pithaya Fruit with Cheese
4 servings

Pithaya is a Colombian fruit that is now found in many other countries and is of great nutritional value and aids in digestion, so be careful not to over eat it! It is delicious and juicy and can be eaten with cheese as we also do with guava paste—we call this delicious combination "*matrimonio*" (marriage).

1 *pithaya* fruit
6 ounces fresh white farmer s cheese
1 lime, cut into quarters

1. Cut the pithaya into fourths lengthwise.

2. Cut the cheese into ¾-inch x 2-inch x ¼-inch slices.

3. Arrange in a dish with lime and serve.

BATIDOS DE FRUTA TROPICALES
Tropical Fruit Smoothies
2 servings

Smoothies have been on Colombian tables forever. We add milk or not, depending on personal preference, and we use a variety of high fiber and sweet fruits to enhance the flavor and texture of the smoothie. This makes for a complete fruit serving for a day served in such a delicious way that kids can enjoy without knowing it is loaded with vitamins. We actually give smoothies to babies in their bottles after they start eating fruit.

1 banana, sliced
1 cup diced papaya
1 cup diced pineapple
1 cup chopped ice
8 mint or spearmint leaves

Place all ingredients in a blender and blend until smooth. Serve immediately.

SALPICÓN

Colombian Fruit Cocktail with Ice Cream
6 to 8 servings

Salpicón or *Tutti Frutti con helado* is a common dessert all around Colombia. We usually use fresh fruit mixed with some orange juice to prevent oxidation of the fruit. The fruit is typically diced small and after an hour or so of being refrigerated, it releases some of its flavor into the orange juice and thickens it a little. The ice cream is what makes it a dessert and to make this even healthier you could serve it with frozen yogurt.

3 bananas, sliced
2 cups diced papaya
2 cups diced pineapple
2 cups diced mango
2 cups orange juice
Sugar (optional)
1 pint vanilla ice cream or
   frozen yogurt
4 blackberries

1. Mix bananas, papaya, pineapple, mango, and orange juice in a non-reactive bowl. Refrigerate for at least 1 hour. Add a little sugar if desired, only if fruits are somewhat acidic.

2. Serve in a tall glass with ice cream or frozen yogurt and a blackberry on top.

ABORRAJADOS: Batter-fried foods.

ACELGA: Chard.

ACHIOTE: Seeds from the Annatto tree that color foods with a reddish yellow tint. They come in red hard capsules. Pre-Columbian Indians used them to dye their skins. *Color* or achiote can be replaced with turmeric, Sazón Goya Color, or saffron powder.

ADOBO: A pre-mixed seasoning powder. There are many different versions, for example with and without pepper or cumin. Goya is one of the largest-selling brands.

AGUARDIENTE: Also called "Firewater," this liquor made from sugarcane is flavored with aniseed. The alcohol content is 28 percent (56 proof); it is dry (not sweet), and served in shot glasses. If you can't find it, you can substitute vodka and aniseed extract, or an anise-flavored liqueur.

AJÍ DULCE: Small sweet peppers that do have some heat, but are definitely the mildest. They look a lot like habaneros, but are many, many times milder: one to three inches in length, with crinkled skin; they are usually sold green. They are basically sweet miniature green and red peppers.

ALMIDÓN DE YUCA: Yuca or cassava starch comes in three types: regular for *pandebonos*, sweet for *panderos*, and sour for *pandeyucas*. They are slightly different, even in appearance: the sweet one is a shade of yellow; the regular is more powdery white; while the sour one is more home made and has large particles in it. The regular one can be used for both *pandebonos* and *pandeyucas* but not for *panderos*; for that you must use the sweet.

AREPA COOKER PAN / ASADOR DE AREPAS: Special flat-surfaced pan made of very thin metal, which has over it another very thin metal rack.

AREPAS: Corn cakes that are made flat or filled, sweet or salted, with or without cheese or butter, fried or cooked on the stove top or coals, from yellow or white precooked cornmeal, dried corn or sweet corn.

ARRACACHA: An Andean root and tuber like *yuca* or cassava, but is slightly sweet and has a purple center. You could say it has a ring of purple color in the center and light orange inside.

BIJAO: Green and large plantain leaves.

BOROJÓ: A fruit from the Chocó region of Colombia, round oval-shaped, four to six inches in diameter, with a dark brown skin and pulp. It has a soft, cracked, and rough peel. The aroma is odd but the juice is very good.

CALDERO: Round cast aluminum pots that come in many sizes, with a cover and two small handles. They are the ideal pot for preparing rice.

CARANTANTAS: The leftover material in the bottom of the pot that is peeled off after cooked corn *masa* is prepared. It is sold as a snack, fried like chips, or sold for the preparation of soup.

CARGAMANTO RED BEANS: A type of pinto bean that is a cream speckled kidney-type red bean, also called cranberry beans.

CIMARRÓN or **CULANTRO:** Also called *recao*, fitweed or long coriander. An herb with a large leaf, two to four inches long, with a pungent aroma.

COLOR: Powdered achiote that colors foods with a reddish-yellow tint. Readily available brands include Goya and Bijol.

COROZO: A tiny dark red fruit with a large pit and a tough papery skin. It comes from a wild palm and is eaten alone with salt or prepared in juice. Alone it is very sour; the juice is sweetened.

CUCHUCO DE MAÍZ: The cut or chopped pieces of dried or dehydrated corn kernels, they are about the size of one-eighth of a kernel.

CUAJADA: A variety of a white farmer's cheese that is prepared with fresh, raw, non-pasteurized milk and eaten alone or with sweets.

CUAJO: Rennet curd tablets.

CUMIN: Seeds and powder. Cumin seeds can be ground in a coffee mill and will be much more aromatic than if bought in powdered form.

CURUBA: A small, oblong (half-an-inch wide by two to three inches long) fruit, with a thick and pale yellowish-green skin and an orange seedy pulp, it is both acidic and astringent in taste.

FARMER'S CHEESE: This cheese is sold in large thirty-pound blocks at the entrance of many supermarkets, fresh for people to buy as much as they want or packaged in the dairy sections. While it is sometimes very salty, the ones packaged and sold abroad are not, and these recipes are adapted to them. If you think your recipes need more salt, go ahead, it depends on the cheese.

FEIJOA: Small guavas with the shape of a strawberry; also called pineapple guavas. When ripe, they are somewhat sweet and delicious, with dark green granular skin on the outside and white seedy pulp in the inside. One to three inches long and oval pear-shaped, they grow in the colder mountains of Antioquia.

FRESH NON-PASTEURIZED MILK: Ask for it at local dairy farms or markets in the United States where the sale is permitted.

FRÍJOL DE CABECITA NEGRA: Black-eyed peas.

GREEN ONIONS: Large, thick scallions; about half-an-inch thick and fourteen inches long.

GROSELLAS: Yellow currants; they are a yellowish green berry that looks more like a miniature green tomato with a large pit in the inside. They range from one-quarter to half-an-inch in diameter, are acid tasting and very intensely flavored. We eat them alone with salt and cooked in syrup. They change to pink-colored after cooking.

GUASCAS: An herb from the Andes in Colombia. It is a green leaf about the size of a large leaf of fresh basil. It is sold fresh in bunches of leaves tied together or dehydrated in bags. Look for it in the spice aisle of specialty and Latino markets.

GUANDÚ or **GUANDUL:** Pigeon peas.

HARINA DE MAÍZ CAPIO: Corn starch made from a yellow corn that has large cobs and grain; can be substituted with corn starch.

HABANERO: A very small, very hot pepper, one to two inches long, with crinkled skin. Sold from green to red in color. Habaneros are said to be the hottest of all peppers.

LONGANIZA: A kielbasa-like sausage from the Bogotá and Andean regions.

LULO: A round fruit with a diameter of one-and-a-half to two inches. Bright orange on the outside when fully ripe, with green pulp. *Lulos* have a tart to acidic flavor. They are called Naranjillas in other Latin American countries.

MAÍZ PETO: Dried yellow or white corn kernels.

MAMEY: A fruit like zapote or caimito, with thick, brown, and granular skin and a large pit. The ripe pulp is orange in color and very fibrous with a characteristic sweet flavor.

MAMONCILLO: A fruit sold in clusters as they grow on the tree, and tied up in hundreds. They are half-an-inch to one inch in diameter, green on the outside, with a very hard outer shell that you crack open in with a fingernail or sharp point. The glistening yellow-beige pulp has an acid sweet taste that is sometimes astringent at the end.

MARACUYÁ: Passion fruit. Round, three to five inches in diameter. A yellow to purple thick yellow fruit with an orange seeded pulp, very acidic and somewhat bitter in flavor,

MARRANITAS O PUERQUITAS: Fritters of thin green plantain slices, filled and then refried.

MASA: Dough.

MASA FLOUR: Specially ground and precooked cornmeal for making doughs for *tamales* and tortillas. Similar to precooked cornmeal.

MOLINO: A corn mill, similar to a food mill, used for grinding whole fresh corn kernels or cooked dried corn.

MONDONGO: Tripe soup.

NÍSPERO: A light brown, hairy-skinned fruit from the tropical forests of Colombia. Our Colombian version of the kiwi, about the same color on the outside but brownish red or yellowish brown on the inside. The pulp has two large black seeds in the center.

ÑAME: *Ñame* is a tuber, like *yuca*, but with a different taste. The size is a lot like *yuca* but some varieties have a rougher skin and some are smoother. Even though it is often translated as "yam," it is not the same. You must ask for it as *ñame* ("nyahmay") in Latin American and specialty supermarkets.

PANELA: A product that comes from sugarcane; it is very sweet and reddish brown in color. Sold in round or square blocks that weigh half or one pound, it is only recently being packaged. You can also purchase it shredded. It has no additives or chemicals and is therefore supposed to be healthier. The flavor is very aromatic and could be replaced with dark brown sugar.

PIANGUA: Cockles, similar to very small clams. They are found on the Pacific coast of Colombia.

PITHAYA: A juicy Colombian fruit that is known to aid with digestion.

PLÁTANOS: Plantains come in many shades of color and ripeness going from green to black in the color of the peel. Use only green plantains for *tostadas, patacones, sancochos,* and *moneditas*. Use the ripest black but firm plantains for *tajadas, torta de plátano, plátano al horno* and *plátano en tentación*. For adding to a soup like coconut soup, you could add plantains that are two days old if you bought them green; they will be only slightly sweet.

POLEO: Mint-like herb grown in the wet and humid forests.

PRECOOKED WHITE or **YELLOW CORNMEAL:** Used to make *arepas, tamales, empanadas* and other corn products; much easier and less time-consuming to use than older versions of cornmeal or corn flour.

RED PINTO BEANS: Speckled dry beans from southwestern states; they can be found under the Camelia bean product line.

SAZÓN: A pre-mixed seasoning powder. There are many different versions, and flavors, with and without coloring. Goya is one of the largest-selling brands.

SOBREBARRIGA: Translates as "over the belly beef," and is actually the piece of meat that surrounds the flank steak; it is a subcutaneous muscle type of flesh. The closest American cut is outer skirt steak or diaphragm.

TOCINO: Fatty part of pork like bacon but sliced thicker.

TOMATE DE ÁRBOL: Also known as *tamarillo* or tree tomatoes, it is a yellowish red fruit with yellow to orange pulp. Oval-shaped and one to two inches in length. The flavor ranges from slightly acid to sweet. It is used mainly for the production of juice. Nowadays there is a cross with berries that produces a more red variety that is also very rich in flavor.

UCHUVAS: Yellow gooseberries. This small and round fruit (about half-an-inch in diameter) has an intense yellow–orange color and somewhat sweet tart flavor. It is covered by a papery casing and full of tiny seeds.

WHITE FARMER'S CHEESE. *See* Farmer's Cheese

YUCA: *Yuca*, cassava, or manioc are some of the names this white root and tuber goes by. It has a thick, brown, bark-looking rough skin, with white fibrous pulp. Somewhat cylindrical, it is two to three inches in diameter. It is used in making starches and many foods as well as eaten alone, baked, fried or stewed.

ZAPALLO: Pumpkin.

INDEX

FROM THE HIPPOCRENE
INTERNATIONAL COOKBOOK LIBRARY

MUY BUENO:
Three Generations of Authentic Mexican Flavor
Yvette Marquez-Sharpnack, Veronica Gonzalez-Smith, and *Evangelina Soza*

"Siéntate a comer, esta muy bueno!" —*Sit down and eat, it's very good!* This was how Jesusita always welcomed guests to her table. The same words served as inspiration for her daughter Evangelina and granddaughters Yvette and Veronica, who wanted to honor her memory and preserve their family's recipes and stories for future generations. They started the Muy Bueno Cookbook blog in 2010 with this idea in mind, and quickly attracted thousands of fans and followers who fell in love with Muy Bueno's flavorful Mexican recipes, heartwarming family stories, and beautiful photography.

Now they open their hearts and kitchens to an even wider audience, sharing memories and over 100 beloved family recipes in their first cookbook. Spanning three generations, *Muy Bueno* offers traditional old-world northern Mexican recipes from Jesusita's kitchen; comforting south of the border home-style dishes from Evangelina; and innovative Latin fusion recipes from Yvette and Veronica.

ISBN 978-0-7818-1304-4 · $22.50 · Fall 2012

Argentina Cooks! *Expanded Edition*
Shirley Lomax Brooks

Argentine cuisine is one of the world's best-kept culinary secrets. As a result, a great variety of foods are available—lamb, an incredible assortment of fish and seafood, exotic fruits, and prime quality beef. Inside are sophisticated culinary offerings like *Pavita Relleno a la Criolla* (Roast Turkey with Persimmon, Sausage, and Jalapeño Stuffing) and *Gaspado de Cazador* (Game Stew with Wild Rabbit, Partridges, Quail, and Gin), as well as home-style favorites like *Gazpacho de Mesopotamia* (Raw Vegetables in Chicken Broth and Fresh Lime Juice). The 190 recipes are all adapted for the North American kitchen. Complete with black-and-white photographs and illustrations.

ISBN 0-7818-0997-5 · $24.95

Brazil: A Culinary Journey
Cherie Hamilton

The largest nation in South America, Brazil is home to vast rain forests, pristine tropical beaches, the Amazon River, and one of the region's most interesting cuisines. The recipes presented in *Brazil: A Culinary Journey* provide a glimpse into the surprisingly diverse repertoire of Brazilian cooking, from the heavily African-influenced cuisine of the Northeast to the Southern cookery. More than 130 recipes range from *Feijoada*, Brazil's national dish of beans, rice, and various meats (in its many regional variations), to lesser-known dishes, such as Shrimp and Bread Pudding, Crab Soup, and Banana Brittle. With more than 130 recipes, this cookbook is features black-and-white illustrations, photographs, and maps.

ISBN 0-7818-1080-9 · $24.95

Aprovecho: A Mexican-American Border Cookbook
Teresa Cordero-Cordell and Robert Cordell

This book will entertain and enlighten readers about life along the Border. In addition to more than 250 recipes, *Aprovecho* includes special sections that relate popular legends such as "La Llorona and the Chupacabra," explain how tequila is made, and provide instructions for making your own festive piñatas. Also included are a glossary of chiles and cooking terms, and a Mexican pantry list so you'll always be prepared for a fiesta! Complete with black-and-white photographs.

ISBN 978-0-7818-1206-1 · $16.95pb

My Mother's Bolivian Kitchen
José Sánchez-H.

More than a cookbook, *My Mother's Bolivian Kitchen* is a memoir of a Bolivian childhood. Along with recipes for everything from *salteñas* (Meat-Filled Pastries) and quinoa soup to *picante de pollo* (Spicy Chicken), Sánchez-H. shares many poignant childhood memories. Come to Aunt Nazaria's sixty-ninth birthday party to feast on *picante de pato con chuño* (Spicy Duck with Freeze-Dried Potatoes); to observe El Día de Todos Santos (All Saints' Day), when traditional shaped breads are baked in honor of the deceased; and camping in the mountains, where the memory of his mother's food leads him home. Complete with black-and-white photographs, illustrations, and maps.

ISBN 0-7818-1056-6 · $24.95

Tasting Chile:
A Celebration of Authentic Chilean Foods and Wines
Daniel Joelson

Despite the ever-growing popularity of Latin American food, little is known about Chilean cuisine. *Tasting Chile* is a comprehensive guide to the culinary treasures of this South American nation, with cultural information, a chapter on Chilean wines, and a Spanish-English dictionary of Chilean fish and shellfish. Try 140 traditional recipes, from spicy salsas and hearty soups to the ubiquitous empanada and *manjar*-based (carmel cream) desserts. The home chef can prepare simple, everyday recipes, as well as more exotic fare, including blood sausage, fried frogs' legs, and rhubarb mousse. Complete with black and white photographs.

ISBN 0-7818-1028-0 · $24.95

Corsican Cuisine
Arthur L. Meyer

Corsican cuisine draws on French, Italian, Spanish, and North African influences while remaining fiercely distinct. Using fresh ingredients to create complex flavors, these 100 authentic recipes make simple and satisfying fare. Try your hand at traditional staples like garlic soup, ragout of game hen with myrtle, and wild boar meatballs with roasted red peppers. Or satisfy your sweet tooth with Chestnut Beignets and sweet cheese-filled turnovers. Also included are a 16 page color photo insert, and a glossary of Corsican foods and culinary terms.

ISBN 978-0-7818-1248-1 · $35.00

Old Havana Cookbook (Bilingual)
Havana is one of the oldest and most picturesque cities of the western hemisphere. It was a popular winter destination for North American tourists in the 1950s, and this cookbook recaptures the spirit of Old Havana—*Habana la vieja*—and its celebrated culinary traditions. Cuban cuisine, though derived from its mother country, Spain, has been modified and refined by locally available foods like pork, rice, corn, beans and sugar, and the requirements of a tropical climate. Fine Gulf Stream fish, crabs, lobsters, tropical fruits also have their places on the traditional Cuban table.

ISBN 0-7818-0767-0 · $14.95

Cuisines of Portuguese Encounters, *Expanded Edition*
Cherie Hamilton

From famous dishes like Spicy Pork Vindaloo from Goa, the classic *bacalhau* of Portugal, and all varieties of *feijoada*, to lesser-known treats like Guinean Oyster Stew and Coconut Pudding from East Timor, this cookbook has something for every adventurous gastronome. The 8-page section of color photographs brings the recipes to life. Menus for religious holidays and festive occasions, a glossary of terms, a section on mail-order resources, and a bilingual index will assist the home chef in celebrating the rich, diverse, and delicious culinary legacy of this age-old empire.

ISBN 978-0-7818-1181-1 · $29.95

Spanish Language Guides from Hippocrene

Mastering Spanish with 2 Audio CDs, *Second Edition*
ISBN 0-7818-1064-7 · $24.95pb

Spanish-English/English-Spanish Pocket Legal Dictionary
ISBN 978-0-7818-1214-6 · $19.95pb

Spanish-English/English-Spanish Children's Picture Dictionary
625 entries · ISBN 0-7818-1130-9 · $14.95pb

Chilenismos-English/English-Chilenismos Dictionary & Phrasebook
1,500 entries · ISBN 0-7818-1062-0 · $13.95pb

Emergency Spanish Phrasebook
ISBN 0-7818-0977-0 · $5.95pb

Hippocrene Children's Illustrated Spanish Dictionary
500 entries · ISBN 978-0-7818-0889-7 · $14.95pb

Spanish-English/English-Spanish (Latin American)
Compact Dictionary
3,800 entries · ISBN 0-7818-1041-3 · $9.95pb

Spanish-English/English-Spanish (Latin American)
Concise Dictionary
8,000 entries · ISBN 0-7818-0261-X · $12.95pb

Spanish-English/English-Spanish Practical Dictionary
35,000 entries · ISBN 0-7818-0179-6 · $14.95pb

Spanish Learner's Dictionary: Spanish-English/English –Spanish
14,000 entries · ISBN 0-7818-0937-1 · $14.95pb

Prices subject to change without prior notice. **To purchase Hippocrene Books** contact your local bookstore, visit www.hippocrenebooks.com, call (212) 685-4373, or write to: HIPPOCRENE BOOKS, 171 Madison Avenue, New York, NY 10016.